Are You Lied *To* *About The* Bible?

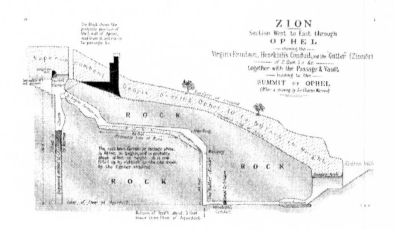

Volume 1

By

Leif A. Werner

ISBN: 1-4107-5842-7 (e-book)
ISBN: 1-4107-5841-9 (Paperback)

This book is printed on acid free paper.

1stBooks – rev. 08/25/03

Information

This book naturally covers only a part, but a very important one, of the whole Word of God. This book is simply meant as an appetizer to drive eager students of the Word, or anyone seeking the Kingdom, deeper into studying the meat of the Word for themselves with available tools or/and with a good teacher. The Word is pregnant so you learn more every time you study it.

All Bible quotes in this book are from the Authorized King James Version of 1611 as published by the Revisers in their 'Parallel Bible' in 1886.

The translation analysis is mostly built on Strong's Exhaustive Concordance of the Bible. I have abbreviated the names of the books of the Bible in large the same way as Strong.

Cover picture

The picture shows the tower of Ophel, where the Nethinims' headquarters were, 'undercut' by the Virgin's Fountain representing the 'Living Water' of Christ. If you read Ezra 8:15 and Neh 3:26-27 you will understand. There were no Levite priests left in the 'church'. There were only Nethinims, mostly Kenites. The Nethinims were only supposed to carry wood and water for the Temple, but they had taken over the leadership of the Temple.

What does God require of us?

Deuteronomy 10:

12 And now, Israel, what doth the Lord thy God require of thee, but to fear (revere) *the Lord thy God, to walk in all His ways, and to love Him, and to serve the Lord thy God with all thy heart and with all thy soul.*

I dedicate

this book to my beloved family, and to whoever is seeking the knowledge of the Word of God.

To Dave
from
Leo
the author

Why This Book Is Written

Table of Contents

The reason this book is written

We need to study the Scriptures chapter by chapter and verse by verse, the way God gave it, and learn to hold on to, and not go away from, the subject, object and article of the text.

The famine in the end times is *'not a famine of bread, nor a thirst for water, but of hearing the words of the Lord'*, Amos 8:11.

We do not know the Word of God. We must learn to study by ourselves, using available tools. God holds us personally responsible for knowing, or not knowing, the word of God. We can not blame somebody else at the judgment day for our Biblical illiteracy.

If you don't know the Word of God you are going to be deceived by false teachers, and in these end times there are lots of them around, Mark 13:

6 For Many shall come in my name, saying, 'I am Christ;' and shall deceive many.

Table of Contents

Chapter I

This Generation Shall Not Pass

Genesis 6:

3 And the Lord said, 'My spirit shall not always strive with man, for that he also is flesh: yet his days shall be an hundred and twenty years.'

So 120 years is a generation.

Numbers 14:

33 And your children shall wander in the wilderness forty years, and bear your whordoms, until your carcasses be wasted in the wilderness.

Here we have 40 years as a generation. 120 years is the longest span of time though for a generation today according to God's decision in Genesis 6:3.

We see here at least two ways to define the length of 'a generation' from the Bible.

Let's now go to Mark 13:

28 Now learn a parable of the fig tree; When her branch is yet tender, and putteth forth leaves, ye know that summer is near:

Jesus is telling us to learn 'the parable of the fig tree'. The parable of the fig tree is written in Jeremiah 24, see below. It has to do with Judah forming a nation again, Israel, May 15, 1948.

29 So ye in like manner, when ye shall see these things come to pass, know that it is nigh, even at the doors.

Jesus tells us, that when we see the things He is explaining in Mark 13, the end is near, that will say, we are close to the 'second advent' = His return.

He is telling us though what is going to happen first, before He returns, and that is important to know, so we don't go wrong, be deceived.

30 Verily I say unto you, that this generation shall not pass, till all these things be done.

'This generation' means the generation of 1948, when Israel became a nation again.

31 Heaven and earth shall pass away: but My words shall not pass away.

Heaven and earth shall not pass away, but this heaven and earth 'age' shall pass away. We know this from other Scriptures, 2 Peter 3:13......*new heavens and a new earth,* where 'new' is the Greek word 'kainos', which means 'rejuvenated'. We also see in the same chapter verse 10......*the elements shall melt,* where 'element' is the Greek word for 'rudiment', 'stoicheion', that will say the 'evil' things, that we do not have to do with total destruction of heaven and earth, but a rejuvenation.

32 But of that day and that hour knoweth no man, no, not the angels which are in heaven, neither the Son, but the Father.

Jesus is saying that no one knows when He is coming back. That is of course true, but we can estimate a little bit I think. He is coming back in the generation He told us, and we talked about. That must be within 120 years from May 15, 1948, which is before or at 1948+120=2068, May 15.

I think Jesus means, that we don't know the day or the our. One thing is certain though. We can discern the season. In other words we can discern when we get closer and closer, because of what's happening in the world and compare that with Jesus' guidelines in Mark 13. That is what Jesus is telling us in Mark 13.

An interesting place in this context is Revelation 11 where we can discern the last three and a half days of this dispensation, that will say, we know when it's three and a half days left to Christ's return. Before this event we can only discern the season. Let's read Revelation 11:

7 And when they shall have finished their testimony, the beast that ascendeth out of the bottomless pit shall make war against them, and shall overcome them, and kill them.

We see here how Satan in the office of Antichrist shall kill the two witnesses. Then verse

11 And after three days and an half the spirit of life from God entered into them, and they stood upon their feet; and great fear fell upon them which saw them.

Three days after they are killed, the seventh trump, the last, sounds. See verse

15 And the seventh angel sounded; and there were great voices in heaven, saying, 'the kingdoms of this world are become the kingdoms of our Lord, and of his Christ; and He shall reign for ever and ever.'

The seventh trump, the last, sounds, and that is when Christ returns, Second Advent. The kingdoms of this world are not Satan's any more. There we have it. We certainly know when it is 3,5 days left to Christ's return.

We have a second witness about all this in Matthew 24:

32 Now learn a parable of the fig tree; When his branch is yet tender, and putteth forth leaves, ye know that summer is nigh:

33 So likewise ye, when ye shall see all these things, know that it is near, even at the doors.

3

34 Verily I say unto you, This generation shall not pass, till all these things be fulfilled.

35 Heaven and earth shall pass away, but My words shall not pass away.

36 But of that day and hour knoweth no man, no, not the angels of heaven, but My Father only.

37 But as the days of Noe were, so shall also the coming of the Son of Man be.

38 For as in the days that were before the flood they were eating and drinking, marrying and giving in marriage, until the day that Noe entered into the ark,

What happened in the times of Noe=Noah? Genesis 6:1-ff. The fallen angels, Nephilim, took women to wives. They came directly down on to earth. They couldn't wait to be born through woman, as was God's plan for this earth age. They committed sin to death of their soul this way, and are reserved by God in everlasting chains under darkness unto the judgment of the great day, Jude 6.
This is going to happen again just before Christ returns, see verse 37 above and Revelation 12:

9 And the great dragon was cast out, that old serpent, called the Devil and Satan, which deceiveth the whole world: he was cast out into the earth, and his angels were cast out with him.

This is the reason why in 1 Corinthians 11:

10 The woman ought to have power on her head because of the angels.

'Power' here is basically knowledge of the Word, the Truth, so she can spot the Nephilim, these fallen angels, when they appear again and are going to try to wholly seduce her, in the end times.

Now Psalms 22:

1 My God, My God, why hast thou forsaken me?......

This is what Christ quoted when he was hanging on the cross. God had not forsaken him, see verse 24. Christ quoted the whole Psalm most likely. I believe this is one of the reasons the centurion said in Mark 15:39......*"Truly this Man was the Son of God."* He heard Jesus quote Psalm 22.

Let's continue in Psalms 22, verse

6 But I am a worm, and no man; A reproach of men, and despised of the People.

'Worm' means 'scarlet'. It comes from the crimson coccus, from which the scarlet dye was obtained. Has to do with Ex 25:4, 26:1. Scarlet is one of the colors of the tabernacle. It means that Christ is Holy.

7 All they that see me laugh me to scorn: They shoot out the lip, they shake the head, saying,

8 'He trusted on the Lord that he would deliver him: Let Him deliver him, seeing He delighted in him.'

Quoted by people at the Cross in Matthew 27:43, Mark 15:29, and Luke 23:35. They didn't know it though. God put the words in their mouth, for them and for us to see, that God's word is true, so if we know the Word, if we study it, we recognize it in the events that happens in this world.

14 I am poured out like water, And all my bones are out of joint: My heart is like wax; It is melted in the midst of my bowels,

15 My strength is dried up like a potsherd; And my tongue cleaveth to my jaws; And Thou hast brought me into the dust of death.

16 For dogs have compassed me: The assembly of the wicked have inclosed me: They pierced my hands and my feet.

'Dogs' means 'enemies'.

17 I may tell all my bones: They look and stare upon me.

18 They part my garments among them, And cast lots upon my vesture.

And they did, see Matthew 27:35.
We see here how The Crucifixion of Christ was prophesied, even to the exactness of what people said and did at the cross, one thousand years before it happened.

24 For he has not despised nor abhorred the affliction of the afflicted; Neither hath He hid His face from him; But when he cried unto Him, He heard.

27 All the ends of the world shall remember and turn unto the Lord: And all the kindreds of the nations shall worship before Thee.

Every knee shall bow at the first day of the Millennium, Isaiah 45:23, Romans 14:11.

28 For the kingdom is the Lord's: And He is the Governor among the nations.

29 All they that be fat upon earth shall eat and worship: All they that go down to the dust shall bow before Him: And none can keep alive his own soul.

'Fat' means in the spiritual sense.

30 A seed shall serve Him; It shall be accounted to the Lord for a generation.

'A seed' are the elect, and they shall serve God in the last generation, 'the generation of the fig tree'.

31 They shall come and shall declare His righteousness unto a People that shall be born, That He hath done this.

'That He hath done this' means: 'It is finished' in the Hebrew language. Cp. John 19:

30 When Jesus therefore had received the vinegar, He said, 'It is finished'.

This, I think, clearly proves that He quoted the whole Psalm. The first and the last of what Christ said on the cross are therefore recorded in the New Testament.

I wanted to bring up Psalm 22 to show, that a prophecy, that will say Psalms 22, thousand years before Christ was crucified foretold the event, and Christ quoted it to stretch the point even more clearly for us. If we go to Mark 13:

23 But take ye heed: behold I have foretold you all things.

We see that Christ has told us all things before they happen. If Psalm 22 came to pass why shouldn't other prophecies come to pass? They will, and exactly as they are written in the Manuscripts. I insert this to sharpen your mind about the mistranslations that are done some times in the translations of the manuscripts.

Now let's go to Jeremiah 24:

1 The Lord shewed me, and, behold, two baskets of figs were set before the temple of the Lord, after that Nebuchadrezzar king of Babylon had carried away captive Jeconiah the son of Jehoiakim king of Judah, and the princes of Judah, with the carpenters and smiths, from Jerusalem, and had brought them to Babylon.

2 One basket had very good figs, even like the figs that are first ripe: and the other basket had very naughty figs, which could not be eaten, they were so bad.

3 Then said the Lord unto me, 'What seest thou, Jeremiah?' And I said, 'Figs; the good figs, very good; and the evil, very evil, that cannot be eaten, they are so evil.'

4 Again the word of the Lord came unto me, saying,

5 'Thus saith the Lord, the God of Israel; 'Like these good figs, so will I acknowledge them that are carried away captive of Judah, whom I have sent out of this place into the land of the Chaldeans for their good.

Here we start to understand that the figs are people, in this case the tribe of Judah, including Benjamin (the ten northern tribes, called Israel, were taken captive by the Assyrians 200 years before this, see 1 Kings 11:28-32, 12:19 and 2 Kings 15:29, 17:6, 23, 19:32-34). God sent Judah out of their home country to Babylon for their best, to wake them up about the truth. This is also a type for the future and alludes to Antichrist's, Satan's, appearance in the end times, which means that the people, that do not know the truth are going to be taken captive by Antichrist, spiritually, they think he is Christ, see 2 Thessalonians 2. They will surely wake up, when they see the true Jesus Christ return just after Antichrist, Satan, has been here 5 months playing Christ, Revelation 9:5,10.

6 For I will set Mine eyes upon them for good, and I will bring them again to this land: and I will build them, and not pull them down; and I will plant them, and not pluck them up.

And now it talks about planting them, Judah, back to their home country, and not pluck them up again. That happened 1948, for the first time since AD 70. It is not talking about when they came back from Babylon, for AD 70 they were dispersed, plucked up again.

7 And I will give them an heart to know Me. That I am the Lord: and they shall be My People, and I will be their God: for they shall return unto Me with their whole heart.

And God will give Judah a heart to know Him. And God will be there. Has God been there yet? Of course not. That happens first in the Millennium, when Christ returns. Has Judah returned to God with their whole heart yet? Of course not. That happens first in the Millennium. See Revelation 20 and 21.

8 And as the evil figs, which cannot be eaten, they are so evil; surely thus saith the Lord, So will I give Zedekiah the king of Judah, and his princes, and the residue of Jerusalem, that remain in this land, and them that dwell in the land of Egypt:

Residue = residents.
The evil figs are the Kenites, the sons of the Devil, Satan. Remember how Christ cursed the fig tree, Matthew 21:19. This has to do with the Kenites, the bad figs. The Kenites always move with Judah, for they are mixed in with them, Matthew 13:24-30, 37-43.
The mountain = nation in Matthew 21:21 is the Kenites and their 'one world system'. We have power over our enemies, Luke 10:19. That's what it means, not moving a literal mountain. Always be alert of the context.

9 And I will deliver them to be removed into all the kingdoms of the earth for their hurt, to be a reproach and a proverb, a taunt and a curse, in all places wither I shall drive them.

'Them' are the Kenites, the bad figs, not Judah.

10 And I will send the sword, the famine, and the pestilence, among them, till they be consumed from off the land that I gave unto them and to their fathers.'

God is going to get rid of the Kenites, them that not repent, of course, for if anyone repents he is a child of God, not of Satan.

Let me now explain the culture of the figs to make you understand how the relationship is between the Jews and the Kenites and other peoples. God always means something with using nature as an analogy, so watch up when you see that in the Bible. A good example is Revelation 9 and the locust, which I explain later in this paper. Now back to the culture of the fig.

Hundreds of tiny female fig flowers are borne on the inside of a fleshy fruit-like receptacle with a small opening at the apex. Smyrna is one edible variety of the figs, one of the best; can be pollinated only by the fig wasp (Blastophaga), which passes its larval stage inside the inedible fruit of a wild variety called the caprifig. In order to produce mature fruit, the cultivated variety is subjected to a process called caprification; flowering branches of caprifig are hung in the tree so that the emerging wasps will transfer caprifig pollen to the edible fig. After entering the receptacle and laying its eggs, the wasp dies and its body and eggs are absorbed by the developing fruit; only the eggs laid inside the caprifig fruit survive.

I am going to let you use your own imagination to figure out how the different parts and stages of this, the fig's, culture represent the Kenites, the Jews and other peoples. Who do you think the wasp represents for example, and the different figs.

Let's go to Matthew 7:

15 Beware of false prophets, which come to you in sheep's clothing, but inwardly they are ravening wolves.

16 Ye shall know them by their fruits. Do men gather grapes of thorns or figs of thistles?

17 Even so every good tree bringeth forth good fruit; but a corrupt tree bringeth forth evil fruit.

18 A good tree can not bring forth evil fruit. Neither can a corrupt tree bring forth good fruit.

19 Every tree that bringeth not forth good fruit is hewn down and cast into the fire.

20 Wherefore by their fruits ye shall know them.

21 Not every one that saith unto Me, 'Lord, Lord,' shall enter into the kingdom of heaven; but he that doeth the will of My Father Which is in heaven.

22 Many will say to Me in that day, 'Lord, Lord, have we not prophesied in Thy name? and in Thy name have cast out devils? and in Thy name done many wonderful works?'

23 And then will I profess unto them, 'I never knew you: depart from Me, ye that work iniquity.'

Talks for itself.

Now to Isaiah 34:

1 Come near, ye nations, to hear; and hearken, ye people: let the earth hear, and all that is therein; the world, and all things that come forth of it.

'Nations' here is 'the one world order', set up by the Kenites, right now. You hear it all the time as 'the one world economy'.
'All' is all the races.

2 For the indignation of the Lord is upon all nations, and His fury upon all their armies: He hath utterly destroyed them, He hath delivered them to the slaughter.

3 Their slain also shall be cast out, and their stink shall come up out of their carcasses, and the mountains shall be melted with their blood.

4 And all the host of heaven shall be dissolved, and the heavens shall be rolled together as a scroll: and all their host shall fall down, as the leaf falleth off from the vine, and as a falling fig from the tree.

This earth age, chapter, is over, 'rolled together as a scroll'.

'Host of heaven' means 'peoples'. We are changed here to the 'celestial' = 'heavenly' body, the flesh is dissolved, cp. 1 Corinthians 15:40, 51-52, and Acts 24:15. It is talking about the last, the seventh trump, Second Advent, Christ's return. We are all going to be 'changed', both the just and unjust, to wait for judgment after the Millennium, Revelation 20. This is also recorded in 1 Thessalonians 4:16-17. So we are in the Millennium here.

The 'falling figs' here are the Biblically illiterate, deceiving preachers, Christians, etc. in Revelation 6:13-16. Revelation 6:

13 And the stars of heaven fell unto the earth, even as a fig tree casteth her untimely figs, when she is shaken of a mighty wind.

'Untimely' because they didn't now the correct order of the events, when Christ would return. They didn't know that Satan, in the office of Antichrist, would come first, five months, Revelation 9:5, 10.

Now back to Isaiah 34:

5 For My sword shall be bathed in heaven: behold, it shall come down upon Idumea, and upon the people of My curse, to judgment.

'Sword' here is 'word', see Revelation 1:16. 'Bathed' means it is going to be a cleansing during the Millennium = disciplined teaching of the word of God, and a lot of 'saving'.

6 The sword of the Lord is filled with blood, it is made fat with fatness, and with the blood of lambs and goats, with the fat of the kidneys of rams: for the Lord hath a sacrifice in Bozrah, and a great slaughter in the land of Idumea.

Bozrah is a place in Edom = Russia, where Esau's descendants, after mixing with other peoples, moved, cp. Genesis 25:30 and 27:39. In 27:39 it should say 'be away from'. It is a mistranslation. It is interesting that the Swedish Bible, for example, has spotted this mistranslation and translates it correct.

'Made fat with fatness' means 'plenty to do'. Idumea is Russia. It comes from Edom which means red, cp. Genesis 25:30. You can read about all this in Ezekiel 38 and 39, where the 'chief prince of Meshech and Tubal' is Russia = Hebrew 'Rosh'. It is talking about the battle, 'the great slaughter' in the valley of Hamon-gog, which I think is Alaska, according to how it is explained in the Scriptures. A subject for another time. USA = part of Israel bought Alaska for this reason, for little more than $7 Millions.

7 And the unicorns, shall come down with them, and the bullocks with the bulls; and their land shall be soaked with blood, and their dust made fat with fatness.

'Unicorn' shall be 'wild ox'. It is a mistranslation.

8 For it is the day of the Lord's vengeance, and the year of recompenses for the controversy of Zion.

The day of the Lord is second Advent, Christ's return, and the Millennium, cp. 2 Peter 3:8.
'The controversy of Zion' means the controversy between God and Satan about who is God.

I have to stop with this now because of the risk of digressing too much from the subject, but it is all about the end times, which have to do with the 'parable of the fig tree'.

Now to Hebrews 3:

9 When your fathers tempted Me, proved Me, and saw My works forty years.

10 Wherefore I was grieved with that generation, and said, They do alway err in their heart; and they have not known My ways.

11 So I sware in My wrath, They shall not enter into My rest.')

12 Take heed, brethren. Lest there be in any of you an evil heart of unbelief, in departing from the living God.

13 But exhort one another daily, while it is called To day; lest any of you be hardened through the deceitfulness of sin.

14 For we are made partakers of Christ, if we hold the beginning of our confidence steadfast unto the end;

15 While it is said, 'To day if ye will hear His voice, harden not your hearts, as in the provocation.'

16 For some, when they had heard, did provoke: howbeit not all that came out of Egypt by Moses.

17 But with whom was He grieved forty years? Was it not with them that had sinned, whose carcasses fell in the wilderness?

18 And to whom sware He that they should not enter into His rest, but to them that believed not?

19 So we see that they could not enter in because of unbelief.

This is the type for the end times, which is now, from the Exodus, the Hebrew people's departing from the captivity in Egypt. More is on the way about this.

1 Corinthians 10:

1 Moreover, brethren, I would not that ye should be ignorant, how that all our fathers were under the cloud, and all passed through the sea;

2 And were all baptized unto Moses in the cloud and in the sea;

3 And did all eat the same spiritual meat;

4 And did all drink the same spiritual drink: for they drank of that spiritual Rock that followed them: and that Rock was Christ.

5 But with many of them God was not well pleased: for they were overthrown in the wilderness.

6 Now these things were our examples, to the intent we should not lust after evil things, as they also lusted.

Here we see that these things were examples, types, for what is going to happen in the future.

7 Neither be ye idolaters, as were some of them; as it is written, 'The people sat down to eat and drink, and rose up to play.'

8 Neither let us commit fornication, as some of them committed, and fell in one day three and twenty thousand.

9 Neither let us tempt Christ, as some of them also tempted, and were destroyed of serpents.

10 Neither murmur ye, as some of them also murmured, and were destroyed of the destroyer.

11 Now all these things happened unto them for ensamples: and they are written for our admonition, upon whom the ends of the world are come.

Here it is again. God foretold us all things, and also made examples for us, so we can see exactly how it is going to happen. The whole Bible is full of examples, types, for the end times.

12 Wherefore let him that thinketh he standeth take heed lest he fall.

13 There hath no temptation taken you but such as is common to man: but God is faithful, Who will not suffer you to be tempted above that ye are able; but will with the temptation also make a way to escape, that ye may be able to bear it.

14 Wherefore, my dearly beloved, flee from idolatry.

15 I speak as to wise men; judge ye what I say.

We can also according to Revelation 9 discern that Christ, most likely, is coming back in September, at the Feast of Tabernacle, I believe, because the time of the locust, Revelation 9:3, which are Satan's guys, is May – September, five months, Revelation 9:5,10. So we also can discern that Antichrist is coming in May, Revelation 9:10-11. We still don't know what year though. We are not supposed to.

1 Thessalonians 5:

3 For when they shall say, 'Peace and safety;' then sudden destruction cometh upon them, as travail upon a woman with child; and they shall not escape.

Do you hear people, and nations, including the United Nations, say peace, peace today? I hope so, for we are in the end times. There we have it pretty much.

Chapter II

Birth of an Age

1 Thess 5:

1 But of the times and the seasons, brethren, ye have no need that I write unto you.

We who know the Word study the situation in the world and can thereby see how we are getting closer to the end of this earth age.

2 For yourselves know perfectly that the day of the Lord so cometh as a thief in the night.

3 For when they shall say, 'Peace and safety;' then sudden destruction cometh upon them, as travail upon a woman with child; and they shall not escape.

We hear a lot about peace today, including the construction of the One World Order, also called the New World Order, heard about as the 'one world economy' for example, and thereby are they trying to achieve that peace. At the same time though we still have wars and rumors of wars, but it's getting less of it, so it hasn't really balanced over yet to be just peace and safety. We still have a while to go to the end therefore.

Matt 24:

3 And as He sat upon the mount of Olives, the disciples came unto Him privately, saying, 'Tell us, when shall these things be and what shall be the sign of Thy coming, and of the end of the world?'

'The end of the world' means 'the end of this present world age', for 'world' is the Greek word 'aion' which means 'age'.

4 And Jesus answered and said unto them, 'Take heed that no man deceive you.

5 For many shall come in My name, saying, 'I am Christ; and shall deceive many.'

We must be getting closer to the end, for there is a lot of deception going on out there. Be very careful and study the Word. Stay in it every day, so you do not be deceived.

6 And ye shall hear of wars and rumours of wars: see that ye be not troubled: for all these things must come to pass, but the end is not yet.

7 For nation shall rise against nation, and kingdom against kingdom: and there shall be famines, and pestilences, and earthquakes, in divers places.

'Famines' are not famines of food but for hearing the word of God, see Amos 8:11. We have pestilences today like aids. I don't know so much about earthquakes, but they say the amount of them is increasing.

8 All these are the beginning of sorrows.

'Sorrows' or 'labor pains' when we go into a new age, the millennium age.

Is 13:

1 The burden of Babylon, which Isaiah the son of Amoz did see.
2 Lift ye up a banner upon the high mountain, exalt the voice unto them, shake the hand, that they may go into the gates of the nobles.

Think about the word of God taught by satellite today for example. That's pretty high.

3 I have commanded My sanctified ones, I have also called My mighty ones for Mine anger, even them that rejoice in My highness.

'My sanctified ones' etc. are the elect, see Rom 8:26-33. They study the Word verse by verse.

4 The noise of a multitude in the mountains, like as of a great people; a tumultuous noise of the kingdoms of nations gathered together: the Lord of hosts mustereth the host of the battle.

'*...the kingdoms of nations gathered together:*' is the 'One World Order'.

5 They come from a far country, from the end of heaven, even the Lord, and the weapons of His indignation, to destroy the whole land.

Preparations for the last battle, to destroy the whole land, which is Babylon, which means confusion, this world, which is confused. Very!

6 Howl ye; for the day of the Lord is at hand; it shall come as a destruction from the ALMIGHTY.

7 Therefore shall all hands be faint, and every man's heart shall melt:

At Christ's return we are going to be changed to our spiritual, celestial, body. The flesh 'melts' away.

8 And they shall be afraid: pangs and sorrows shall take hold of them; they shall be in pain as a woman that travaileth: they shall be amazed one at another; their faces shall be as flames.

'Flames' means 'ashamed'. 'They' are the deceived ones. If you know the truth and have repented from your sins, you do not have to be afraid.

9 Behold, the day of the Lord cometh, cruel both with wrath and fierce anger, to lay the land desolate: and He shall destroy the sinners thereof out of it.

We who have repented from our sins do not have to fear anything though. God is not angry at us. We have the seal of God in our foreheads, Rev 7:3 and 9:4.

10 For the stars of heaven and the constellations thereof shall not give their light: the sun shall be darkened in his going forth, and the moon shall not cause her light to shine.

Christ shall shine brighter than all this, so they are going to fade away compared to it.

11 And I will punish the world for their evil, and the wicked for their iniquity; and I will cause the arrogancy of the proud to cease, and will lay low the haughtiness of the terrible.

12 I will make a man more precious than fine gold; even a man than the golden wedge of Ophir.

13 Therefore I will shake the heavens, and the earth shall remove out of her place, in the wrath of the Lord of hosts, and in the day of His fierce anger.

The earth shall move back to where it was in the first earth age before the katabole, most likely. There will be no more 90 miles discrepancy between the geographical and the magnetic poles, as it is now.

14 And it shall be as the chased roe, and as a sheep that no man taketh up: they shall every man turn to his own people, and flee every one into his own land.

15 Every one that is found shall be thrust through; and every one that is joined unto them shall fall by the sword.

'Sword' means 'word'. The 'word' of God, the truth, shall convict.

16 Their children also shall be dashed to pieces before their eyes; their houses shall be spoiled, and their wives ravished.

'Ravished' by the fallen angels of Gen 6 and Jude 6. It is going to be as in the time of Noah, Matt 24:37-38

Ps 48:

1 Great is the Lord, and greatly to be praised
  In the city of our God, in the mountain of His holiness.

2 Beautiful for situation, the joy of the whole earth,
  Is mount Zion, on the sides of the north,
  The city of the great King.

Read Is 14:11-16 and see how Antichrist, Satan, is going to 'sit in the sides of the north', God's favorite place.

3 God is known in her palaces for a refuge.

4 For, lo, the kings were assembled,
  They passed by together.

The 'assembled kings' is the One World Order.

5 They saw it, and so they marveled;
  They were troubled, and hasted away.

They saw the end of this earth age.

6 Fear took hold upon them there,
And pain, as of a woman in travail.

7 Thou breakest the ships of Tarshish
With an east wind.

'Ships of Tarshish' are the Kenites' 'trade ships'. Tarshish was an important trade center in Spain. It alludes to the destruction of the Old World Order, which is led by the Kenites. The east wind is hot, for it comes from the desert countries east of Palestine. It's like 'hell'. It's Hebrew 12:29 **For our God is a consuming fire.** It is the lake of fire of Rev 20:15.

8 As we have heard, so have we seen
In the city of the Lord of hosts, in the city of our God:
God will establish it for ever. Selah.

'Selah' means 'stop and meditate on it'.

9 We have thought of Thy lovingkindness, O God,
In the midst of Thy temple.

10 According to Thy name, O God,
So is Thy praise unto the ends of the earth:
Thy right hand is full of righteousness.

11 Let mount Zion rejoice,
Let the daughters of Judah be glad,
Because of Thy judgments.

12 Walk about Zion, and go round about her:
Tell the towers thereof.

23

Zion is our Father's favorite place in the universe.

13 Mark ye well her bulwarks,
   Consider her palaces;
   That ye may tell it to the generation following.

14 For this God is our God for ever and ever:
   He will be our guide even unto death.

'Even unto' shall be 'over'. Here we see a typical scribe falsification of the Word, cp. 1 Chr 2:55, where we see that the Kenites are the scribes. This is a deliberate falsification of the Word by a Kenite.

Is 26:

1 In that day shall this song be sung in the land of Judah; We have a strong city; salvation will God appoint for walls and bulwarks.

In that day, cp. Rev 1:10. It is Christ's return, the Lord's day.

2 Open ye the gates, that the righteous nation which keepeth the truth may enter in.

'The righteous nation' are 'the elect'.

3 Thou wilt keep him in perfect peace, whose mind is stayed on Thee: because he trusteth in Thee.

4 Trust ye in the Lord for ever: for in THE LORD JEHOVAH is everlasting strength:

'Jehovah' is a polluted name for God. It is not God's name. **God's name is YHVH (YAHAVEH).**

5 For He bringeth down them that dwell on high; the lofty city, He layeth it low; He layeth it low, even to the ground; He bringeth it even to the dust.

6 The foot shall tread it down, even the feet of the poor, and the steps of the needy.

7 The way of the just is uprightness: Thou, most upright, dost weigh the path of the just.

'The just' are the 'elect', the 'zedek' or 'zadok' in the English, but more correct 'tsaddiyq' in the Hebrew. Cp. Melchizedek, which means and is the King of the just, that will say Christ.

8 Yea, in the way of Thy judgments, O Lord, have we waited for Thee; the desire of our soul is to Thy name, and to the remembrance of Thee.

9 With my soul have I desired Thee in the night; yea, with my spirit within me will I seek Thee early: for when Thy judgments are in the earth, the inhabitants of the world will learn righteousness.

This is about the millennium.

10 Let favour be shewed to the wicked, yet will he not learn righteousness: in the land of uprightness will he deal unjustly, and will not behold the majesty of the Lord.

'The wicked' is Satan.

11 Lord, when Thy hand is lifted up, they will not see: but they shall see, and be ashamed for their envy at the people; yea, the fire of Thine enemies shall devour them.

'Hand' is 'fist'. 'The people' are 'the elect'.

12 Lord, Thou wilt ordain peace for us: for Thou also hast wrought all our works in us.

13 O Lord our God, other lords beside Thee have had dominion over us: but by Thee only will we make mention of Thy name.

'Other lords' are the Kenites.

14 They are dead, they shall not live; they are deceased, they shall not rise: therefore hast Thou visited and destroyed them, and made all their memory to perish.

'Deceased' is a proper name, Rephaim, and should not have been translated. Rephaim are the progeny of the fallen angels of Gen 6, Jude 6, and 1 Pet 3:19, they are in chains, 2 Pet 2:4, reserved unto judgment. They shall not rise. They are actually the seven thousand men perishing in Rev 11:13.

15 Thou hast increased the nation, O Lord, Thou hast increased the nation: Thou art glorified: Thou hadst removed it far unto all the ends of the earth.

There are more saved now in this earth age than in the first earth age. That means that God is increasing His people together with them.

16 Lord, in trouble have they visited Thee, they poured out a prayer when Thy chastening was upon them.

17 Like as a woman with child, that draweth near the time of her delivery, is in pain, and crieth out in her pangs; so have we been in Thy sight, O Lord.

18 We have been with child, we have been in pain, we have as it were brought forth wind; we have not wrought any deliverance in the earth; neither have the inhabitants of the world fallen.

'Wind' is 'ruach', spirit.

Rev 12:

1 And there appeared a great wonder in heaven; a woman clothed with the sun, and the moon under her feet, and upon her head a crown of twelve stars:

2 And she being with child cried, travailing in birth, and pained to be delivered.

This is how the birth pangs were at the age change from the first to the second earth and heaven age. It's going to be much like that with the change between the second and the third age, which we are approaching rapidly now.

Chapter III

Rapture and More

What is 'the rapture'?

It is the taking away of the church when Christ returns. The belief that this is going to take place is widely spread over the world among Christians, but it is a lie. It originates from a false, evil 'prophecy', 'revelation' if you wish, 1830, by a Ms. Margaret Macdonald of Port Glasgow, Scotland. It is also called the pre-trib revelation. You can read about it in the book 'The Incredible Cover-up' by Dave MacPehrson. He investigated what happened in 1830 in Great Britain when Margaret Macdonald had her so called revelation about the 'rapture'.

Basically Margaret Macdonald was a mental ill person who was most likely possessed by evil spirits.

What she said or 'prophesied' is not true and it is not written in God's Word.

Let us start to analyze the so called 'rapture theory' with the help of the Word of God, the Bible.

The 'rapturists', that is they who believe in the 'rapture', believe that Christ is going to return a first time to take, rapture, the church out from the earth up in the sky, heaven, before the tribulation and then come back again to stay. This is not true according to the Word.

The 'rapturists' are using several Scriptures as evidence. Let us start with 1 Thess 4:

17 Then we which are alive, and remain, shall be caught up together with them in the clouds to meet the Lord in the air: and so shall we ever be with the Lord.

Who are we that are alive? We who live on earth when Christ returns.

Who are 'them'? We have to go to the previous verses 14, 15 and 16 to find the answer.

16 For the Lord Himself shall descend from heaven with a shout, with the voice of the archangel, and with the trump of God: and the dead in Christ shall rise first:

'Them' are the dead in Christ who shall rise first. What does 'rise first' means? We see in verse

14 For if we believe that Jesus died and rose again, even them also which sleep in Jesus will God bring with Him.

that like Jesus died and rose so also they who died in Christ rose. They went to be with God, like we all do when we die the flesh death, the first death.

This might be shocking to some, but let us read 1 Cor 15:

51 Behold, I show You a mystery; We shall not all sleep, but we shall all be changed.

Changed to what? Put on our celestial, heavenly body.

What does **all** mean? Let's go to Acts 24:

15 And have hope toward God, which they themselves also allow, that there shall be a resurrection of the dead, both of the just and unjust.

'Resurrection' here means 'rise', like in 1Thess 4:14 and 16. It can not mean resurrection of the soul, for the unjust's soul can not be resurrected, unless they repent, and all will not, but they can put on an incorruptible body, and they will, as in 1Cor 15:

53 For this corruptible must put on incorruption, and this mortal must put on immortality.

Incorruption is about the body. That happens when Christ returns. We will all, just and unjust, put on the celestial, heavenly, body then.

We are all going to be changed. That body everyone, just and unjust, is going to have through the millennium. There will be teaching by Christ and his elect during the millennium, for there are going to be a lot of people saved then. They are, thereafter, going to be tested by Satan when he is loosed a little season after the millennium, Rev 20:3 and 7-8. They will be judged according to their works, Rev 20:12-13. We are judged by faith now, for we can not see Christ. In the millennium we can. There is a difference here.

Immortality is about the soul. That happens for some, they who are going to teach during the millennium, at the first resurrection, Rev 20:6, and for others at the white throne judgment, after the testing mentioned above, Rev 20:11-15.

So we learn from this, that there is a difference between 'to rise' and 'to resurrect'.

Read in Rev 20:

5 But the rest of the dead lived not again until the thousand years were finished. This is the first resurrection.

The word for 'dead' here is the Greek, with Article, 'hoi nekroi', which means dead bodies in the grave apart from their personality they once had. 'Live' is the Greek word 'anazao', which means 'to recover life', 'revive' and 'live again'. It means that the rest of the people that have died the flesh death are not going to live spiritually until after the millennium, if they overcome of course.

Those spiritually dead are those that have not overcome yet, but have a chance, their first, in the millennium, the thousand years. You see, God, our Father, is fair. Most people donít have a chance now, because of the lack of true teaching of the Word of God.

Now let's go back to 1 Thess 4:

15 For this we say unto you by the word of the Lord, that we which are alive and remain unto the coming of the Lord, shall not prevent them which are asleep.

We see here that we who are alive when Christ returns can not prevent them that are asleep, they who are dead in the flesh, because they are already with God. 2 Cor 5:

8......to be absent from the body,...is......to be present with the Lord.

Think about that when you want to comfort somebody, when their nearest have died. Eccl 12:

7 Then shall the dust return to the earth as it was: and the spirit shall return unto God Who gave it.

is giving the same message. This is of course one place from where Paul got his message. So, when we die, our spirit = Hebr. ruach, that will say we, our soul, because the spirit is the intellect of the soul, and they can therefore not be separate, goes back to God to await judgment, and the body goes back to dust, in the grave, or is burned, cremated. The body is only a 'bunch' of minerals used as our suit for this earth age only. You should read Eccl 12: 5-6 in your Bible to get the context.

1Thess 4:17 is really talking about Christ's return, but it is not saying that we are going to 'fly away' from earth. That is because of the following.

There are two words that play an important role here in the misunderstanding of this Scripture.

Paul was a Hebrew scholar, but not a Greek scholar so he spoke and wrote 'street Greek'. The word 'clouds' means 'crowds' and this we can see from Hebr 12:1, where Paul is talking about 'a cloud of witnesses.' He means of course a crowd.

The word 'air' in verse 17 is from the Greek word 'aer' from 'aemi', that means 'the breath of life' or 'spirit'. It does not mean 'sky' which is another word in the Greek, 'ouranos'.

The verse is communicating the same thing as 1 Cor 15:

52 In a moment, in the twinkling of an eye, at the last trump; for the trumpet shall sound, and the dead shall be raised incorruptible, and we shall be changed.

The last trump is the seventh. We are going to be changed into our spiritual body when Christ returns. The flesh body is done away with, so remember that if you are still in the flesh, Christ is not here yet. Read in 1 Cor 15:

40 There are also celestial bodies, and bodies terrestrial: but the glory of the celestial is one, and the glory of the terrestrial is another.

Celestial is heavenly and terrestrial is earthly.
1 Cor 15 and 1 Thess 4 are basically teaching about where the dead are.

Paul wrote a second letter to the Thessalonians. He did that to make certain that they had understood what he taught them in the first letter. 2 Thess 2:

1 Now we beseech you, brethren, by the coming of our Lord Jesus Christ, and by gathering together unto Him.

2 That ye be not soon shaken in mind, or be troubled, neither by spirit, nor by word, nor by letter, as from us, as that the day of Christ is at hand.

3 Let no man deceive you by any means: for that day shall not come, except there come a falling away first, and that man of sin be revealed, the son of perdition,

4 Who opposeth and exalteth himself above all that is called God, or that is worshipped; so that he as God sitteth in the Temple of God, showing himself as God.

So what do we have here? Paul is saying that before Christ returns people are going to fall away from the truth. The Greek word used here is 'apostasia', apostasy in the English. Then shall the 'son of perdition' come. The Greek text here is 'apoleia'. If we read Rev 9:

11 And they had a king over them, which is the angel of the bottomless pit, whose name in the Hebrew tongue is Abaddon, but in the Greek tongue hath his name Apollyon.

we see that one of Satan's names is Apollyon, which comes from 'apollumi' which means to destroy fully, which comes from 'apo', that means separation or departure or completion and 'olethros', which means destroy or ruin or death or punishment or destruction. The words 'apoleia', 'apollumi' and 'Apollyon' are from the same roots.

We can also read about 'the son of perdition' in John 17:

12......,and none of them is lost, but the son of perdition;......

The 'son of perdition' is not Judas for he repented, Matt 27:

3 Then Judas, which had betrayed Him, when he saw that He was condemned, repented himself,......

Judas did not commit suicide. He was murdered for you can not 'burst asunder in the midst and your bowels gush out' if you commit suicide. Somebody has cut you up. The Kenite priests did, for they didn't want Judas to witness about what had happened. The Jews did not murder Judas. Acts 1:

18......; and falling headlong, he burst asunder in the midst, and all his bowels gushed out.

Judas is not going to perish in the lake of fire.

I don't think there is any doubt that 2 Thess 2:3 is talking about Satan who is condemned by God in Ez 28:

18 Thou hast defiled thy sanctuaries by the multitude of thine iniquities, by the iniquity of thy traffick; therefore will I bring forth a fire from the midst of thee, it shall devour thee, and I will bring thee to ashes upon the earth in the sight of them that behold thee.

Traffick is alluding to the trade and business of the Kenites, Satan's sons, even to all four of the hidden dynasties: economy, education, religion and politics.

'To bring forth a fire from the midst and devour and bring to ashes' is a Hebrew idiom that means fully destroy.

19 All they that know thee among the people shall be astonished at thee: thou shalt be a terror, and never shalt thou be any more.

Satan shall perish in the lake of fire, be blotted out and be no more, Rev 20:

10 And the devil that deceived them was cast into the lake of fire and brimstone, where the beast and the false prophet are, and shall be tormented day and night for ever and ever.

after the millennium, the thousand year reign by Christ and His elect, after His return. Read Rev 20 and Ez 44, which both are about the millennium.

As you see in Ez 28:19 Satan shall not be any more. If he is not going to be any more how can he be tormented in 'hell' for ever if he is not supposed to exist. Well the answer is pretty simple.

There is no 'hell'. Hell is a teaching from the traditions of men, not the Scriptures. 'Hell' originates from a misunderstanding and consequently a mistranslation of the Hebrew word 'sheol' that has nothing to do with the blotting out process of souls in Rev 20, after The Judgment Day.

The first occurrence of this word is in Gen 37:35, where it is rendered 'grave'. It occurs sixty-five times in the Hebrew of the Old Testament; and only by studying each passage by itself can the student hope to gather the Biblical usage of the word. All heathen or traditional usages are not only worthless, but mischievous.

There is no place called 'hell' and there is not going to be one either. The devil and his followers are going to be blotted out as never existed, at the judgment day, after the millennium, see Rev 20:10 and 15.

This is what the idiom tormented day and night for ever and ever means. God is the consuming fire, Hebrew 12:29.

After the lake of fire, the blotting out process of all evil, including death and hell (grave), in Rev 20, comes Rev 21:

4 And God shall wipe away all tears from their eyes; and there shall be no more death, neither sorrow, nor crying, neither shall there be any more pain: for the former things are passed away.'

How can there be a 'hell' with pain, and crying, and death, and sorrow, etc., when this is not going to exist any more? It can't. There is no 'hell' as it is taught by traditions of men.

It makes sense too, for what kind of Father do we have, if He is going to allow us to look at people screaming and yelling from 'hell' through the eternity? He will not allow this of course. 'Hell' doesn't exist. It is a creation by traditions of men and a misunderstanding of the Scriptures.

The parable told in Luke 16 is talking about the two separate places in heaven, on each side of the 'gulf', where they are who made it, and they who did not make it. We still have the millennium, when they who do not have a chance to make it, be saved, now, because of the lack of true teaching of the Word, are going to have a chance, their first, from the teaching by Christ and the elect, Rev 20:

6......,but they shall be priests of God and of Christ, and shall reign with Him a thousand years'.

'They' are the elect.

This is about anybody, who do not have a chance now.

Then we can also, specifically, read in Ez 44:

25 And they shall come at no dead person to defile themselves: but for father, or for mother, or for son, or for daughter, for brother, or for sister that hath had no husband, they may defile themselves.

This means that the elect can go to their family members, who are spiritually dead, in the millennium and pull them over to the 'Right' side of the 'gulf' with a good Bible lesson. This is happening in the millennium and we are not in flesh then.

The beast and the false prophet in Rev 20:10 are the one world system (or order) that is being created now in the world by the Kenites and it is Satan's office as false prophet, antichrist (playing Christ), from Rev 19:

20 And the beast was taken, and with him the false prophet that wrought miracles before him, with which he deceived them that had received the mark of the beast, and them that worshipped his image. These both were cast alive into a(the) lake of fire burning with brimstone.

The beast and the false prophet are very well connected as we see in Rev 13. There are two beasts there. The first is the one world order, and the second is Satan, antichrist; the same as here mentioned and in the same order.

Read the whole chapter of Rev 13. To have the mark of the beast is to believe that antichrist, Satan, is Christ during the five months period he is going to be here before the True Christ, Jesus, returns. The mark of the beast in their forehead (their brain, thinking process, belief system) or in their right hand (work for Satan) is not a bar-code or a chip or like, stamped on your skin or placed in your skin. Satan is smarter that that. Don't you think?

The lake of fire with burning brimstone is an idiom that means consumed and blotted out by God, for He is a consuming fire, Hebr 12:

29 For our God is a consuming fire.

Another reference against 'the rapture' is Ez 13:

17 Likewise, thou son of man, set thy face against the daughters of thy People, which prophesy out of their own heart; and prophesy thou against them,

20 Wherefore thus saith the Lord God; Behold, I am against your pillows, wherewith ye there hunt the souls to make them fly, and I will tear them from your arms, and will let the souls go, even the souls that ye hunt to make them fly.

So God doesn't like 'rapture' doctrines? That's right!
Margaret Macdonald is an example of 'the daughters of thy People'. 'Fly' is of course alluding to 'rapture', which false prophecy God knew would come in the latter days, now.

In Mark 13, Matt 24, Luke 12 and 21 and Rev 6 through 11 we can read about the seven events, or steps, or seals and trumps, consummating this earth age, the seventh event being Christ's return, Rev 11:

15 And the seventh angel sounded; and there were great voices in heaven, saying, "The kingdoms of this world are become the kingdoms of our Lord, and of His Christ; and He shall reign for ever and ever."

Because Rev 12 and 13 are close ups of events we have to go to Rev 14 to read the continuation of the seventh event, Rev 14:

1 And I looked, and lo, a Lamb stood on the mount of Sion,......

Let us look in Mark 13 and see what Jesus is Himself teaching about His return. Watch carefully and you will see there is no 'rapture' or the like mentioned in His teaching.

Read verses 1 through 13 for your self so you get the full context.

Jesus' disciples are asking Him what the signs shall be of His coming (return) and the end of the world ('age' is a better translation for it is the Greek word 'aion') and when it shall happen. I have quoted here from Matt 24 which is about the same event. Continue with Mark 13:

14 But when ye shall see the abomination of desolation, spoken of by Daniel the prophet, standing where it ought not, (let him that readeth understand,) then let them that be in Judaea flee to the mountains.

The 'abomination of desolation' is better translated the 'abominable desolator' and 'it' is better translated 'he'. The Greek works that way. Who is 'he'? Satan of course. He is going to stand where he ought not. This is what Paul is saying in 2 Thess 2:4.

See also that Jesus is giving Daniel credentials as prophet here.

Read on for yourself verses 15 through 17. Verse

18 And pray ye that your flight be not in the winter.

Winter is the wrong season for harvest. So if you would be flying away, 'raptured' in the winter you are harvested out of season. You are taken by antichrist, the 'abominable desolator' above; the first taken in Matt 24:

40 Then shall two be in the field; the one shall be taken, and the other left.

41 Two women shall be grinding at the mill; the one shall be taken, and the other left.

The subject here is "taken" which we see from Matt 24:

38 For as in the days that were before the flood they were eating and drinking, marrying and giving in marriage, until the day that Noe entered into the ark,

39 And knew not until the flood came, and took them away; so shall also the coming of the Son of man be.

Who do you think were taken? They who knew the truth or they who did not? They who did not of course. The others were on the ark. That's where you shall be also in the end times, now, not taken by deception. You are supposed to stay or stand and wait till the true Christ returns. You are supposed to be here like everybody else through the first tribulation, which is when Satan is here for 5 months, see Rev 9:

5 And to them it was given that they should not kill them, but that they should be tormented five months:.......,

10 And they had tails like unto scorpions, and there were stings in their tails: and their power was to hurt men five months.

Let's read on in Mark 13:

19 For in those days shall be affliction, such as was not from the beginning of the creation which god created unto this time, neither shall be.

20 And except that the Lord had shortened those days, no flesh should be saved: but for the elect's sake, whom He has chosen, He hath shortened the days.

Satan is going to be pretty convincing if you are Biblically illiterate. He looks like Jesus almost. He does not have long red underwear, a pitch fork and a tail. He is a very beautiful cherub see Ez 28:

12......"Thou sealest up the sum, full of wisdom, and perfect in beauty.

14 Thou art the anointed cherub that covereth;......

Satan was the protector of the mercy seat.

We continue in Mark 13:

21 And then if any man shall say to you, 'Lo, here is Christ;' or, 'lo, He is there;' believe him not:

22 For false Christs and false prophets shall rise, and shall show signs and wonders, to seduce, if it were possible, even the elect.

23 But take ye heed: behold, I have foretold you all things.

It is all in the Bible.

24 But in those days, after that tribulation, the sun shall be darkened, and the moon shall not give her light,......

26 And then shall they see the Son of man coming in the clouds with great power and glory.

Read for your self all the text I have left out. You may check that I haven't left any 'rapture' out. I have not as you can see.

It is very simple. First comes Satan playing Christ, the first tribulation 5 months, and then Christ returns.

There is no 'rapture' and we are not going any where. We are going to be here on earth all the time, even through the millennium, see Rev 5:

10 And hast made us unto our God kings and priests, and we shall reign on the earth."

and Rev 20:

6 Blessed and holy is he that hath part in the first resurrection: on such the second death hath no power, but they shall be priests of God and of Christ, and shall reign with Him a thousand years.

Now let's go back to this earth age.

We have the armour of God to stand against antichrist, Eph 6:

13 Wherefore take unto you the whole armour of God, that ye may be able to withstand in the evil day, and having done all, to stand.

We are supposed to stand, not fly away, or "rapture" out of here or escape the evil day, that is Satan's tribulation mentioned above.

Now let's take another place that the 'rapturists' use as evidence of 'the rapture'. Rev 4:

1 After this I looked, and behold, a door was opened in heaven: and the first voice which I heard was as it were of a trumpet talking with me, which said, "Come up hither, and I will shew thee things which must be hereafter."

2 And immediately I was in the Spirit: and behold, a throne was set in heaven, and One sat on the throne.

The 'rapturists' say this is the church 'raptured' into heaven. I say, it is not so according to the Scriptures, but it is John's spirit looking into, or taken if you wish, to the third heaven age. It says 'I looked' and 'I heard' and 'I was'. That is John. I don't see 'church' or the like anywhere. If you are somewhat knowledgeable about the Scriptures, you understand that to say this is 'a rapture' of the church is an ignorant statement.

Let's continue with more evidence that the 'rapture' is a lie and now from the Old Testament. Isaiah 10:

3 And what will ye do in the day of visitation, and in the desolation which shall come from far? To whom will ye flee for help? and where will ye leave your glory?

God would use the Assyrian to straighten His children out. Why? He was filled with righteous indignation. The Assyrian is a type of antichrist. What is a type? Let us read 1 Cor 10:

11 Now all these things happened unto them for ensamples: and they are written for our admonition, upon whom the ends of the world are come.

The prophecies in the Old testament are examples of what is going to happen in the end times, even to God's people, for most do not understand that Satan, antichrist is coming first, playing Christ five months, before the True Christ, Jesus, returns. Is 10:

4 Without me they shall bow down under the prisoners, and they shall fall under the slain. For all this His anger is not turned away, but His hand is stretched out still.

5 O, Assyrian! The rod of Mine anger, and the staff in their hand is Mine indignation.

The rod of God's anger and His indignation is the Assyrian, 'ensample' or example, type of antichrist. God will use antichrist to express His anger and indignation toward his children that don't study His Word enough to know the false messiah from the True Messiah. Is 10:

6 I will send him against an hypocritical nation, and against the People of My wrath will I give him a charge, to take the spoil, and to take the prey, and to tread them down like the mire of the streets.

7 Howbeit he meaneth not so, neither doth his heart think so; but it is in his heart to destroy and cut off nations not a few.

Antichrist is blind to the fact that God is using him. Antichrist will think he is in control. Is 10:

8 For he saith, 'Are not my princes altogether kings?

9 Is not Calno as Carchemish? Is not Hamath as Arpad? Is not Samaria as Damascus?

Satan actually believes he is good enough to defeat God. Remember, it is God who is allowing his success. Is 10:

10 As my hand hath found the kingdom of the idols, and whose graven images did excel them of Jerusalem and of Samaria;

11 Shall I not, as I have done unto Samaria and her idols, so do to Jerusalem and her idols?"

These last two verses will be the words of antichrist. Let us continue with Is 10:

12 Wherefore it shall come to pass, that when the Lord hath performed His whole work upon mount Zion and on Jerusalem, I will punish the fruit of the stout heart of the king of Assyria, and the glory of his high looks.

At the end of the millennium, Satan will go into the lake of fire and be destroyed. Is 10:

13 For he saith, "By the strength of my hand I have done it, and by my wisdom; for I am prudent: and I have removed the bounds of the people, and even robbed their treasures, and I have put down the inhabitants like a valiant man:

14 And my hand hath found as a nest the riches of the people: and as one gathereth eggs that are left, have I gathered all the earth; and there was none that moved the wing, or opened the mouth, or peeped."

None of those deceived, including deceived Christians, will peep. They think they are doing right by worshipping antichrist. With the aid of the Holy Spirit, many of you, the elect, will be doing some peeping at this time, see Luke 12:

11 And when they bring you unto the synagogues, and unto magistrates, and powers, take ye no thought how or what thing ye shall answer, or what ye shall say:

12 For the Holy Spirit shall teach you in the same hour what ye ought to say."

The synagogues are the synagogues of Satan or the churches that are teaching falsehood.

The same is written in Mark 13:11. The synagogues of Satan are written about in Rev 2:

9......, and I know the blasphemy of them which say they are Jews, and are not, but are the synagogue of Satan.

They who say they are Jews, but are not, are the Kenites, the sons of Cain whose father is Satan.

and Rev 3:

9 Behold I will make them of the synagogue of Satan, which say they are Jews, and are not, but do lie;......

Let us now go to Hosea 11:

5 He shall not return into the land of Egypt, but the Assyrian shall be his king, because they refused to return.

The Assyrian here is of course a type of antichrist in the end times and 'he' is Ephraim, the ten northern tribes that were taken captive by the Assyrian and then scattered all over the world and became the 'Christian nations'. They are not going to return geographically, but antichrist is going to deceive them where they are now, because they refused to return to God.

6 And the sword shall abide on his cities, and shall consume his branches, and devour them, because of their own counsels.

They don't ask for God's counsel but trust their own. Just as it is today. They don't study the Word but follow traditions of men.

7 And My People are bent to backsliding from me: though they called them to the Most High, none at all would exalt Him.

They don't know that antichrist, Satan, is coming first, so they will think he is Christ and worship him as Christ.

8 How shall I give thee up, Ephraim? How shall I deliver thee, Israel? how shall I make thee as Admah? How shall I set thee as Zeboim? Mine heart is turned within me, My repentings are kindled together.

Israel, in this case, like Ephraim is the ten scattered northern tribes. Admah and Zeboim were allies to Sodom and Gomorrah.

9 I will not execute the fierceness of Mine anger, I will not return to destroy Ephraim: for I am God, and not man; the holy One in the midst of thee: and I will not enter into the city.

10 They shall walk after the Lord: He shall roar like a lion: when He shall roar, then the children shall tremble from the west.

God is going to be tough to Israel in the end, with antichrist and so on, but they shall finally come home again, to God. They are living in the west, the western Christian nations, so they will naturally come trembling from the west.

11 They shall tremble as a bird out of Egypt, and as a dove out of the land of Assyria: and I will place them in their houses, saith the Lord.

Egypt and Assyria are once again types of antichrist. It is prophecy, ensamples.

12 Ephraim compasseth Me about with lies, and the house of Israel with deceit: but Judah yet ruleth with God, and is faithful with the saints.

Verse 12 is a little bit mistranslated. It is:

and Judah yet wondereth without God and is away from the faithfulness of God and His saints.

Israel is teaching falsehoods and Judah is not following God either.

As we know from 1 Kings 12:19 the ten northern tribes were split from Judah and Benjamin, and in Ez 37 we see that they are not going to join until Christ returns. The ten northern tribes are called Israel or Ephraim; Judah and Benjamin are called Judah after the split. We can read more of this, a little earlier, in 1 Kings 11:28-37. You have to read that for yourself.

The saints are the elect, they who stood up for God in the first earth age at the katabole, that is when Satan rebelled (see Ez 28), from Rom 8:

29 For whom He foreknow,......

30......whom He did predestinate,......

Hosea 12:

1 Ephraim feedeth on wind, and followeth the east wind: he daily increaseth lies and desolation; and they do make a covenant with the Assyrians, and oil is carried into Egypt.

Feedeth on the wind means that they are listening to Biblically illiterate teachers, so called 'wind bags, blowing hot air', the east wind, for an hour or more instead of teaching the word of God, chapter by chapter and verse by verse. In other words, this is talking about false teachers. The oil is alluding historically to the Camp David Accords. Remember? It is prophecy.

2 The Lord hath also a controversy with Judah, and will punish Jacob according to his ways; according to his doings will He recompense him.

Jacob is the natural seed of all 12 tribes.

What I am trying to show you are Scriptures that are talking about how God is going to chastise His own people, the Christians and Jews, for their disobedience and rebellion against Him. They do not study the Word of God but traditions of men, so they are going to be deceived by antichrist and worship him instead of waiting for the True Christ. The Hebrew people have always been rebellious against God, ungrateful, and too lazy to study the Word, by running to other gods, from the beginning. Because they do not study the Word but listen to traditions of men, they do not understand about antichrist. Their belief is therefore going to be a stumbling block for them. They will believe in the false christ. They do not know the difference. See what will happen when they realize they believed in the wrong christ, Rev 6:

15 And the kings of the earth, and the great men, and the rich men, and the chief captains, and the mighty men, and every bondman, and every free man, hid themselves in the dens and in the rocks of the mountains;

16 And said to the mountains and rocks, "Fall on us, and hide us from the face of Him That sitteth on the throne, and from the wrath of the Lamb:

17 For the great day of His wrath is come; and who shall be able to stand?"

It is not the unsaved that He is talking about here. We can see this clearly in Rom 11:

7 What then? Israel hath not obtained that which he seeketh for; but the election hath obtained it, and the rest were blinded.

8 (According as it is written, "God hath given them the spirit of slumber, eyes that they should not see, and ears that they should not hear';) unto this day.

'Slumber' here is 'stupor' in the Greek, katanuxis. If God puts a stupor on people that they can not see or hear, they can not be responsible for their actions so God can not judge them according to their actions. Why is God doing that? To protect weak-minded souls that can not stand against antichrist, Satan, during his five months reign on earth, just before Christ returns. We take care of them in the millennium, and teach them the truth then, when we all have our full mind function, are not living in the flesh, and when there is no evil present, for Satan is bound in the pit, Rev 20:

1 And I saw an angel come down from heaven, having the key to the bottomless pit and a great chain in his hand.

2 And he laid hold on the dragon, that old serpent, which is the Devil, and Satan and bound him a thousand years,

3 And cast him into the bottomless pit, and shut him up, and set a seal upon him, that he should deceive the nations no more, till the thousand years should be fulfilled: and after that he must be loosed a little season.

Satan is loosed a little season after the millennium, so the 'new' Christians can be tested, for God to see if their faith and works can stand his deception. In the millennium salvation is by works and not by faith as now, for we see Christ then, but not now, see Rev 20:

12......:and the dead were judged out of those things which were written in the books, according to their works.

Dead here means spiritually dead of course, for they have not overcome yet.

13......: and they were judged every man according to their works.

Read the whole thing for your self from the Bible.

Another place that proves that the 'rapture' is false is Acts 1:

9 And when he had spoken these things, while they beheld, He was taken up; and a cloud received Him out of their sight.

10 And while they looked steadfastly toward heaven as He went up, behold, two men stood by them in white apparel;

'Men' are 'angels'.

11 Which also said, "Ye men of Galilee, why stand ye gazing up into heaven? This same Jesus Which is taken up from you into heaven, shall so come in like manner as ye have seen Him go into heaven."

12 Then returned they unto Jerusalem from the mount called Olivet, which is from Jerusalem a sabbath day's journey.

The distance is about 2000 English yards. That's what you could walk on a sabbath.

Olivet is the same as Olive, the mount of Olives, the same mountain as in Zech 14, where Christ returns.

Christ is going to return, we are gathering together unto Him, one time. There are no 'in-between times'. The 'rapturists' say, that Christ first is going to 'take' or 'rapture' the church 'out of here' before the tribulation and then come back again a final time. That is a lie from the Devil, it is a no-no. It is not written in the Word of God. I really hope that you can see that now. Read Zech 14:4 and on. Zech 14:

4 And His feet shall stand in that day upon the mount of Olives, which is before Jerusalem on the east, and the mount of Olives shall cleave in the midst thereof toward the east and toward the west, and there shall be a very great valley; and half of the mountain shall remove toward the north, and half of it toward the south.

Conclusion:

What I am trying to document here is written all over the Bible. As Jesus said, 'I have foretold you all things', Mark 13:23, and He really has, over and over, and over again. There are types everywhere in the Old Testament. That's going to be another chapter I am going to write.

A few words about Bible studying here I think are not misplaced.

Beyond the New Testament you are not going to get the real understanding of the Scriptures until you have made a serious study of the Old Testament. To really get a grip you also need to brake it back to the Hebrew and Caldee. You can do that with the help of a Strongs Exhaustive Concordance, for example.

I have read the Swedish Bible, some of the English ones and even checked certain Scriptures out in the German, Italian and French Bibles, and found they are all mis-translated many places. You can read the preface to the King James Version 1611 for example and there see that the translators warn us to believe everything they have translated. They say that they don't understand everything and are uncertain of many translations they have done. They have made mistakes they say. That's very natural, isn't it. The Hebrew, Caldee and Greek manuscripts though are accurate enough.

This is in part because these languages are more exact than English and other modern languages. Ezra and Nehemiah also did the Massorah around 400 years before Christ was born. The Massorah is a text around the Scriptures that locks it in, so it can not be misunderstood.

The Companion Bible is a good study tool also, I think the best available, although it has flaws.

No one is perfect though. If you have a good Bible teacher at hand it's wonderful, but they are very few and far in between. I mean very few. But don't just listen to man, this man or any other man.

You have to check it out for yourself, with the help of the best tools to find, for you are personally responsible for your soul. No one stands between you and Father God at the Judgment Day. Remember: we all fall short and that's why we have repentance.

Study on! Study on! It becomes more interesting the more you study. Promise!

Just before I leave you, I would like to mention something interesting.

We all know what 'the day of the Lord' is. It is when Christ returns and the millennium, the thousand year period of teaching, Rev 20:6. But what is 'the night of the Lord' written in Ex 12:

42 It is a night to be much observed unto the Lord for bringing them out from the land of Egypt: this is that night of the Lord to be observed of all the children of Israel in their generations.

? It is, or a type of, when Antichrist, Satan, is here five months 'playing' Christ.

It is for Israel to observe 'the night of the Lord' in their generations. Don't forget it. Don't be deceived. Don't receive the 'mark of the beast', Rev 13, which is Satan's lies about a 'rapture'.

Satan *had the power of death,* Hebr 2:14, just like the *destroyer* of Ex 12:23, but if we are armed with the truth, that is, believe in the true Christ, not the fake, Antichrist, that is, know the difference, because we love the truth, the Word, enough to study It, the *destroyer,* that is, Satan, Antichrist, can not touch us, that is, deceive us to believe he is Christ.

So we see the Scriptures are entwined together, and we have types for the end already in the beginning of history, and recorded in the Word, because there is only One Author, The Living God, and He is in control.

You should be 'entwined' too with the Word. That's what 'wait' means in Is 40:

31 But they that wait upon the Lord shall renew their strength; they shall mount up with wings as eagles; they shall run, and not be weary; and they shall walk, and not faint.

and in Ps 25, and 27. It is the word 'qavah' in the Hebrew, that means 'bind together, collect, gather together, entwine, twist together.' It does not mean sit and wait doing nothing. It means study the Word and pray to 'entwine' yourself with the Lord and His Word, because He, Jesus, is the Living Word, John 1:1.

Chapter IV

Antichrist Documented

Who is antichrist? Let's go to John 17:

12 While I was with them in the world, I kept them in Thy name: those that Thou gavest Me I have kept, and none of them is lost, but the son of perdition; that the scripture might be fulfilled.

In the Greek Manuscripts 'son of perdition' is 'apoleia' from the word 'apollumi' from 'apo' and 'olethros'. 'Apo' is a primary particle 'off', i.e. 'away' (from something near, in various senses of place, time or relation); it denotes separation, departure. 'Olethros' means punishment, death destruction, ruin.

The Greek word 'Apollyon' meaning 'a destroyer', i.e. Satan, used in Rev 9:

11 And they had a king over them, which is the angel of the bottomless pit, whose name in the Hebrew tongue is Abaddon, but in the Greek tongue hath his name Apollyon.

is from the same root as 'apoleia'. 'Abaddon' is the Hebrew name for Satan as we see. And guess who the angel of the bottomless pit is?! You only have one guess. Did you make it? Yes! That is Satan. Well done!

So what do we have now? We are starting to understand, that 'the son of perdition' is Satan. Let's go to 2 Thess 2:

1 Now we beseech you, brethren, by the coming of our Lord Jesus Christ, and by our gathering together unto Him,

Talking about Christ's return of course.

2 That ye be not soon shaken in mind, or troubled, neither by spirit, nor by word, nor by letter, as from us, as that the day of Christ is at hand.

Paul wrote the second letter to the Thessalonians to make sure they didn't misunderstand his first.

3 Let no man deceive you by any means: for that day shall not come, except there come a falling away first, and that man of sin be revealed, the son of perdition,

It is saying that you shall be very careful, so no one deceive you. Don't trust any man, including this man. Check it out in the Scriptures yourself. That means in fact even, don't totally trust any Bible translation. Read the preface to the 1611 King James Bible, where the translators warn the reader to believe everything they translated, because they say, they don't understand everything and have therefore most certainly mistranslated things here and there. You have to check it out from the Manuscripts. You can do that with a Strong's Concordance for example. You have to be a little familiar with the Hebrew, Caldee (Aramaic) and Greek, and the Massorah.

Falling away here is the Greek word 'apostasia' = apostasy. In the Greek manuscripts 'perdition' here is 'apoleia', the same as mentioned above. So it is talking about Apollyon, which is one of Satan's names. It is talking about Satan. Satan is going to be here before Christ returns. What is he going to be doing here? Let's read on.

4 Who opposeth and exalteth himself above all that is called God, or that is worshipped; so that he as God sitteth in the Temple of God, shewing himself that he is God.

He is going to sit in God's Temple and play God.

5 Remember ye not, that, when I was yet with you, I told you these things?

Paul discussed these things with the Thessalonians when he was with them.

6 And now ye know what withholdeth that he might be revealed in his time.

Michael is holding him, Satan, back.

7 For the mystery of iniquity doth already work: only he who now letteth will let, until he be taken out of the way.

'The mystery of iniquity doth already work' is talking about the deception by the Kenites and their 'four hidden dynasties': education, religion, economics and politics. The Kenites are Cain's children, which is Satan's child from the Garden of Eden. Cain and Kenites is the same Hebrew word 'Qayin' in the Manuscripts.
'Letteth' is the Greek word 'katecho' = hold fast, as verse 6. Supply the Ellipsis by 'there is one who holds fast', instead of by repeating the verb 'will let'. But 'katecho' is a transitive verb, and an object must be supplied too. See all the occ. verse 6. If the subject be Satan, the object must be his position in the heavenlies, Eph 6:12, from which he will be ejected by Michael, Rev 12:7-9. Believe it or not, it is Satan, it is talking about.

8 And then shall that wicked be revealed, whom the Lord shall consume with the spirit of His mouth, and shall destroy with the brightness of His coming:

'The wicked' is of course Satan. We just talked about it. The rest is self explanatory.

9 Even him, whose coming is after the working of Satan with all power and signs and lying wonders.

Satan, when he is here five months just before Christ returns, Rev 9:5, 10, is going to perform 'wonders', Rev 13:13. He can do it. He is not in flesh. He is a cherub, Ez 28:

14 Thou art the anointed cherub that covereth;......

Satan was the protector of the Mercy Seat. That's what 'covereth' means.

and Ez 28:

12......king of Tyrus,...... 'Thou sealest up the sum, full of wisdom, and perfect in beauty.

There is more about 'the king of Tyrus' in Ez 28 than can be attributed to a human being. The words can be understood only of the mightiest and most exalted supernatural being that God ever created.

The king of Tyrus is Satan before his fall. Tyrus, Hebrew, 'Tzor' (now the modern town Sur, is a little island, now a peninsula because of landfill out to the Island, the way the Island once was concurred, outside the cost of Israel, where the Kenites started there trade business 6000 years ago; now we have the World Trade Center in New York, with the same people, the Kenites, ruling it) means 'a rock'. Satan is the false rock though. Christ is the True. Look in the song of Moses in Deut 32:4 and 31, for example. The song of Moses is the song we are singing, who have the victory over Satan and his political system, Rev 15:3.

To understand who 'a man' is in Ez 28:2 let's go to Is 14:

12 How art thou fallen from heaven, O Lucifer, son of the morning! How art thou cut down to the ground, which didst weaken the nations!

Lucifer is one of Satan's names. It means 'morning-star' and worshipped by the Assyrians as male at sunrise and female at sunset.

Lucifer is deceiving people and nations everywhere.

13 For thou hast said in thine heart, 'I will ascend into heaven, I will exalt my throne above the stars of God: I will sit also upon the mount of the congregation, in the sides of the north:

Antichrist, Satan, is coming by the north gate. He likes that place for the Throne of God is there. Christ is coming by the east gate, Zech 14:

4 And His feet shall stand in that day upon the mount of Olives, which is before Jerusalem on the east,......

Back to Is 14:

14 I will ascend above the heights of the clouds; I will be like the MOST HIGH.'

15 Yet thou shalt be brought down to hell, to the sides of the pit.

16 They that see thee shall narrowly look upon thee, and consider thee, saying, 'Is this the man that made the earth to tremble, that did shake kingdoms;

Now back to the comments on Ez 28:12.

Satan is using his wisdom wickedly.
Satan is beautiful. He looks like Jesus almost. He does not have horns, a pitch fork in his hand and long red underwear. That's why so many can't 'see' the difference. You need to know the Scriptures to 'know' the difference. You have to study the Word.
Read the whole chapter 28 in Ezekiel, and you will understand. Use your Strong's Concordance and look up words that you don't understand. Just a little home assignment.

Now back to 2 Thess 2:

10 And with all deceivableness of unrighteousness in them that perish; because they received not the love of the truth, that they might be saved.

The believe in the Rapture Theory for example.

11 And for this cause God shall send them strong delusion, that they should believe a lie:

If you don't love the truth, God is going to help you to be deceived. Sounds hard but that's how it is. I mean to love the truth is to really dig and scrape and do everything that's in your power to find it.

You see, you can not play church. You have to be serious about God's Word.

12 That they all might be damned who believed not the truth, but had pleasure in unrighteousness.

13 But we are bound to give thanks alway to God for you, brethren beloved of the Lord, because God hath from the beginning chosen you to salvation through sanctification of the Spirit and belief of the truth:

Paul talking about the Thessalonians and himself.

Now let's go to Rev 12:

1 And there appeared a great wonder in heaven; a women clothed with the sun, and the moon under her feet, and upon her head a crown of twelve stars;

The woman here is Israel in the zodiacal signs, representing the nation in embryo. The stars are numbered and named. That's what the Zodiac is. There are twelve signs of the Zodiac, called 'the stars' in

Gen 37:9 (eleven of which bowed down to Joseph's, the twelfth). The word Zodiac means the 'degrees' or 'steps', which mark the stages of the sun's path through the heavens, corresponding with the twelve months. The stars were all named by God (Ps 147:4). They are for signs, Gen 1:14. The whole Bible is written in the stars. God did that so man can not change it. I can not go in deeper about this here for I will digress then.

2 And she being with child cried, travailing in birth, and pained to be delivered.

The child is Christ.

3 And there appeared another wonder in heaven; and behold, a great red dragon, having seven heads and ten horns, and seven crowns upon his heads.

The dragon is of course Satan. He has his power structure with him. That is what heads and horns and crowns mean.

4 And his tail drew the third part of the stars of heaven, and did cast them to the earth: and the dragon stood before the women which was ready to be delivered, for to devour her child as soon as it was born.

We see here that this is happening in the first earth age, at Satan's rebellion, the katabole, at the foundation of the world, this earth age (explained in my chapter Sealing), Ez 28, for Satan took a third of the souls, 'stars', about 4 Billion, with him in his rebellion. In this earth age, Satan, antichrist, is going to have a little different power structure, Rev 13:1, ten in stead of seven crowns. Then we jump right in to the second earth age, the one we have now, when Satan is trying to murder Christ. Herod murdered every child, two years or younger, in trying to get 'The new born King of the Jews' killed. You have read about this in Matt 2 and other places. See also the prophecy in Jer 31:15.

Now we go to Rev 17:

1 And there came one of the seven angels which had the seven vials, and talked with me, saying unto me, 'Come hither; I will shew unto thee the judgment of the great whore that sitteth upon many waters:

The 'whore' is the deceived church. The reason they are called 'whore' is that they believe that Satan, antichrist, is the true Christ. We saw in 2 Thess 2 that Satan is coming before Christ returns. Most Christians don't know that, so when Satan is cast out of heaven into the earth, they think he is Christ and worship him as if he were Christ. That is to be 'whoring', when you, because of ignorance, do not know to wait for the true Bridegroom, Christ. Cp. Mark 13:

17 But woe unto them that are with child, and to them that give suck in those days!

Which means that they are with a sucking child, spiritually, with the wrong husband, Satan, when Christ returns.

Back to Rev 17:

2 With whom the kings of the earth have committed fornication, and the inhabiters of the earth have been made drunk with the wine of her fornication.'

I think this is pretty much self explanatory. Fornication is of course spiritually, and thereby religiously 'drunken'.

3 So he carried me away in the Spirit into the wilderness: and I saw a woman sit upon a scarlet coloured beast, full of names of blasphemy, having seven heads and ten horns.

The wilderness is the confused world, and specifically, with Satan, antichrist, playing God, and with the 'one world order' with the 'four hidden dynasties': religion, education, politics and economics. This is the tool, to deceive the world, of the Kenites, who are the children of Cain, Satan's son from the Garden of Eden. This is the negative part of God's plan. This is how God is testing us, if we really love Him and study His Word enough to know the whole truth and nothing but the truth. If we don't, we fall into the traps of the Kenites, and most people and churches are there, unfortunately. The Scriptures are in fact prophesying this also, Rev 13:3, where it says that *'all the world wondered after the beast'.* The 'beast' here is the 'one world order'. Just one example of many addresses about this.

Again, horns and heads is the political power structure. Blasphemy talks for itself.

4 And the woman was arrayed in purple and scarlet colour, and decked with gold and precious stones and pearls, having a golden cup in her hand full of abominations and filthiness of her fornication:

I mean, she is dressed up like a real whore.

This is talking for itself pretty much. The golden cup is written about also in Jer 51:7.

5 And upon her forehead was a name written, MYSTERY, BABYLON THE GREAT, THE MOTHER OF HARLOTS AND ABOMINATIONS OF THE EARTH.

This verse should be read: 'And upon her forehead (she had) a name written, a secret symbol (musterion), BABYLON THE GREAT, the mother of the harlots and the abominations of the earth'. The name of the woman is therefore a secret sign or symbol of 'that great city' which she personifies (verse 18).
It is talking about the confused, deceived, church in the end times. 'Babylon' means 'confusion'.

6 And I saw the woman drunken with the blood of the saints, and with the blood of the martyrs of Jesus: and when I saw her, I wondered with great admiration.

The 'woman' persecutes the Christians that know the whole truth. Remember, we are talking here about confused Christians persecuting Christians that know the truth. Has it happen yet? Well, it is about there.

'Admiration' here is a poor translation. It shall be 'astonishment'.

7 And the angel said unto me, 'Wherefore didst thou marvel? I will tell thee the mystery of the woman, and of the beast that carried her, which hath the seven heads and ten horns.

Here we can see that Satan and the Kenites' 'one world order' is carrying the 'woman', the 'whore', the confused church, the 'rapture'-people more specifically.

8 The beast that thou sawest was, and is not; and shall ascend out of the bottomless pit, and go into perdition: and they that dwell on the earth shall wonder, whose names were not written in the book of life from the foundation of the world, when they behold the beast that was, and is not, and yet is.

Satan, the beast here, is affiliated with the 'one world order' as we know now. That the beast, Satan, was, and is not, and yet is, means that he is condemned to perish, that's why 'perdition', but still lives and have more to accomplish, until he is cast into the lake of fire, Rev 20, which is the blotting out of him, Ez 28:18-19.

The 'foundation of the world' is the 'katabole', the casting down of Satan in the first earth age, at his rebellion against God, also written about in Ez 28. Read the whole chapter. I have explained this in my chapter called 'Sealing'.

9 And here is the mind that has wisdom. The seven heads are seven mountains, on which the woman sitteth.

Mountains are countries, in this case continents. The 'woman' sits on the whole earth in other words. There are seven continents on this earth.

10 And there are seven kings: five are fallen, and one is, and the other is not yet come; and when he cometh, he must continue a short space.

Five of Satan's roles are fallen, and two are still to come: Antichrist and the testing after the millennium, Rev 20:7-8.

11 And the beast that was, and is not, even he is the eighth, and is of the seven, and goeth into perdition.

Satan has things to accomplish after the millennium, Rev 20:7-8, and this is what 'he is the eighth' means. Then he goes into perdition, Rev 20:10. He is blotted out as never existed. That's what the idioms *'......tormented day and night for ever and ever.'* and *'......bring forth a fire from the midst of thee, it shall devour thee, and I will bring thee to ashes upon the earth......, and never shalt thou be any more'*, Ez 28:18-19, mean.

12 And the ten horns which thou sawest are ten kings, which have received no kingdom as yet; but receive power as kings one hour with the beast.

'Horns' means 'power'. We see here a political power structure that is going to receive power first when Satan is here as antichrist, five months, Rev 9:5,10, = one hour, 'the hour of temptation'.

Cp. Daniel 7:7.

13 These have one mind, and shall give their power and strength unto the beast.

The political system 'one world order' has one mind of course, and they are going to give the 'one world order' to Satan, antichrist, when he is here.

14 These shall make war with the Lamb, and the Lamb shall overcome them: for He is Lord of lords, and King of kings: and they that are with Him are called, and chosen, and faithful.'

They shall try to defeat Christ of course when He returns. That doesn't work, naturally. The called, and chosen, and faithful are the elect, Rom 8:26-33.

15 And he saith unto me, "The waters which thou sawest, where the whore sitteth, are peoples, and multitudes, and nations, and tongues.

The whole world in other words.

Let's now go to what Paul is saying in 2 Cor 11:

1 Would to God ye could bear with me a little in my folly: and indeed bear with me.

2 For I am jealous over you with godly jealousy: for I have espoused you to one husband, that I may present you as a chaste virgin to Christ.

'Espoused' means 'engaged'.
The 'husband' is Christ of course. Paul doesn't want the Corinthians to be deceived, by anybody.

3 But I fear, lest by any means, as the serpent beguiled Eve through his subtlety, so your minds should be corrupted from the simplicity that is in Christ.

'Beguiled' here is the Greek word 'exapataho', which only meaning is 'wholly seduced'.
That's what happened in the Garden of Eden when Satan, the serpent, 'wholly seduced' Eve, and Cain was conceived, from where the Kenites come. Remember that 'Cain' and 'Kenites' is the same word 'Qayin' in the Hebrew Manuscripts. Also remember that 'touch'

in Gen 3:3 is the Hebrew word 'naga', which means 'lie with a women' when it is used in an euphemistic way, which means used as a nicer word than the real one.

4 For if he that cometh preacheth another Jesus, whom we have not preached, or if ye receive another spirit, which ye have not received, or another gospel, which ye have not accepted, ye might well bear with him.

5 For I suppose I was not a whit behind the very chiefest apostles.

6 But though I be rude in speech, yet not in knowledge; but we have been throughly made manifest among you in all things.

12 But what I do, that I will do, that I may cut off occasion from them which desire occasion; that wherein they glory, they may be found even as we.

13 For such are false apostles, deceitful workers, transforming themselves into the apostles of Christ.

14 And no marvel; for Satan himself is transformed into an angel of light.

The word 'transformed' here is a very poor translation. It shall be 'disguised' instead, for it is the Greek word 'metaschematizo'. Satan is going to 'disguise' himself to Christ, five months, just before Christ returns, 2 Thess 2. Antichrist means 'instead of Christ' in the Greek. The same way Satan's preachers 'disguise' themselves, also, to true Christians, but they are false.

15 Therefore it is no great thing if his ministers also be transformed as the ministers of righteousness; whose end shall be according to their works.

We know where they are going if they are aware of what they are doing.

16 I say again, Let no man think me a fool; if otherwise, yet as a fool receive me, that I may boast myself a little.

17 That which I speak, I speak it not after the Lord, but as it were foolishly, in this confidence of boasting.

Now let's continue in Rev 12:

7 And there was war in heaven: Michael and his angels fought against the dragon; and the dragon fought and his angels,

8 And prevailed not, neither was their place found any more in heaven.

9 And the great dragon was cast out, that old serpent, called the Devil and Satan, which deceiveth the whole world: he was cast out into the earth, and his angels were cast out with him.

We see here how Satan is cast out of heaven, by Michael, into the earth. This is when he is going to be here five months, playing Christ, the first tribulation, 2 Thess 2. We also see that *'his angels were cast out with him'.* What angels? The fallen angels, *'the sons of God',* of Gen 6 and Jude 6: they who couldn't wait to be born in the flesh, but came to earth anyway and took *'the daughters'* to wives, and giants were born. That's why the end times, just before Christ returns, is going to be as in the time of Noe (Noah), Gen 6, Matt 24:37-38: *they were…marrying and giving in marriage,* to the fallen angels. That's why a woman shall cover her head, with Christ, the Truth, have power on her head, 1 Cor 11:10, to protect herself from being deceived, wholly seduced, by these angels, 'Nephilim' in the Hebrew tongue.

10 And I heard a loud voice saying in heaven, "Now is come salvation, and strength, and the kingdom of our God, and the power of His Christ: for the accuser of our brethren is cast down, which accused them before our God day and night.

Satan cast down into the earth.

11 And they overcame him by the blood of the Lamb, and by the word of their testimony; and they loved not their lives unto the death.

'They' are the elect, who are overcoming Satan with their testimony, in the way it is written in Mark 13:

9 But take head to yourselves: for they shall deliver you up to councils; and in the synagogues ye shall be beaten: and ye shall be brought before rulers and kings for My sake, for a testimony against them.

10 And the gospel must first be published among all nations.

11 But when they shall lead you, and deliver you up, take no thought beforehand what ye shall speak, neither do ye premeditate: but whatsoever shall be given you in that hour, that speak ye: for it is not ye that speak, but the Holy Ghost (Holy Spirit).

These three verses need to be explained.

The elect, the ones that are sealed in Rev 7:3, are going to be brought up into the synagogues of Satan, cp. Rev 2:9 and 3:9, the deceived, false church, the church that believe in the 'rapture', and that Satan is Christ, 2 Thess 2, and be browbeaten there, while they are witnessing about Christ. They will also be brought up before rulers and kings for the sake of Christ and witness about Him for them.

This is how the Gospel really is going to be spread over the world. Not the way it is done now by evangelists and missionaries and others. It is, as we see in the next verse, through the tongue written in Acts 2. Everybody in the world can understand that tongue in his own home dialect, Acts 2:8, even if only one person is talking. That is the evidence of the presence of the Holy Spirit, when several languages can be heard at the same time from only one person talking.

In Luke 12:10-12 and 21:12-15 we can see the same future event recorded by Luke. See specifically Luke 21:

15 For I will give you a mouth and wisdom, which all your adversaries shall not be able to gainsay nor resist.

See also Luke 12:

10......: but unto him that blasphemeth against the Holy Spirit it shall not be forgiven.

To blaspheme the Holy Spirit, is for the elect to refuse to let the Holy Spirit talk through them, when they are brought up in the synagogues as mentioned above, when Satan is here during the five months, the first tribulation, playing Christ. It has not happened yet and can only be committed by the elect. So only the elect can commit the unforgivable sin. All other sins are forgivable.

The elect will not commit this sin, for they don't love their lives in the flesh enough, *'they loved not their lives unto death'*, to be tempted by Satan, in any way, during this time. Satan is coming......*peaceably*......and...*by flatteries...*, as we know from Dan 11:21, and...*he shall scatter among them the prey, and spoil, and riches:......*, Dan 11:24;......*and he shall destroy wonderfully, and shall prosper,......*, Dan 8:24;......*he shall cause craft to prosper......and by peace shall destroy many:......*, Dan 8:25.

Let's go back now to Rev 12:

12 Therefore rejoice, ye heavens, and ye that dwell in them. Woe to the inhabiters of the earth and of the sea! For the devil is come down unto you, having great wrath, because he knoweth that he hath but a short time."

Satan only has the five months before Christ returns and a little season after the Millennium, Rev 20:3,7.

13 And when the dragon saw that he was cast unto the earth, he persecuted the woman which brought forth the man child.

The woman is Israel with her elect.

14 And to the woman were given two wings of a great eagle, that she might fly into the wilderness into her place, where she is nourished for a time, and times, and half a time, from the face of the serpent.

The 'wilderness' is the world. A time, and times, and half a time, is 3,5 years. This is shortened, Mark 13:20, by Christ, to five months, Rev 9:5,10.

They who have the seal of God in their forehead, Rev 7:3, are protected from being hurt by Satan, during the first, Satan's, tribulation, Rev 9:4.

15 And the serpent cast out of his mouth water as a flood after the woman, that he might cause her to be carried away of the flood.

The flood is a flood of lies, trying to deceive of course, Is 59:

19......When the enemy shall come in like a flood, the spirit of the Lord shall lift up a standard against him.

Remarkable is that this flood, of lies, is as long as Noah's flood.

Back to Rev 12:

16 And the earth helped the woman, and the earth opened her mouth, and swallowed up the flood which the dragon cast out of his mouth.

'The earth opened her mouth, and swallowed up' here is the 'lift up a standard', which is the elect witnessing against Satan as mentioned above: the Holy Spirit talking through the elect.

17 And the dragon was wroth with the woman, and went to make war with the remnant of her seed, which keep the commandments of God, and have the testimony of Jesus Christ.

The dragon is Satan, and I don't think I have to mention that again.

The remnant is the elect, witnessing, giving the testimony of Christ, with the Holy Spirit talking through them as mentioned above.

Now we are going to Mark 13: (same is recorded in Matt 24 and Luke 12 and 21)

14 But when ye shall see the abomination of desolation, spoken of by Daniel the prophet, standing where it ought not, (let him that readeth understand,) then let them that be in Judaea flee to the mountains:

When Christ is saying: 'let him that readeth understand', He is addressing the elect.
'The abomination of desolation' is better translated 'the abominable desolater'. Of this follows that 'it' shall be 'him' instead. Who is 'he'? Satan of course! Do as Christ is saying in this verse, go to Dan 9:

27......and for the overspreading of abominations he shall make it desolate, even until the consummation, and that determined shall be poured upon the desolate.'

This is better translated: on the wings of an eagle, with abominations, Satan, antichrist, the instead of Christ, the little horn in Dan 7:8, 8:9, shall make the Temple of God desolate, defile the sanctuary. *'Until the consummation'* means 'unto a full end'. The reference is Is 10:22-23.
'That determined', which simply is God's plan, *'shall be poured upon'* has to do with the consummation of this earth age. The end, which is part of God's plan, shall take care of Satan, the desolater.

70

Christ takes care of Satan when He returns, as we ought to know at this point.

15 And let him that is on the housetop not go down into the house, neither enter therein, to take any thing out of his house:

16 And let him that is in the field not turn back again to take up his garment.

This is a figure of speech, that it is not much time left of this earth age. It is only five months left.

17 But woe to them that are with child, and to them that give suck in those days!

This doesn't mean literary being with child and give suck, but alludes to that the deceived have jumped in bed with Satan, spiritually, the wrong husband.

18 And pray ye that your flight be not in the winter.

If the 'flight', which is a figure of speech, or an analogy if you wish, is in the winter, it is out of season. Harvest is not in the winter. Therefore it can not be the True Christ, but the false.

19 For in those days shall be affliction, such as was not from the beginning of the creation which God created unto this time, neither shall be.

20 And except that the Lord had shortened those days, no flesh should be saved: but for the elect's sake, whom He has chosen, He hath shortened the days.

It is talking about the first tribulation: see verse 24. We are all going to be here. The so called 'rapture' is a lie, which I have documented from the Scriptures in 'Rapture and more'. In fact this very chapter, Mark 13, is one of the many, many documentations.

It's going to be a rough time, spiritually, because of deception. They, who believe Satan is Christ, are going to have a great revival with Satan. Remember here, that it is not a rough time, physically, but spiritually. As we know from Dan 11:24, Satan is entering peaceably and prosperously, so most people, including the deceived Christians, the 'whore', are going to think they are OK. I mean, they think Christ is here and everything goes well for them: all debts paid off, a chicken in every pot, etc.

They who have the seal of God in their forehead, Rev 7:3, the elect and the very elect, are protected, Rev 9:4-5, from deception. Why? If you know the truth, who can deceive you? No one, of course! But they are going to be persecuted, browbeaten, Mark 13:9.

Here we also see that the Lord has shortened this tribulation, from 3,5 years, 42 months, to 5 months, Rev 9:5,10. That it's going to be a rough time, we can see from, that even the elect would be deceived if the time was not shortened: see verse 22. We know from other scripture that the very elect will not fall away, but the elect will, for a little while, and then come back again to the truth, during the five months tribulation. A subject for an other time.

Remember, that as long as You have a flesh body, Christ is not here. We are changed to our celestial, heavenly, body when Christ returns, 1 Cor 15:40, 52, 1 Thess 4:17, both the just and the unjust people, Acts 24:15.

21 And then if any man shall say to you, 'Lo, here is Christ;' or, 'lo, He is here;' believe him not:

22 For false Christs and false prophets shall rise, and shall shew signs and wonders, to seduce, if it were possible, even the elect.

Antichrist, Satan, is coming, and 'all the world', Rev 13:3, are going to think it is Christ, Messiah.

We have to be careful so we are not deceived by false teachers. There are lots of them today. Many people, because they are Biblically illiterate don't see that: I would say most people, for the Scriptures say so, Rev 13:3, and I can witness to it from my own little life experience. Cp. 2 Pet 3:2-3 and many other places.

23 But take ye heed: behold, I have foretold you all things.

We have to study the Scriptures in depth, so we are not deceived. We are foretold everything there. Don't listen to any man, including this one: me. I could be wrong, but I hope not. Check every teacher out, carefully.

24 But in those days, after that tribulation, the sun shall be darkened, and the moon shall not give her light,

25 And the stars of heaven shall fall, and the powers that are in heaven shall be shaken.

26 And then shall they see the Son of man coming in the clouds with great power and glory.

Here we see that after the first tribulation, the Son of man (Quoted from Dan 7:13, cp. Joel 2:31; this title, when used of Christ, always has the Article; and the word for man is 'anthropos'), which is Christ of course, is coming. This is the second tribulation: a very short period in the very beginning of the Second Advent. This is the real rough time for those who thought Christ was here already, when they see the true Christ coming. A lot of disappointments I think, Rev 6:

15 And the king s of the earth, and the great men, and the rich men, and the chief captains, and the mighty men, and every bondman, and every free man, hid themselves in the dens and in the rocks of the mountains;

16 And said to the mountains and rocks, 'Fall on us, and hide us from the face of Him That sitteth on the throne, and from the wrath of the Lamb:

17 For the great day of His wrath is come; and who shall be able to stand?

The elect will stand. For others: 'there shall be weeping and gnashing of teeth', Matt 24:51. Now back to Mark 13:

27 And then shall he send His angels, and shall gather together His elect from the four winds, from the uttermost part of the earth to the uttermost part of the heaven.

Self explanatory.

28 Now learn a parable of the fig tree: When her branch is yet tender, and putteth forth leaves, ye know that summer is near:

The 'parable of the fig tree' is from Jer 24. It is about how Judah (Judah and Benjamin, not the other ten tribes, Israel; for they are split now from Judah, see 1 Kings 11:28, 31-32, 12:19, 2 Kings 17:23, 19:32. They join again when Christ returns, Ez 37:15-28) returns when Israel becomes a nation again, which happened May 1948. With Judah returns also the false Jews, the Kenites, the bad figs. Read Jer 24. Christ just told you to learn it.

29 So ye in like manner, when ye shall see these things come to pass, know that it is nigh, even at the doors.

So when we see these things happening, we know that the Second Advent is near.

30 Verily I say unto you, that this generation shall not pass, till all these things be done.

In the generation of the fig tree, in the generation when Israel became a nation again, all these things are going to happen, including Christ's return. How long time is that? Well! The Scriptures have three different time spans for a generation: 40, 70 or 120 years. Within these time spans Christ is back; 40 has already past: that was 1988, so it is either before 2018 or 2068.

Conclusion:

This is one way to document antichrist. He is mentioned so many places in the Old Testament, it would take a much longer chapter, than this, to document all that. I might do it some time. If you look at Satan's names below, you may with a Strong's Concordance find the places, through the whole Bible, where Satan is addressed, and that way you can make your own study.

Satan has many names, or 'offices' if you will:

little horn = a horn of small beginnings; this identifies the vision with those of Dan 8,9,11,12. The first of twelve titles given to the power commonly known as 'the Antichrist': it is used again in Dan 8:9; Cp. Dan 11:21-30.

Note the other titles:

'the king of Babylon', Is 14:4; 'the Assyrian', Is 14:25; 'Lucifer, son of the morning', in opposition to 'the bright and morning star', Is 14:12; 'the Prince that shall come', Dan 9:26; 'the king of fierce countenance', Dan 8:23; 'the vile person', Dan 11:21; 'the willful king', Dan 11:36; 'the man of sin', 2 Thess 2:3; 'the son of perdition', 2 Thess 2:3; 'that wicked (or lawless) one', 2 Thess 2:8, Rev 13:18;

More names for Satan:

'the Devil', 'that old serpent', 'the great dragon', Rev 12:9, Gen 3:1; 'the tree of knowledge of good and evil', Gen 2:17; 'beast with two horns like a lamb', Rev 13:11; 'king, the angel of the bottomless pit', 'Abaddon', and 'Apollyon', Rev 9:11; '666 is his number, for he appears in the sixth seal, sixth trump and the sixth vial', Rev 13:18, 'false prophet', Rev 19:20; 'the beast that was, and is not, and yet is', Rev 17:8; 'the eighth' and 'of the seven', Rev 17:11; King of Babylon the type in Daniel; desolater (in the Manuscriptes), KJV = the abomination of desolation, Mark 13:14; destroyer, 1 Cor 10:10; father, one of them in Malachi 4:6, the other One is YHVH, God.

I have left some of them out, but you can find them in the Scriptures.

Chapter V

Three World Ages

Peter is in his 2:nd epistle saying in chapter 3:

5 For this they willingly are ignorant of, that by the word of God the heavens were of old (Gr. Ekpalai=in time past through the idea of retrocession, to cede or give back territory, again, ancient), *and the earth standing out of the water and in the water:*

6 Whereby the world that then was (1:st earth age), *being overflowed with water, perished:*

'Perished' is not by the flood of Noah for perished is the Gr. 'apollumi' which means destroy fully. At Noah's flood the world, or earth, was not destroyed fully which is the same root as in 'son of perdition', cp. 2 Thess 2, where the Gr. Scriptures use 'apoleia' for 'perdition'.

7 But the heavens and the earth which are now (=2:nd world age=2:nd heaven and earth age), *by the same word are kept in store, reserved unto fire* (Hebr 12:29) *against the day of judgment and perdition of ungodly men.*

Let us go to Jer 4:

23 I beheld the earth, and, lo, it was (Hebr. 'hayah'='became', in this case) *without form, and void* (tuhu va bohu); *and the heavens, and they had no light.* See now what happened after this, Gen 1:2......*and darkness was upon the face of the deep* and Gen 1:3 *And God said, 'Let there be light:'......).*

There was light all the time during and after Noah's flood, so this is not Noah's flood, but the katabole.

24 I beheld the mountains, and, lo, they trembled, and all the hills moved lightly.

The hills didn't move and the mountains didn't tremble at Noah's flood. They were only covered with water, so this is not Noah's flood but the katabole.

25 I beheld, and, lo, there was no man, and all the birds of the heavens were fled.

There were birds and men left at Noah's flood; on the ark, Noah himself for example: cp. Gen 8:11.

26 **I beheld, and, lo, the fruitful place was** (Hebr. 'hayah'='became', in this case) **a wilderness, and all the cities thereof were broken down at the presence of the Lord, and by His fierce anger.**

Yes, there were cities in the first earth age. Cities were not broken down at Noah's flood. They were just covered with water a few months.

27 **For thus hath the Lord said, "The whole land shall be desolate: yet will I not make a full end.**

The land was not desolate after Noah's flood as you see in other places in this chapter.

An interesting fact is that the flood is mentioned in the Chinese History books. Noah's flood was not necessarily world wide, but could have been limited to a certain area, where the fallen angels, Gen 6, operated, wholly seducing the Adamic people, by order from Satan of course, trying to destroy the lineage from where Christ was going to be born. Just like Satan tried in the Garden with Eve. That was the whole purpose with the flood, to destroy the fruit of this mixing.

Let us take some more references: Is 45:

18 For thus saith the Lord That created the heavens; God Himself That formed the earth and made it: He hath established it, He created it not in vain (tuhu), *He formed it to be inhabited: "I am the Lord; and there is none else.*

God didn't form the earth 'without form and void', 'tohu va bohu' in the Hebrew. God created the earth perfect, *to be inhabited.* It became 'tohu va bohu' at Satan's overthrow = the 'katabole' in the first earth age, Ez 28. God destroyed the first earth age.

Gen 1:

1 In the beginning God created the heaven and the earth.

That was millions of years ago. Science has proved that enough, so it is true.

2 And the earth was (Hebr. 'hayah'='became', in this case, at the overthrow of Satan=the katabole) *without form, and void* (tohu va bohu); *and darkness was upon the face of the deep.*

You see that the same word 'tuhu' is used in both Is 45:18 (vain) and Gen 1:2 (without form). There would be a contradiction here if 'hayah' in this case is not translated 'became'. Do you see that? The world can not be <u>not</u> 'tuhu' and 'tohu' at the same time.
Gen 8:

11 And the dove came in to him in the evening; and, lo, in her mouth was an olive leaf pluckt off: so Noah knew that the waters were abated from off the earth.

The dove came back with an olive leaf, which shows that this is not what it is talking about in Jer 4, where the whole land was desolate. An olive tree can not grow a leaf in days as was the time available here at the flood, if the land is desolate. It takes months or even years. There were no birds like here in Jer 4 either, and ***there was no man.*** That means that Jer 4 is not talking about Noah's flood but about the situation at the overthrow of Satan, which was before the foundation of this earth age, which begins in Gen 1:3. All the cities were broken down also. Ps 104 has this recorded too, where it says in verse

7 At Thy rebuke they fled; At the voice of Thy thunder they hasted (this is direct; the flood took several months) ***away.***

2 Pet 3:

1 This second epistle, beloved, I now write unto you: in both which I stir up your pure minds by way of remembrance (this is talking about the minds of the elect and reminding them about what happened in the first earth age);

The elect are people (souls) that stood up for God in the first earth age, when Satan rebelled and was overthrown, which is the katabole, which was before the foundation of this earth age, the age in which we live in a flesh body, Gen 1:

26 And God said, "Let Us (God and the souls=we) ***make man*** (adam=man kind=flesh man) ***in our image, after Our likeness:......***

28......"Be fruitful, and multiply, and replenish the earth,......

Why <u>re</u>plenish? Because we lived here before, in the first earth age, but not in flesh as now. See Gen 6:

3 And the Lord said, "My spirit shall not always strive with man (Adam, with article), ***for that he also*** (the animals were flesh in the first earth age, but not we) ***is flesh:......***

When Christ returns and the millennium starts, we are back into a spiritual, or celestial, body again.

79

6 *And it repented the Lord that He had made man on earth,......*

'Man on earth' means 'flesh man', cp. the expression 'under the sun' in the book of Ecclesiastes.

Eph 1:

4 *According as He hath chosen us* (the elect) ***in him before the foundation*** (Gr. katabole, from kataballo=throw down, from Gr. kata=down and Gr. ballo=throw; this is the overthrow of Satan in the first earth age before this earth age, Ez 28, which was before the 'foundation' of the present earth age) ***of the world, that we should be holy and without blame before Him in love:***

Some of the souls stood up for God in the first earth age against Satan at his rebellion and were rewarded by being chosen by God, for God can trust them; they earned it. These are the elect.

5 *Having predestinated us unto the adoption of children by Jesus Christ to Himself,*

Rom 8:

28 *And we know that all things work together for good to them that love God, to them who are the called according to His purpose.*

29 *For whom He did forknow* (from the first earth age)***, he also did predestinate to be conformed to the image of His Son, that He might be the firstborn among many brethren.***

30 *Moreover whom He did predestinate, them He also called: and whom He called, them He also justified* (cp. Rev 20:6 'they' = the elect, who take part in the first resurrection: on such the second death hath no power): ***and whom He justified, them He also glorified.***

33 *Who shall lay anything to the charge of God's elect? It is God That justifieth.*

Rev 19:

7 *Let us be glad and rejoice, and give honour to Him: for the marriage of the Lamb is come, and His wife* (not the bride here because it is talking about the elect) ***hath made herself ready."***

The elect were already 'married' to Christ, spiritually of course, in the first earth age, while the rest of the Christians are still a bride.

The reason God created the flesh man, us, living in flesh in this second earth age, was that He didn't want to destroy a third of His children, the third of the stars (souls) that followed Satan at his rebellion, Rev 12:4. He destroyed the first earth age instead, as explained above, and let us be born through woman (born from above, commonly called 'born again', and mostly misunderstood), through the water in the womb, innocent, that will say the memory from the first earth age erased (otherwise we wouldn't be innocent), cp. 2 Pet 3:1, to make our choice between God and Satan in this earth age, the second earth age. When Christ returns this second earth age is finished, and the third and the last begins, and we are not going to be in a flesh (terrestrial) body any more but in a spiritual (celestial) body. We are changed, cp. 1 Cor 15:51-52 and 1 Thess 4:17. Observe that the word <u>air</u> in 1 Thess 4:17 is the Greek word <u>aer</u> from <u>aemi = spirit, the breath of life,</u> and <u>not</u> the Greek word <u>ouranos = sky,</u> cp. Ez 13:17-20. This has to do with the 'rapture theory', which is a deception, and is a subject for an other time.

The beginning of the third and last earth age is the thousand year period, the millennium, see Rev 20. During the millennium are more people going to be saved than ever before. The reason is that most people are deceived now, cp. Rev 13:3, where it says that......***all the world wondered after the beast.*** This beast is the 'one world system or order', which is Satan's (the second beast in the same chapter, Rev 13:11) system for deception, set up for him by the Kenites = his sons, before he is booted out on earth, Rev 12:9.

Also, observe 'behemoth' – 'dinosaurs (and brontosaurs)' in Job 40:15-17 ***He moveth his tale like a cedar:......***They lived in the first earth age, long before we became men in flesh. We existed but in a celestial body. The earth's axis was 'straight up' at that time. When God destroyed the first earth age at the katabole, God moved the axis to a leaning position. The temperature fell drastically, where the dinosaurs were, because of it, and they became deep frozen in a hurry. The geographical poles are today 90 miles off the magnetic poles for this reason, and we have ice in the polar areas, and we have changes of seasons in this earth age. The scientists' (who dug the dinosaurs up from the tundra) dogs could eat the flesh of the dinosaurs after cooking it, so well was the meat preserved in the frozen tundra. When the dinosaurs lived on the tundra, in the first earth age, the climate was much warmer on that latitude. There was no ice. Therefore they found buttercups in the dinosaurs' mouths. There could be additional reasons for the dramatic fall of temperature at the katabole. For example, if a big meteor plunged into the earth, a lot of dust and more would have been stirred up, and would have prohibited the rays from the sun to reach the earth for a while.

We read in Jer 4:

23 I beheld the earth, and, lo, it was without form, and void; and the heavens, and they had no light.

28 For this reason shall the earth mourn, and the heavens above be black:......

29 The whole city shall flee for the noise of the horsemen and bowmen; they shall go into thickets,......

'Bowmen' is the Hebrew 'ramah', which means 'to hurt, to shoot, to delude or betray (as if causing to fall), beguile, deceive, throw.' Satan does all that. 'Thickets', is 'thick cloud', of dust, or of whatever, including deception. This is of course a type for the end times with Antichrist, cp. Rev 6:2, where we have......*a white horse: and he that sat on him had a bow;......*

The 'bow' here is the Greek 'toxon', which is a cheap imitation of the simplest fabric, symbolizing false glory, which shows it is talking about Antichrist, Satan, on the horse, and not Jesus as in Rev 19:11 with His Shekinah Glory. Satan is a copy cat and loves to disguise himself to Christ and be worshipped, 2 Cor 11:14, where 'transformed' should have been translated 'disguised', for it is 'metaschematizo' in the Greek text.

We know about the darkness, Rev 9:2......*there arose a smoke out of the pit, as the smoke of a great furnace; and the sun and the air were darkened by reason of the smoke......*, that will say the deception, and the *flood* of lies in the end times of this present, the second, earth age by Satan and his people, Rev 12:15......*the serpent cast out of his mouth water as a flood......that he might cause......to be carried away of the flood,* and 16 *And the earth helped......and the earth opened her mouth, and swallowed up the flood which the dragon cast out of his mouth.* We see here how within the Scriptures are woven ensamples, 1 Cor 10:11. Here is the change between the first and the second earth ages woven with the change between the second and the third (the approaching) earth ages.

Now, when the dust, we talked about, successively settled onto the earth, the ice that had frozen under it, on a large part of the earth, melted and created the first flood, 2 Pet 3:6, which was <u>not</u> Noah's flood, see above. The ice in the tundra didn't melt though, because of the leaning axis of the earth and consequential seasons.

There are of course more references in the Bible for the three earth ages.

Remember that God always works in natural ways, he uses the elements, because He is super natural, which means He is more natural than we are.

Chapter VI

The Four Hidden Dynasties

The Four Hidden Dynasties are: Religion, Education, Politics, and the Economy. Dynasty is a rule that a family holds. What a family do we have here? Satan's, through his children the Kenites. Let's see what the Bible has to say about this.

Ezekiel 22:

23 And the word of the Lord came unto me, saying,

'Me' is Ezekiel.

24 'Son of man, say unto her, 'Thou are the land that is not cleansed, nor rained upon in the day of indignation.'

'Her' is Jerusalem. This is a type for the countries where the 12 tribes live and rule today, basically western Europe and the Americas, USA and Canada. The latter rain, the word of God in the end times, is not falling on her. It is a famine for hearing the Word, Amos 8:11-13.

25 There is a conspiracy of her prophets in the midst thereof, like a roaring lion ravening the prey; they have devoured souls; they have taken the treasure and precious things; they have made her many widows in the midst thereof.

'Prophets' here are 'false Bible teachers'. 'Widows' because they don't understand, that Antichrist is Satan coming first, five months, playing Christ, 2 Thess 2, so they believe that he is Christ.

26 Her priests have violated My law, and have profaned Mine holy things: they have put no difference between the holy and profane, neither have they shewed difference between the unclean and the clean, and have hid their eyes from My sabbaths, and I am profaned among them.

First we have the priests, so we have the church, the Religious Dynasty. Think about Easter for example, which has nothing to do with Passover. Easter is a heathen festival concerning sexual orgies. Passover was mistranslated one time in the King James, done by a false scribe, and all churches, almost, celebrates Easter in stead of Passover, with symbols of fertility rites, eggs, and everything, and mixing it with Christ. Isn't that strange so what?

27 Her princes in the midst thereof are like wolves ravening the prey, to shed blood, and to destroy souls, to get dishonest gain.

Second we have the princes=the Government=the Political Dynasty.

28 And her prophets have daubed them with untempered mortar, seeing vanity, and divining lies unto them, saying, 'Thus saith the Lord God,' when the Lord has not spoken.

The priests are lying about God talking with them.

29 The People of the land have used oppression, and exercised robbery, and have vexed the poor and needy: yea, they have oppressed the stranger wrongfully.

Here we have the ripping off, financially, of as many as possible, the Economical Dynasty. Look at credit cards, for example, with interest of 24%, and how much is interest, and how much is principal when you pay off your house? We have the International Monetary Fund, IMF, and how they rip Governments off with usury etc., lending money to them, that the Government, we, gave them in the first place.

30 And I sought for a man among them, that should make up the hedge, and stand in the gap before Me for the land, that I should not destroy it: but I found none.

31 Therefore have I poured out Mine indignation upon them: I have consumed them with the fire of My wrath: their own way have I recompensed upon their heads, saith the Lord God.

Let's go to Daniel 1:

3 And the king spake unto Ashpenaz the master of his eunuchs, that he should bring certain of the children of Israel, and of the king's seed, and of the princes;

4 Children in whom was no blemish, but well favoured, and skillful in all wisdom, and cunning in knowledge, and understanding science, and such as had ability in them to stand in the king's palace, and whom they might teach the learning and the tongue of the Chaldeans.

Here we have the Hidden Dynasty of Education in process, when Daniel and his friends were in captivity school in Babylon. Now to Deuteronomy 28:

48 Therefore shalt thou serve thine enemies which the Lord shall send against thee, in hunger, and in thirst, and in nakedness, and in want of all things: and he shall put a yoke of iron upon thy neck, until he have destroyed thee.

49 The Lord shall bring a nation against thee from far, from the end of the earth, a swift as the eagle flieth; a nation whose tongue thou shalt not understand;
The 'nation' are the Kenites.

50 A nation of fierce countenance, which shall not regard the person of the old, nor shew favour to the young:

51 And he shall eat the fruit of thy cattle, and the fruit of thy land, until thou be destroyed: which also shall not leave thee either corn, wine, or oil, or the increase of thy kine, or flocks of thy sheep, until he have destroyed thee.

Here we see how God is letting the evil, in fact the Kenites in large part, punish us if we do not obey God. He is using this to wake us up, and the ultimate wake up call will be when Christ returns, and all the world, as it is written in Revelation 13:3, have worshipped the 'beast' = the One World System or Order, and Antichrist, Satan, for five month. Read what is going to happen then in Revelation 6:

15 And the kings of the earth and the great men, and the rich men, and the chief captains, and the mighty men, and every bondsman, and every free man, hid themselves in the dens and in the rocks of the mountains;

16 And said to the mountains and rocks, 'Fall on us, and hide us from the face of Him That sitteth on the throne, and from the wrath of the Lamb:

17 For the great day of His wrath is come; and who shall be able to stand.

Only the ones that know the truth are going to be able to stand. Cp. Ephesians 6:

13 Wherefore take unto you the whole armour of God, that ye may be able to withstand in the evil day, and having done all, to stand.

14 Stand therefore, having your loins girt about with truth, and having on the breastplate of righteousness;

15 And your feet shod with the preparation of the gospel of peace;

16 Above all, taking the shield of faith, wherewith ye shall be able to quench all the fiery darts of the wicked.

17 And take the helmet of salvation, and the sword of the Spirit, which is the word of God:

18 Praying always with all prayer and supplication in the Spirit, and watching thereunto with all perseverance and supplication for all saints.

You can't go around deceiving or ripping people off if you do this. The understanding of the word of God is the best protection against the Four Hidden Dynasties. If you know the truth you can't be deceived.

Now to Zechariah 1:

18 Then lifted I up mine eyes, and saw, and behold four horns.

Horn means power. These horns are the Kenites power of the 'Four Hidden Dynasties'. The Kenites are the sons of Cain, who is the son of Satan and Eve from the Garden of Eden, Genesis 3 and 4. The Hebrew Manuscripts has the same word for Cain and Kenites, 'Qayin'. See my chapters about this, Antichrist Documented, Rapture And More, and The Beginning Of This Earth age etc.

19 And I said unto the angel that talked with me, 'What be these?' And he answered me, 'These are the horns which have scattered Judah, Israel, and Jerusalem.'

God allowed the rulers of this world, this way to scatter, or confuse, Judah and Israel, because they disobeyed God's word. The same thing happens to us if we disobey God's word. We are going to be confused, or as it says in 2 Thessalonians 2:

10 And with all deceivableness of unrighteousness in them that perish; because they received not the love of the truth, that they might be saved.

11 And for this cause God shall send them strong delusion, that they should believe a lie:

Is God sending strong delusion, that will say false teachers to teach us, if we don't want to seek the truth, or better as it says in the Word, if we don't love the truth? Yes.

Back to Zechariah 1:

20 And the Lord shewed me four carpenters.

'Carpenters' here is actually 'blacksmiths', and they represent God's 'elect'.

21 Then said I, 'What come these to do?' And he spake, saying, 'These are the horns which have scattered Judah, so that no man did lift up his head: but these are come to fray them, to cast out the horns of the Gentiles, which lifted up their horn over the land of Judah to scatter it.'

The first 'these……horns' are the Four Hidden Dynasties. The second 'these' are the blacksmiths = the elect. 'Fray' is a short form of 'affray' = terrify.

Well, we know that the ten northern tribes = Israel were scattered around 600 BC and Judah and Benjamin 200 years later, but this is what is happening also now in a spiritual sense through deception, which leads to confusion. Now Revelation 6:

8 And I looked, and behold, a pale horse: and his name that sat on him was Death, and Hell followed with him. And power was given them over the fourth part of the earth, to kill with sword, and with hunger, and with death, and with the beasts of the earth.

Who is death? One guess! Satan of course, and in this case in the office of Antichrist. Beasts of the earth are different deception tools belonging to the Four Hidden Dynasties.

Here we see how God is giving power to the Kenites, 'them', to deceive with words = 'kill with sword' them who don't love the truth enough to study God's Word. If you know the Word, you can not be deceived. No one can 'kill' you spiritually. This is part of the conspiracy between God's children and Satan's children. It is there for a test for us, so God can learn to know us, if we stand up for Him, and if we 'deserve' to have eternal life, that will say to live with God for ever. God won't allow any 'crooks' in the eternity. We all fall short, but repentance through Christ makes us not guilty. If we do not believe that, we will not be excepted.

Now to Zechariah 4:

7 Who art thou, O great mountain? before Zerubbabel thou shalt become a plain: and he shall bring forth the headstone thereof with shoutings, crying, 'Grace, grace unto it.'

The 'great mountain' is the Kenites and their Four Hidden Dynasties. We have power over them though, Matthew 21:

21 Jesus answered and said unto them, 'verily I say unto you, If ye have faith, and doubt not, ye shall not only do this which is done to the fig tree, but also if ye shall say unto this mountain, 'Be thou removed, and be thou cast into the sea; 'it shall be done.

The 'mountain' here is not a literal mountain but the Kenites. Mountain means 'nation', and the Kenites are called a 'nation' in the Scriptures, see above. Now Luke 10:

19 Behold, I give unto you power to tread on serpents and scorpions, and over all the power of the enemy: and nothing shall by any means hurt you.

Christ is saying, that he has given us power over all our enemies.

Revelation 9:

4 And it was commanded them that they should not hurt the grass of the earth, neither any green thing, neither any tree; but only those men which have not the seal of God in their forehead.

This is when Satan and his lieutenants are here trying to deceive people. If You know the truth, written in next verse Rev 7:3, you can not be deceived. We see they are people for they are not supposed to hurt grass, trees, and any green thing. Locust do, but not Satan's children. We can see in Rev 9:8 that they had hair as the hair of women, and their teeth were as the teeth of lions. They are people all right. Hair of women because they behave, outwardly, gentle like women, but they rip and tare like lions, spiritually = deceive.

Revelation 7:

3 Saying, 'Hurt not the earth, neither the sea, nor the trees, till we have sealed the servants of our God in their foreheads.

Here we see how God wants to seal the truth in the foreheads of his servants before the deception is coming, by Satan, in Revelation chapter 9.

Let's go to Luke 1:

68 "Blessed be the Lord God of Israel; for He hath visited and redeemed his people,

69 And hath raised up an horn of salvation for us in the house of His servant David;

70 As He spake by the mouth of His holy prophets, which have been since the world began:

71 That we should be saved from our enemies, and from the hand of all that hate us;

72 To perform the mercy promised to our fathers, and to remember His holy covenant;

73 The oath which He sware to our father Abraham,

74 That He would grant unto us, that we being delivered out of the hand of our enemies might serve Him without fear.

75 In holiness and righteousness before Him, all the days of our life.

76 And thou, child, shalt be called the prophet of the Highest: for thou shalt go before the face of the Lord to prepare His ways;

We have here Zacharias, filled with the Holy Spirit, talking to his son John the Baptist.

77 To give knowledge of salvation unto His people by the remission of their sins,

78 Through the tender mercy of our God; whereby the dayspring from on high hath visited us,

The only way to stand against the deception from Satan and his lieutenants is to obey God, and study his Word with understanding. It is not enough just to believe, more than for salvation, and that is wonderful, but the Scriptures say, *My people are destroyed for lack of knowledge,* and *wisdom and knowledge shall be the stability of the times,* Hosea 4:6 and Isaiah 33:6.

Rev 17:

12 And the ten horns which thou sawest are ten kings, which have received no kingdom as yet; but receive power as kings one hour with the beast.

Here we see the Political Dynasty. Read on:

13 These have one mind, and shall give their power and strength unto the beast.

They have 'one' mind because they are the 'One' World System or Order, and they give the system to Satan, Antichrist, when he comes here five months playing Christ just before the true Christ returns. It is called the first tribulation, or 'the our of temptation' if you will, and called 'one hour' in verse 12 above.

14 These shall make war with the lamb, and the Lamb shall overcome them: for He is Lord of lords, and King of kings: and they that are with Him are called, and chosen, and faithful.'

The Lamb is Christ, of course. The chosen and called are the elect.

15 And he saith unto me, 'The waters which thou sawest, where the whore sitteth, are peoples, and multitudes, and nations, and tongues.

The whore is the deceived, Biblically illiterate, Christian church. Most churches are Biblically illiterate, and they 'sit' on the population of the world.

16 And the ten horns which thou sawest upon the beast, these shall hate the whore, and shall make her desolate and naked, and shall eat her flesh, and burn her with fire.

The One World Order hates the church and rips her off spiritually.

17 For God hath put in their hearts to fulfill His will, and to agree, and give their kingdom unto the beast, until the words of God shall be fulfilled.

The One World Order is given to Antichrist.

18 And the woman which thou sawest is that great city, which reigneth over the kings of the earth.'

At this time Antichrist is in Jerusalem playing Christ, so Jerusalem is the leading city in the world.

Daniel 8:

23 And in the latter time of their kingdom, when the transgressors are come to the full, a king of fierce countenance, and understanding dark sentences shall stand up

The king is Antichrist, Satan, the son of perdition naturally.

24 And his power shall be mighty, but not by his own power: and he shall destroy wonderfully, and shall prosper, and practice, and shall destroy the mighty and the holy People.

'Destroy' is not 'kill'.

Satan has no power of his own. God gives him the power. He is going to be flattering, paying everybody's debts etc., if you worship him. He wants to be worshipped as God. He is beautiful and prideful, see Ezekiel 28:12, 17. Satan is not coming to kill people, but to deceive, trying to get as many as he can with him to 'hell'. He is basically God's tool to test us, to find out if we love God or Satan. Make the right choice.

25 And through his policy also he shall cause craft to prosper in his hand; and he shall magnify himself in his heart, and by peace shall destroy many: he shall also stand up against the Prince of princes; but he shall be broken without hand.

The One World System and Antichrist are coming in very prosperous, and they are going to deceive many through their policy of peace, but it's not real peace, and thereby destroy, deceive, many spiritually, and lead them away from the truth, so they think Antichrist is the true Christ. Antichrist shall be broken by Christ with out hand, see 2 Thessalonians 2:

8 And then shall the wicked be revealed, whom the Lord shall consume with the spirit of His mouth, and shall destroy with the brightness of His coming:

No hand involved.

Back to Daniel 8:

26 And the vision of the evening and the morning which was told is true: wherefore shut thou up the vision; for it shall be for many days.

'Many days' means it is going to happen in the latter days = end times, which is now, this generation, the generation of the fig tree, Mark 13:28 and Jeremiah 24, the generation of 1948, when Israel became a nation again.

We just studied the Hidden Dynasty of the Economy in these verses, and more we have in

Daniel 11:

21 And in his estate shall stand up a vile person, to whom they shall not give the honour of the kingdom: but he shall come in peaceably, and obtain the kingdom by flatteries.

Satan, in the office of Antichrist, is not going to kill people. He is coming to 'save' people to 'hell'.

Here we see again how Antichrist, Satan, is going to act during the five months he is here, see Revelation 9.

22 And with the arms of a flood shall they be overflown from before him, and shall be broken; yea, also the prince of the covenant.

This is the flood of lies from Satan, Revelation 12:15.

23 And after the league made with him he shall work deceitfully: for he shall come up, and shall become strong with a small people.

The 'small people' are the Kenites, Cain's children, Satan's children from the Garden of Eden.

24 He shall enter peaceably even upon the fattest places of the province; and he shall do that which his fathers have not done, nor his fathers' fathers; he shall scatter among them the prey, and spoil, and riches: yea, and he shall forecast his devices against the strong holds, even for a time.

Satan is going to do everything he can to deceive, 'save' as many as he can to 'hell'. 'For a time' = 'five months', Revelation 9:5, 10.

32 And such as do wickedly against the covenant shall he corrupt by flatteries: but the people that do know their God shall be strong, and do exploits.

They who know the Word are going to win people over for the kingdom of God, but they who don't, Satan is going to win over to himself, with flatteries.

Revelation 13:

11 And I beheld another beast coming up out of the earth; and he had two horns like a lamb, and he spake as a dragon.

This is Satan playing Christ. He looks like the Lamb, Christ, but he is deceiving people. This is the Hidden Dynasty of Religion.

12 And he exerciseth all the power of the first beast before him, and causeth the earth and them which dwell therein to worship the first beast, whose deadly wound was healed.

'The first beast' is the One World Order or System, from verse 3 in the same chapter.

13 And he doeth great wonders, so that he maketh fire come down from heaven on the earth in the sight of men.

Satan is going to have a lot of 'sideshows', and that way try to convince people that he is Christ.

14 And deceiveth them that dwell on the earth by the means of those miracles which he had power to do in the sight of the beast: saying to them that dwell on the earth, that they should make an image to the beast, which had the wound by a sword and do live.

15 And he had power to give life unto the image of the beast, that the image of the beast should both speak, and cause that as many as would not worship the image of the beast should be killed.

'Killed' doesn't mean physically, but spiritually.

16 And he causeth all, both small and great, rich and poor, free and bond, to receive a mark in their right hand, or in their foreheads:

This 'mark of the beast' is an idiom, and means that people are deceived in their mind, in their forehead, as to who is the true or false Christ. They who have 'the mark of the beast' believe that Satan, Antichrist, is the true Christ. They will work for Antichrist, which is to have the mark in the right hand. They are in other words Biblically illiterate. They can't discern the difference.

17 And that no man might buy or sell save he that had the mark, or the name of the beast, or the number of his name.

This problem I believe is only going to last for ten days for they who are lacking the mark, that will say know the truth. The reason is what is written in Revelation 2:

10 Fear none of those things which thou shalt suffer: behold, the devil shall cast some of you into prison, that ye may be tried; and ye shall have tribulation ten days: be thou faithful unto death, and I will give thee a crown of life.

Back to Revelation 13:

18 Here is wisdom, Let him that hath understanding count the number of the beast: for it is the number of a man; and his number is Six hundred threescore and six.

The word 'count' here is a very interesting word. It is the Greek word 'psephizo' = to use pebbles in enumeration, i.e. to compute. The word is from the word 'psephos' = a pebble (as worn smooth by handling), i.e. (by impl. of use as a counter or ballot) a verdict (of acquittal) or ticket (of admission); a vote. This word comes from the word 'pselaphao' = to manipulate, i.e. verify by contact; fig. to search for. What it means is that we have to search for the beast, who he is, from the beginning of time, and then find, that he is the serpent and the tree of the knowledge of good and evil (Gen 2 and 3), and the king and prince of Tyrus and the covering cherub (Ez 28), and Satan, and the Devil, and the dragon, etc., etc. He has many, many, many names. I made a little inventory in Antichrist Documented.

The reason the number is 666 is that Satan appears in the 6th Seal, the 6th Trump, and the 6th Vial.

I am going to end with Psalms 43:

1 Judge me, O God, and plead my cause against an ungodly nation: O deliver me from the deceitful and unjust man.

'An ungodly nation' here is the 'one world order', and 'the deceitful and unjust man' is of course Satan himself.

Luke 10:

17 And the seventy returned again with joy, saying, 'Lord, even the devils are subject unto us through Thy name.'

18 And He said unto them, 'I beheld Satan as lightning fall from heaven.

See Revelation 12:9 where Satan and his angels are cast out of heaven into the earth.

19 Behold, I give unto you power to tread on serpents and scorpions, and over all the power of the enemy: and nothing shall by any means hurt you.

Observe it says 'over all the power of the enemy' and 'nothing shall by any means hurt you'. It means that if you know the truth, if you have the seal of God, see below, nothing, or nobody, can deceive you, for it is all about deception in the end times. Not physical violence. You also have all other kind of power over your enemy through prayer and actions in the name of Jesus, if you believe it, not otherwise.

Consequently, this doesn't mean serpents and scorpions literary, but is a figure of speech. Serpents and scorpions don't read the Bible, so if you tread on them, they will bite you. Be careful.

One of Satan's names is 'the serpent', and it is alluding to him here. Locusts like scorpions we have in Revelation 9, and they are Satan's guys. Revelation 9:

7......their faces were as the faces of men.

because they are men. Revelation 9:

4 And it was commanded them that they should not hurt the grass of the earth, neither any green thing, neither any tree; but only those which have not the seal of God in their foreheads.

Because they are 'men' and not real locusts, Revelation 9:3, they don't hurt grass, and trees, or any green thing. They are the fallen angels of Genesis 6 and Jude 6, and the kenites.

To have the 'seal of God' is to know the truth, see Revelation 7:3.

So it says that if you know the truth you can not be hurt, which here means deceived.

If you go to Revelation 9:

11 And they had a king over them, which is the angel of the bottomless pit, whose name in the Hebrew tongue is Abaddon, but in the Greek tongue hath his name Apollyon.

you see that Satan is their boss.

Now back to Luke 10:

20 Notwithstanding in this rejoice not, that the spirits are subject unto you; but rather rejoice, because your names are written in heaven.'

Speaks for itself.

Let's look at the Kenites and the 'four hidden dynasties' in Isaiah 23;

1 The burden of Tyre. Howl, ye ships of Tarshish; for it is laid waste, so that there is no house, no entering in: from the land of Chittim it is revealed to them.

Tarshish is in Andalusia Spain. They had big ocean going ships that transported silver, iron, lead and tin.

Tyre is the little rocky island outside the cost of Lebanon today, which controlled by the Kenites was the most important commercial center in the east Mediterranean, noted for silk, glass, and Tyrean purple dye; excavations since 1947 have uncovered remains of Crusader, Arab, Byzantine, and Graeco-Roman cities; several Roman remains, including one of the largest hippodromes of the Roman period. Today the island is deserted except for a few fishermen. Today the Kenites are operating from places like The World Trade Center, IMF and the Federal Reserve Bank.

Chittim is a name for Cyprus, but even used as a name for the cost lands of the Mediterranean. Tyre fell after the concurrer had filled the waters between the cost and the island with dirt, on which the concurrer went. Tyre was impossible to concur from the water.

2 Be still, ye inhabitants of the isle; thou whom the merchants of Zidon, that pass over the sea, have replenished.

The merchants are the Kenites.

3 And by great waters the seed of Sihor, the harvest of the river, is her revenue; and she is a mart of nations.

Sihor is the Nile, through which the merchandise from the far east came, right up to Tyre. When you see 'mart' think about K-Mart or Wal-Mart. That's what Tyre became for people at that time.

4 Be thou ashamed, O Zidon: for the sea hath spoken, even the strength of the sea, saying 'I travail not, nor bring forth children, neither do I nourish up young men, nor bring up virgins.'

Zidon was a seaport, the mother city of Phoenicia, the granary of Egypt's harvests.

5 As at the report concerning Egypt, so shall they be sorely pained at the report of Tyre.

6 Pass ye over to Tarshish; howl, ye inhabitants of the isle.

7 Is this your joyous city, whose antiquity is of ancient days? Her own feet shall carry her afar off to sojourn.

The Kenites can not farm, so they have to live on trades, be merchants. God cursed their soil, Genesis 4:12.

8 Who hath taken this counsel against Tyre, the crowning city, whose merchants are princes, whose traffickers are the honourable of the earth?

The Kenites are very powerful people, for money talks. They are so powerful they even appoint kings and princes. They are the leaders of this earth age.

9 The Lord of hosts hath purposed it. To stain the pride of all glory, and to bring into contempt all the honourable of the earth.

God has purposed it to be this way to make a point, as in this verse. Read on.

10 Pass through thy land as a river, O daughter of Tarshish: there is no more strength.

11 He stretched out his hand over the sea, He shook the kingdoms: the Lord hath given a commandment against the merchant city, to destroy the strong holds thereof.

12 And He said, 'Thou shalt no more rejoice, O thou oppressed virgin, daughter of Zidon: arise, pass over to Chittim; there also shalt thou have no rest.'

13 Behold the land of the Chaldeans; this people was not, till the Assyrian founded it for them that dwell in the wilderness: they set up the towers thereof, they raised up the palaces thereof; and He brought it to ruin.

14 Howl, ye ships of Tarshish: for your strength is laid waste.

15 And it shall come to pass in that day, that Tyre shall be forgotten seventy years, according to the days of one king: after the end of seventy years shall Tyre sing as an harlot.

'One king' here is more 'a unit' than a 'person.' Tyre shall sing as an harlot because of harlotry, committing fornication with the world. Read on.

16 Take an harp, go about the city, thou harlot that hast been forgotten; make sweet melody, sing many songs, that thou mayest be remembered.

17 And it shall come to pass after the end of seventy years, that the Lord will visit Tyre, and she shall turn to her hire, and shall commit fornication with all the kingdoms of the world upon the face of the earth.

Tyre here representing the 'the four hidden dynasties' has ever since committed 'fornication' with the whole world through its lying systems in education, politics, the economy and religion.

18 And her merchandise and her hire shall be holiness to the Lord: it shall not be treasured nor laid up; for her merchandise shall be for them that dwell before the Lord, to eat sufficiently, and for durable clothing.

All the Kenites' wealth shall be turned over to the people that revere God.

Chapter VII

Christ was born in September, for Christ became flesh when Mary conceived December 25th

Does this sounds provoking? May be so, but read and learn the truth of the matter. Traditions of men have destroyed a lot of truths over the years.

Luke 1:

5 There was in the days of Herod, the king of Judaea, a certain priest named Zacharias, of the course of Abia: and his wife was of the daughters of Aaron, and her name was Elisabeth.

If Elisabeth was of Aaron, she was a Levite. And so was Zacharias of course, for he was a priest.

The course of Abia is named in 1 Chr 24:10, and Neh 12:17. Out of the four who returned from Babylon twenty-four courses were formed (by lot) with the original names. The second ministration of Abia fell on 12-18 Sivan=June 13-19. This ministration was Zacharias' priest duty. Gabriel's announcement recorded in Luke to Zacharias therefore was June 13-19.

Let's read on in Luke about this. Luke 1:

7 And they had no child, because that Elisabeth was barren, and they both were now well stricken in years.

8 And it came to pass, that while he executed the priest's office before God in the order of his course,

9 According to the custom of the priest's office, his lot was to burn incense when he went into the Temple of the Lord.

11 And there appeared unto him an angel of the Lord standing on the right side of the altar of incense.

12 And when Zacharias saw him, he was troubled, and fear fell upon him.

13 But the angel said unto him, 'Fear not, Zacharias: for thy prayer is heard; and thy wife Elisabeth shall bear thee a son, and thou shall call his name John.

14 And thou shalt have joy and gladness; and many shall rejoice at his birth.

15 For he shall be great in the sight of the Lord, and shall drink neither wine nor strong drink; and he shall be filled with the Holy Ghost (Spirit), even from his mother's womb.

16 And many of the children of Israel shall he turn to the Lord their God.

17 And he shall go before Him in the spirit and power of Elias (Elijah), to turn the hearts of the fathers to the children, and the disobedient to the wisdom of the just; to make ready a people prepared for the Lord.'

We see here that the son will be John the Baptist.

18 And Zacharias said unto the angel, 'Whereby shall I know this? For I am an old man, and my wife well stricken in years.'

19 And the angel answering said unto him, 'I am Gabriel, that stands in the presence of God; and am sent to speak unto thee, and to shew thee these glad tidings

20 And, behold, thou shalt be dumb, and not able to speak, unto the day that these things shall be performed, because thou believest not my words, which shall be fulfilled in their season.'

23 And it came to pass, that, as soon as the days of his ministration were accomplished, he departed to his own house.

Zacharias lived about thirty miles from Jerusalem, and for an old man that would take at least a couple of days. He could not leave Jerusalem on the 19th of Sivan=June 20, for that day was a Sabbath. So he left the 21 of June. He arrived at his house, possibly in Juttah, around the 22-23 of June.

24 And after those days his wife Elisabeth conceived, and hid herself five months, saying,

She hid herself, after the conception, obviously until the 25th of November.

25 'Thus hath the Lord dealt with me in the days wherein He looked on me. To take away my reproach among men.'

Elisabeth conceived most likely on the 25th of June.

26 And in the sixth month the angel Gabriel was sent from God unto a city of Galilee, named Nazareth,

Sixth months counted from when John was conceived in Elisabeth, June 25. This must be the 25th of December same year.

27 To a virgin espoused to a man whose name was Joseph, of the house of David; and the virgin's name was Mary.

28 And the angel came in unto her, and said, 'Hail, thou that art highly favoured, the Lord is with thee: blessed art thou among women.'

29 And when she saw him she was troubled at his saying, and cast in her mind what manner of salutation this should be.

30 And the angel said unto her, 'Fear not, Mary: for thou has found favour with God.

31 And, behold, thou shalt conceive in thy womb, and bring forth a Son, and shalt call His name JESUS.

So if we think a little bit, we see here, that Jesus was conceived December 25. He became flesh this day, and was born 9 months later in September.

If we study what happened when Christ was born we get a second witness about this. The **shepherds** are not **abiding in the field, keeping watch over their flock by night,** Luke 2:8, in the winter, in this area, the hill country. It is too cold. It says they were, so September is a better month for that.

32 He shall be great, and shall be called the Son of the Highest: and the Lord God shall give unto Him the throne of His father David.

33 And he shall reign over the house of Jacob for ever; and of His kingdom there shall be no end.'

34 Then said Mary unto the angel, 'How shall this be, seeing I know not a man?'

35 And the angel answered and said unto her,'The Holy Ghost (Spirit) shall come upon thee, and the power of the Highest shall overshadow thee: therefore also that holy Thing Which shall be born of thee shall be called the Son of God.

36 And, behold, thy cousin Elisabeth, she hath also conceived a son in her old age: and this is the sixth month with her, who was called barren.

Here we have the sixth month again, so it was sixth months after Elisabeth conceived, that Mary conceived. In other words, John the Baptist was six months older than Jesus Christ, and they were cousins, of course.

37 For with God nothing shall be impossible.'

38 And Mary said, 'Behold the handmaid of the Lord; be it unto me according to thy word.' And the angel departed from her.

39 And Mary arose in those days, and went into the hill country with haste into a city of Juda;

40 And entered into the house of Zacharias, and saluted Elisabeth.

41 And it came to pass, that, when Elisabeth heard the salutation of Mary, the babe leaped in her womb; and Elisabeth was filled with the Holy Ghost (Spirit):

'Ghost' is a bad translation. It shall be 'spirit' instead. God is not a 'spook'.

We see here how John the Baptist leaps, when he is approached by Christ in Mary's womb. Jesus is there. Mary has conceived.

42 And she spake out with a loud voice, and said, 'Blessed art thou among women, and blessed is the fruit of thy womb.

43 And whence is this to me, that the mother of my Lord should come to me?

44 For, lo, as soon as the voice of thy salutation sounded in mine ears, the babe leaped in my womb for joy.

45 And blessed is she that believed: for there shall be a performance of those things which were told her from the Lord.'

Let us leap to verse

56 And Mary abode with her about three months, and returned to her own house.

57 Now Elisabeth's full time came that she should be delivered; and she brought forth a son.

59 And it came to pass, that on the eighth day they came to circumcise the child; and they called him Zacharias, after the name of his father.

60 And his mother answered and said, 'Not so; but he shall be called John.

That's what Gabriel had told her.

61 And they said unto her, 'There is none of thy kindred that is called by this name.'

62 And they made signs to his father how he would have him called.

63 And he asked for a writing table, and wrote, saying, 'His name is John.' And they marveled all.

64 And his mouth was opened immediately, and his tongue loosed, and he spake, and praised God.

65 And came on all that dwelt round about them: and all these sayings were noised abroad throughout all the hill country of Judaea.

66 And all they that heard them laid them up in their hearts, saying, 'What manner of child shall this be!' And the hand of the Lord was with him.

67 And his father Zacharias was filled with the Holy Ghost (Spirit), and prophesied, saying,

68 'Blessed be the Lord God of Israel; for He hath visited and redeemed His people,

69 And hath raised up an horn of salvation for us in the house of His servant David;

70 As He spake by the mouth of His holy prophets, which have been since the world began:

71 That we should be saved from our enemies, and from the hand of all that hate us;

72 To perform the mercy promised to our fathers, and to remember His holy covenant;

73 The outh which He sware to our father Abraham,

74 That He would grant unto us, that we being delivered out of the hand of our enemies might serve Him without fear,

75 In holiness and righteousness before Him, all the days of our life.

76 And thou, child, shalt be called the prophet of the Highest: for thou shalt go before the face of the Lord to prepare His ways;

77 To give knowledge of salvation unto His people by the remission of their sins,

78 Through the tender mercy of our God; whereby the dayspring from on high hath visited us,

79 To give light to them that sit in darkness and in the shadow of death, to guide our feet into the way of peace."

80 And the child grew, and waxed strong in spirit, and was in the desert till the day of his shewing unto Israel.

Don't you think this proves that Christ was conceived December 25 and born in September. I think so.

So Christmas is celebrated correctly except for, that we celebrate His conception and not His birth. Christ started dwelling among us, Immanuel = with us (is) God, at His conception.

Chapter VIII

Sealing

Revelation 7:

1 And after these things I saw four angels standing on the four corners of the earth, holding the four winds of the earth, that the wind should not blow on the earth. Nor on the sea, nor on any tree.

'Wind' is 'spirit', and 'four' is pertaining to the earth. It is about what the Holy Spirit, God, is going to do in the end times, to end this earth age. See Ezekiel 37:

9 Then said He unto me, "Prophesy unto the wind, prophesy. Son of man, and say to the wind, 'Thus saith the Lord God; 'Come from the four winds, O breath, and breathe upon these slain, that they may live.'"

These are the same four winds of the end times, as above.

See also Daniel 7:

2 Daniel spake and said, "I saw in my vision by night, and, behold, the four winds of the heaven strove upon the great sea.

'Sea' here is peoples, Rev 17:

15 And he saith unto me, "The waters which thou sawest, where the whore sitteth, are peoples, and multitudes, and nations, and tongues.

The whore is the deceived Christian church, they who believe in the 'rapture'.

Now back to Rev 7:

2 And I saw another angel ascending from the east, having, the seal of the living God: and he cried with a loud voice to the four angels, to whom it was given to hurt the earth and the sea,

3 Saying, "Hurt not the earth, neither the sea, nor the trees, till we have sealed the servants of our God in their foreheads."

The seal is the truth, the Word of God.

To seal here means to educate God's servants in the true Word of God so they become knowledgeable enough to understand the chronological order of the end time events. That is, so they will not be deceived by antichrist's, Satan's, lies. This is the opposite of, if you will, the mark of the beast from Rev 13:16 and 20:4, which means Satan's deception that he is Christ, the first one coming, 2 Thess 2.

Let's go to Ezekiel 9:

1 He cried also in mine ears with a loud voice, saying, "Cause them that have charge over the city to draw near, even every man with his destroying weapon in his hand.

2 And, behold, six men came from the way of the higher gate, which lieth toward the north, and every man a slaughter weapon in his hand; and one man among them was clothed with linen, with a writer's inkhorn by his side: and they went in, and stood beside the brasen altar.

Six men are six angels. Angels are often called men. These angels are mentioned in Ez 37 also.

One of the men, with an inkhorn, represents the angel that is going to see to that the elect get sealed with the truth, the Word of God. It is an idiom, that the man, the angel, makes the mark with the ink.

The higher gate is the gate between the outer and the inner court in the Temple. The linen was woven from righteous works, Rev 14:

13......' Blessed are the dead which die in the Lord......that they may rest from their labors; and their works do follow them.'"

You have to work for the Lord; the more the better linen.

and 19:

7......for the marriage of the Lamb is come, and His wife hath made herself ready."

8 And to her was granted that she should be arrayed in fine linen, clean and white: for the fine linen is the righteousness of saints.

The wife is God's elect, the just = 'zadok' in Hebrew, the souls that stood up for God in the first earth age when Satan rebelled, the katabole. It is not the same as the bride. A bride is not married yet. A wife is married. The bride are they, who become Christians in this earth age. See Romans 8:

29 For whom He did foreknow, He also did predestinate......

Foreknow from the first earth age.

30 Moreover whom He did predestinate, them He also called: and whom He called, them He also justified: and whom He justified, them He also glorified.

Justified means judged. God judged the elect already in the first earth age. Therefore they have not free will any more. That is why Jesus could struck Paul down on the way to Damascus, and put him into the right track. Paul didn't volunteer. He earned his election in the first earth age. God could lead him wherever He wanted, and He did.

How about you? Do you feel lead? I don't know! Only you and God knows, and can answer.

and Eph 1:

4 According as he hath chosen us in Him before the foundation of the world, that we should be holy and without blame before Him in love:

5 Having predestinated us unto the adoption of children by Jesus Christ to Himself, according to the good pleasure of His will,

The elect are the ones that have part in the first resurrection, Rev 20:

6 Blessed and holy is he that hath part in the first resurrection: on such the second death has no power,......

Why doesn't the second death has any power on 'such'? They are already justified, that is, judged in the first earth age after they stood up for God at the katabole, Ez 28, which was before the foundation of the world, the foundation of this earth age, the age we are living in now.

What is the 'katabole' and the 'foundation' of the world?

To truly understand the meaning of this expression, we must note that there are two words translated 'foundation' in the New Testament: 1, 'themelios', and 2, 'katabole'.

The Noun, 'themelios' is never used of the 'world' (kosmos) or the 'earth' (ge). The corresponding Verb 'themelioo' is only used once of the 'earth'.

A comparison of these passages will show, that these are proper and regular terms for the English words 'to found', and 'foundation'.

The Noun, 'katabole' and the Verb 'kataballo' will at a comparison, especially in 2 Cor 4:9 and Rev 12:10, show that they are not the proper terms for foundation, but the correct meaning is 'casting down', 'or overthrow'.

Consistency, therefore, calls for the same translation in Heb 6:1, where, instead of 'not laying again', the rendering should be 'not casting down'. That is to say, the foundation already laid, of repentance, &c., was not to be cast down or overthrown, but to be left—and progress made unto the perfection.

Accordingly, the Noun 'katabole', derived from, and cognate with the Verb, ought to be translated 'disruption' or 'ruin'.

The remarkable thing is that in all occurrences, except Heb 11:11, the word is connected with 'the world'= 'cosmos' in the Greek, and therefore the expression should be rendered 'the disruption, or ruin, of the world', clearly referring to the condition indicated in Gen 1:2, and described in 2 Pet 3:5-6. For the earth was not created 'tohu', Is 45:18, but became so, as stated in the Hebrew of Gen 1:2 and confirmed by 2 Pet 3:6, where 'the world that then was by the word of God', Gen 1:1, perished, and 'the heavens and the earth which are now, by the same word' were created, Gen 2:4, and are 'kept in store, reserved unto fire against the day of judgment', 2 Pet 3:7, which shall usher in the 'new heavens and the new earth' of 2 Pet 3:13.

'The disruption of the world' is an event forming a great dividing line in the dispensations of the ages. In Gen 1:1 we have the 'founding' of the world, Heb 1:10=themelioo, but in Gen 1:2 we have its 'overthrow'.

This is confirmed by a further remarkable fact, that the phrase, which occurs ten times, is associated with the preposition 'apo'=from, seven times, the former refers to the kingdom, and is connected with the 'counsels' of God; the latter refers to the Mystery or Secret and is connected with the 'purpose' of God, see John 17:24, Eph 1:4, 1 Pet 1:20.

Ample new Testament testimony is thus given to the profoundly significant fact recorded in Gen 1:2, that 'the earth became tohu and bohu, that is, waste and desolate; and darkness was on the face of the deep', before the creation of 'the heavens and the earth which are now', 2 Pet 3:7.

Among 'such' people in Rev 20:6 are also they who died in Christ, not being of the elect, and are asleep now, that is, are dead in the flesh. Also are there those that are 'saved' now and are alive when Christ returns.

They who are believers in Christ now but are deceived by antichrist and the false teaching, now and during the first tribulation, the 5 months reign by antichrist just before the True Christ returns, have no part in the first resurrection. They have to wait until after the millennium to be resurrected, if they overcome the test by Satan, when he is loosed a short while, after the millennium teaching by Christ and His elect, Rev 20:3, 7 and

6......,but they shall be priests of God and of Christ, and shall reign with Him a thousand years.
What do priests do? They teach the truth, God's Word.

This is not a second chance for them, for they don't have a chance now, because of the lack of true teaching of the Word. On some of those last people God has put a 'slumber' = 'stupor' = 'katanuxis' in the Greek, so they can't see and hear, Rom 11:

8 (According as it is written, "God hath given them the spirit of slumber, eyes that they should not see, and ears that they should not hear";) unto this day.

This is to protect them, for they are too weak-minded to stand against Satan during his 5 months tribulation. God saves those for the millennium-teaching.

Read also Ez 44:17.

Back to Ez 9:

3 And the glory of the God of Israel was gone up from the cherub, whereupon He was, to the threshold of the house. And He called to the man clothed with linen, which had the writer's inkhorn by his side;

Here God leaves the Mercy seat. It is future or actually happening right now, because we are in the end times, and most likely in the 5:th Trump. The sealing of the elect is taking place right now.

4 And the Lord said unto him, "Go through the midst of the city, through the midst of Jerusalem, and set a mark upon the foreheads of the men that sigh and that cry for all the abominations that be done in the midst thereof."

The 'mark' here is of course the 'seal' of God in Rev 7:3. The Hebrew word used is 'tav'=signature, desire, mark.

5 And to the others He said in mine hearing, "Go ye after him through the city, and smite: let not your eye spare, neither have pity:

6 Slay utterly old and young, both maids, and little children, and women: but come not near any man upon whom is the mark; and begin at My sanctuary." Then they began at the ancient men which were before the house.

They with the mark, or seal, = they who know the truth, can naturally not be touched. They can not be deceived.

The ancient men here are the priests in chapter 8, that teach falsehood, the false teachers today, by ignorance or otherwise. God is ticked.

Smite and slay means of course 'spiritually'. We see that the priests are going to be judged first, for God starts in the sanctuary. He starts with the teachers.

7 And He said unto them, 'Defile the house, and fill the courts with the slain: go ye forth.' And they went forth, and slew in the city.

8 And it came to pass, while they were slaying them, and I was left, that I fell upon my face, and cried, and said, "Ah Lord God! Wilt Thou destroy all the residue of Israel in Thy pouring out of Thy fury upon Jerusalem?"

The residue are the elect. God is not going to destroy the residue, see verse 6 above and Rev 9:

4 And it was commanded them that they should not hurt the grass of the earth, neither any green thing, neither any tree; but only those men which have not the seal of God in their foreheads.

Satan can only hurt those who have not the seal, or mark, of God, naturally because they don't know the truth. They are deceived.

Because they are not to hurt trees, green things or grass, shows that they are not real locust, but men. They are Satan's little evil army.

5 And to them it was given that they should not kill them, but that they should be tormented five months:......

When does God's fury spills over? At the 7:th Trump, which is the second tribulation, which is when Christ returns. This is right after the false christ, antichrist, Satan, the son of perdition, Apollyon, has been here for 5 month, the first tribulation, see 2 Thess 2:3-4, Mark 13:14-24, Matt 24:15-26 and many other places, not least in the Old Testament, from where the New Testament is drawn.

9 Then said He unto me, "The iniquity of the house of Israel and Judah is exceeding great, and the land is full of blood, and the city full of perverseness: for they say, 'The Lord hath forsaken the earth, and the Lord seeth not.'

Blood is not literally, but spiritually. The Lord has not forsaken the earth, and He sees everything. Be so sure.

10 And as for Me also, Mine eye shall not spare, neither will I have pity, but I will recompense their way upon their head."

11 And, behold, the man clothed with linen, which had the inkhorn by his side, reported the matter, saying, "I have done as Thou hast commanded me."

Can we say we have done that? It is talking about us, at least in part, the very elect.

What has God planned? Let's continue in Ez 10:

1 Then I looked, and behold, in the firmament that was above the head of the cherubims there appeared over them as it were a sapphire stone, as the appearance of the likeness of a throne.

This is God and His throne.

Read on in Ez 10 from the Scriptures. I will just make some notes here.

Coals of fire in verse 2 are alluding to Hebr 12:29, that is, God is a consuming fire. That's a wonderful spiritual fire for us, but not for the false teachers etc. Let's, for a moment, go to Deut 24:

7 If a man be found stealing any of his brethren of the children of Israel, and maketh merchandise of him, or selleth him; then that thief shall die; and thou shalt put evil away from among you.

Apply this in a spiritual sense, which I think is quite possible, and think about preachers steeling souls through false teaching. It is going to be pretty rough for the false teachers.

In verse 3, 'house' is of course church and the cloud is the presence of God.

In verse 6, we see that it is a spiritual fire for the linen does not burn. Just to keep you awake! OK!

The wheels in verses 6-12 are four small 'UFO' ships and one mother ship. I call them 'IFOs', for they are identified, not unidentified. We see in the following verses that they are round because they didn't turn when they went in a new direction. They had eyes = windows. Cp. Ez 1 and 2.

In verse 14 the for faces are the flags or symbols representing the four corners of Israel's camp.

In verse 16 and 17 we see the cherubims were inside the wheels, the 'IFOs', behind the windows, for they went with the vehicle when it moved. It in fact says 'for the spirit of the living creature was in them.'

In verse 19 it is talking about the east gate. When you look toward east from the east gate, you can see the river Chedron and the mount of Olives, see Zechariah 14:4-ff.

Read on in Ez 11. I make some notes.

Verse 1: Christ is coming back by the east gate. Antichrist, Satan is coming by the north gate.

Jaazaniah (means heard from God) son of Azur (helpful), Pelatiah (saved) son of Beniah (YA has built) and the princes of the people are a political structure, the 'one world order' of the Kenites, Satan's sons, and the ones they have deceived to participate. The ancient priests, are the false teachers of the 'Word'. Both very much in effect right now.

In verse 3, 'caldron' means iron pot.

Verse 6: 'Slain' means in the spiritual sense, not in the flesh.

In verses 8 and 9, 'a sword' is Satan's lies, see 2 Thess 2, and 'strangers' is the 'one world order'.

'Fall' in verse 10 is fall spiritually, be deceived and therefore jump in Satan's bed, see Mark 13:

17 But woe to them that are with child, and to them that give suck in those days.

They jumped in Satan's bed, spiritually, the wrong father, or husband if you wish, or bridegroom, believing he is Christ. They believe in the 'rapture', for example. They don't understand the difference between antichrist and Christ. They are Biblically illiterate. Back to Ez 11.

Verses 16 and 18 are talking about the elect among the 10 northern tribes and how God is a little sanctuary for the 10 northern tribes 'in the countries where they shall come', that is, Europe and the Americas, basically.

Verse 19-20 is future from now. The tribe of Judah (the good figs) with the Kenites (the evil figs), the parable of the Fig Tree in Jeremiah 24, also mentioned by Christ in Mark 13:28, has partly moved back to Israel, the present nation Israel, but this is not the same thing as when the 10 tribes, also called Israel, are going to return.

That is still future. That is going to happen first when Joshua our Lord and Savior returns, Ez 37:17. Judah and Israel are going to be united again then. Chaldea in verse 24 is Babylon.

Chapter IX

Satan's New Plan

Rev 12:

1 And there appeared a great wonder in heaven; a woman clothed with the sun, and the moon under her feet, and upon her head a crown of twelve stars:

Heaven is wherever God is.

The woman here is the type of mother Israel, or Mary, in the first earth age. Twelve stars are the 12 tribes, in the zodiacal signs, representing the Israel nation in embryo.

2 And she being with child cried, travailing in birth, and pained to be delivered.

The birth of the present earth age.

3 And there appeared another wonder in heaven; and behold, a great red dragon, having seven heads and ten horns, and seven crowns upon his heads.

Crowns = dominion with a ruler. The 7 crowns are upon 7 heads here, not 10 crowns upon 10 horns as in Rev 13:1.

Horns mean power. The red dragon is Satan in the first earth age. Heads, horns and crowns are 'signs' of universality of earthly power. We see that Satan had the same power structure here, as he is going to have in the end times, when he is here 5 months 'playing' Christ before the True Christ returns, 2 Thess 2, except 10 crowns, Rev 13:

1 And I stood upon the sand of the sea, and saw a beast rise up out of the sea, having seven heads and ten horns, and upon his horns ten crowns, and upon his heads the name of blasphemy.

This beast is the 'one world order' system of the Kenites, Satan's sons through Cain, of the end times, which is now. Examples: the International Monetary Fund (IMF), the Federal Reserve Bank (getting more international in these end times, of course), United Nations, European Union, the mergings of the big companies, like Chrysler-Mercedes Benz, merging Banks, the Asian, American, European etc. markets are 'internally' interrelated, the laundering of money from IMF through Russian and American banks, etc., etc., = 'the consummation' of the Kenites' 'four hidden dynasties', economy, education, politics and religion. We see that the power structure has <u>10</u> crowns, not <u>7</u> crowns, as in Rev 12:3, and the 10 crowns are on the 10 horns, and not on the 7 heads, as the 7 crowns.

Also observe that 'heads' is in plural, and so we can see that it is a power structure, not an individual. An individual does not have more than 'one' head. Our father is very natural. He is in fact 'supernatural', which means 'more' natural, and naturally he is more natural than we are.

Sea means people, the population of the world, cp. Rev 17:15, waters.

Let's go back to Rev 12:

4 And his tail drew the third part of the stars of heaven, and did cast them to the earth: and the dragon stood before the woman which was ready to be delivered, for to devour her child as soon as it was born.

The woman is Mary delivering Christ, and then we have the attempts to murder Christ. In a wider sense it symbolizes Israel born into this earth age through the Adamic peoples, from which lineage Christ would come. As we know from Gen 3, Satan tried to destroy that also. Cain and his sons, the Kenites, were the offspring.

But first we have Satan deceiving a third of the about 12 billion (my own estimate) souls God created in the beginning, Gen 1:1, millions of years ago. It happened in the first earth age, and God 'overthrew' Satan, judged him to perish, be blotted out, after the millennium, Rev 20, because of it. It is called the 'katabole'. It is written about in Ez 28. Read the whole chapter, where 'the prince of Tyrus' is Satan. Satan's name was 'the king of Tyrus' before he fell, which means he was judged by God, as it says in Ez 28:

14 Thou art the anointed cherub that covereth; and I have set thee so: thou wast upon the holy mountain of God; thou hast walked up and down in the midst of the stones of fire.

Satan was the protecting cherub of the 'Mercy Seat', Christ's Seat, part of God's Throne.

15 Thou wast perfect in thy ways from the day that thou wast created, till iniquity was found in thee.

Satan loved God, and God blessed him, until he wanted to be God himself.

16 By the multitude of thy merchandise they have filled the midst of thee with violence, and thou hast sinned: therefore I will cast thee as profane out of the mountain of God: and I will destroy thee, O covering cherub, from the midst of the stones of fire.

When you feel that the 'merchandising' today is to much, your are very healthy, because you are feeling the abomination of Satan's nature and of his children, the Kenites, for they are ruling this world, this present earth age.

17 Thine heart was lifted up because of thy beauty, thou hast corrupted thy wisdom by reason of thy brightness: I will cast thee to the ground, I will lay thee before kings, that they may behold thee.

Compare, read more about this in Is 14:

9 Hell from beneath is moved for thee to meet thee at thy coming: it stirreth up the dead for thee, even all the chief ones of the earth; it hath raised up from their thrones all the kings of the nations.

'Hell' is the Hebrew word 'sheol', which simply means 'grave' or 'pit' or a 'low place', in this figure of speach. The same word is used in verse 11 translated grave.

10 All they shall speak and say unto thee, 'Art thou also become weak as we? Art thou become like unto us?'

This is when Satan is in the pit, Rev 20:1-3, in the beginning of the millennium, and we are in spiritual bodies, not in flesh any more. People are passing the pit, looking into it.

11 Thy pomp is brought down to the grave, and the noise of thy viols: the worm is spread under thee, and the worms cover thee.

'Worms' is of course a figure of speech, not literary. It means Satan is soon going to be blotted out, gone for ever, after his last job, to test the new Christians after the millennium, Rev 20:7-8.

12 How art thou fallen from heaven, O Lucifer, son of the morning! how art thou cut down to the ground, which didst weaken the nations!

Satan is the fake morning star. 'Weaken' means draw people away from God.

13 For thou hast said in thy heart,' I will ascend into heaven, I will exalt my throne above the stars of God: I will sit also upon the mount of the congregation, in the sides of the north:

'The sides of the north' is where God's throne is. Satan likes that place, where he can play God.

14 I will ascend above the heights of the clouds; I will be like the MOST HIGH.'

Satan wanted to be God. But see what God says about that.

15 Yet thou shalt be brought down to hell, to the sides of the pit.

"Hell" here again meaning a 'low place' = the pit.

16 They that see thee shall narrowly look upon thee, and consider thee, saying, 'Is this the man that made the earth to tremble, that did shake kingdoms;

We see here Satan in the pit, as mentioned above, and how people look down into the pit and on Satan and make their comments.

17 That made the world as a wilderness, and destroyed the cities thereof; that opened not the house of the prisoners?'

Back to Ez 28:

18 Thou hast defiled thy sanctuaries by the multitude of thine iniquities, by the iniquity of thy traffick; therefore will I bring forth a fire from the midst of thee, it shall devour thee, and I will bring thee to ashes upon the earth in the sight of all them that behold thee.

'Traffick' means that Satan and his sons, the Kenites, have always been traders, money makers, and first of all through usury. It started on the little rock island Tyrus.

'Bring to ashes' is a figure of speech again, for Satan is not in flesh; has never been and will never be.

19 All they that know thee among the people shall be astonished at thee: thou shalt be a terror, and never shalt thou be any more.'

Satan shall not be any more. So there is no 'hell', where Satan and his people are going to scream and yell for ever. It is all a figure of speech, meaning the blotting out process, of Rev 20, the lake of fire. Remember we are not in flesh at the time of the lake of fire. God is the consuming fire, 1 Cor 12:29. He blots out all the evil souls, Rev 20:15, 2 Pet 3:3, 10-13.

Compare Rev 21:

4 And god shall wipe away all tears from their eyes; and there shall be no more death, neither sorrow, nor crying, neither shall there be any more pain: for the former things are passed away.'

With all this passed away, how can there be a 'hell'. It can't. It makes sense too, for what kind of Father would we have if He would allow us to look at people creaming and yelling from 'hell' all through eternity?

Now to Rev 13:

1 And I stood upon the sand of the sea, and saw a beast rise up out of the sea, having seven heads and ten horns, and upon his horns ten crowns, and upon his heads the name of blasphemy.
The 'sea' is the peoples of the world, cp. Rev 17:15......*'The waters which thou sawest, where the whore sitteth, are peoples, and multitudes, and nations, and tongues.*

So the beast is rising up out from the peoples of the world. That makes sense. The beast is the 'one, or new, world order, or system', mentioned before. It is the Kenites' 'four hidden dynasties', and their effort to 'unite' the whole world, and trying to create peace. It is happening right now before our eyes.
We see here now that 'this system' has ten crowns, not seven as in Rev 12:3. So the power structure Satan has in this earth age is a little bit different from the power structure he had in the first earth age. That brings in a time element, so we can see and understand the scripture, divide the Word correctly.

'Blasphemy' means that the system is existing under false premises. The system claims the living God, our Father, as the 'boss', when their 'boss' is Satan.

2 And the beast which I saw was like unto a leopard, and his feet as the feet of a bear, and his mouth as the mouth of a lion; and the dragon gave him his power, and his seat, and great authority.

'Leopard' is used to 'figure' multi-faceted. As we now know, it's the Kenites' 'four hidden dynasties': education, religion, politics and the economy, and 'bear' to 'figure' 'cumbersome'. It's all over the world. It's the 'one world order'. It's powerful, almost not moveable.

A lion's mouth rip and tare, here meant spiritually of course, a figure of speech again. We are talking about deception to death = Satan = the dragon; spiritual death. Satan is going to give his power to this system. Satan is the father of it, for it is his children, umbilical cord to umbilical cord from Cain, the Kenites, that has created it.

3 And I saw one of his heads as it were wounded to death; and his deadly wound was healed: and all the world wondered after the beast.

The 'one world order' is going to have a problem of some kind. I think this could be that they can not agree over a certain issue, for example.

The wound is healed though, by Satan of course, when he is 'booted' out on earth, Rev 12:9, 2 Thess 2:3-4, and ALL the world wondered after the 'beast' = the 'one world order'. How many are that? ALL means all, and it can only mean one thing. A lot of people, the very majority of the world's population is going to be, actually is already, deceived by 'Antichrist'= Satan and his 'one world order'. This is the 'mark of the beast', Rev 13:16 *And he causeth all, both small and great, rich and poor, free and bond, to receive a mark in their right hand* (=work for Satan), *or in their foreheads* (in their brains, be deceived), and 19:20. Antichrist, Satan, is not here yet, but he is coming, 2 Thess 2. The 'one world order' is already here, and is quickly developing all over the world, with corporate globalization, actually working toward a 'higher unity through cooperation toward holy and just ends'. Most people swallow it, 'hook, line and sinker'. This is how Satan's children work. Makes it more believable if you involve 'holy and just' in the process, the hidden dynasty of 'religion', including Christianity. Viewers have been watching the peace process on TV for years now. It is also called the 'new world order' by some, but is the same thing. United Nations, IMF, the International Monetary Fund, et al, are working everything into a 'one world system', trying to create peace, involving the political hidden dynasty. It is going to fail, for only Christ can bring peace, when He returns. But most people don't know, that Satan is coming as Antichrist before this, and is going to sit in the temple of God and play Christ, 2 Thess 2. Most of the people in the world have the mark of the beast = are deceived and work for Satan. But they don't know it. They think they work for our Father. They are Biblically illiterate.

4 And they worshipped the dragon which gave power unto the beast: and they worshipped the beast, saying, "Who is like unto the beast? Who is able to make war with him?"

The elect are able, and will, by their witnessing with the Holy Spirit talking through them, Mark 13:10-11, Matt 24:14, Luke 21:12-15, 12:11-12, Acts 2.

All the world, including the deceived Christians, the whore, Rev 17:1, 15, 16, 19:2, are going to worship Antichrist, Satan, who is going to give power to the 'one world order'. Satan can do that for he is not in the flesh but in a celestial body. He is super natural, a cherub, Ez 28:14. Satan never had a flesh body and is not going to have that, ever.

Nobody can make war, if we have a 'one world order'. It is 'one world'. There are no enemies except the elect.

5 And there was given unto him a mouth speaking great things and blasphemies; and power was given unto him to continue forty and two months.

Satan's time table is always given in 'months', God's in 'days'.

The 42 months are shortened as we know, to 5 months, Mark 13:

20 And except that the Lord had shortened those days, no flesh should be saved: but for the elect's sake, whom He hath chosen, He hath shortened the days.

Observe here that it says 'no flesh should be saved', not soul. What does it mean? We are in flesh when Antichrist, Satan, is here 5 months. This time period is coming to pass, to wake the sleepy up to be able to recognize the True Christ from the false. When our Lord and Savior returns 'every knee shall bow'. Isaiah 45:

22 Look unto Me, and be ye saved, all the ends of the earth: for I am God, and there is none else.

23......, That unto me every knee shall bow,......

Rom 14:

11 For it is written, "As I live, saith the Lord, every knee shall bow to me, and every tongue shall confess to God."

How about shortened to five months?

Rev 9:

5......, but that they should be tormented five months:......

10......: and their power was to hurt men five months.

There we have it!

Of course Satan's sons, the Kenites, and their followers, are going to speak proudly, bragging and blasphemies things. They think they have it together. But boy what they are going to be disappointed, when the True Christ returns, Rev 6:

15......man, hid themselves in the dens and in the rocks of the mountains;

16 And they said to the mountains and rocks, "Fall on us, and hide us from the face of Him That sitteth on the throne, and from the wrath of the Lamb:

17 For the great day of His wrath is come; and who shall be able to stand?"

Well? Who do you think can stand? They who know the truth of course.

OK! Back to our subject. Dan 11:

36 And the king shall do according to his will: and he shall exalt himself, and magnify himself above every GOD, and shall speak marvelous things against the GOD of gods, and shall prosper till the indignation be accomplished: for that that is determined shall be done.

The king here is Satan during his 5 months reign, the first tribulation, 2 Thess 2, 'that that is determined', meaning God's plan has to come to pass.

37 Neither shall he regard the God of his fathers, nor the desire of women, nor regard any GOD: for he shall magnify himself above all.

'The desire of women' is alluding to the virgin bride = the elect, the wife in Rev 19:7. Remember the statement in Mark 13:17 *But woe to them that are with child, and to them that give suck in those days!* This means, they, the bride, the Biblically illiterate Christians, not the

132

elect of course, have taken Antichrist as husband, believing he is Christ, instead of waiting for the true Christ.

38 But in his estate shall he honor the God of forces: and a god whom his fathers knew not shall he honor with gold, and silver, and precious stones, and pleasant things.

This has to do with the 'one world order', which main issue always is money, riches etc.

39 Thus shall he do in the most strong holds with a strange god, whom he shall acknowledge and increase with glory: and he shall cause them to rule over many, and shall divide the land for gain.

This means 'all that acknowledge him'. Gain is 'price'. It is talking about the 'one world order' = strange god.

40 And at the time of the end shall the king of the south push at him: and the king of the north shall come against him like a whirlwind, with chariots, and with horsemen, and with many ships; and he shall enter into the countries, and shall overflow and pass over.

Ships are the ships of Chittim of Dan 11:30, which are the elect, the ones that know the truth.

Whirlwind is the Holy Spirit, and here it is the Holy Spirit talking through the elect as it is written in Mark 13:

11 But when they shall lead you, and deliver you up, take no thought beforehand what ye shall speak, neither do ye premeditate: but whatsoever shall be given you in that hour, that speak ye: for it is not ye that speak, but the Holy Ghost.

'Holy Ghost' is better translated 'Holy Spirit'. God is not a 'spook'.

and in Luke 12:

11 And when they bring you unto the synagogues, and unto magistrates, and powers, take ye no thought how or what thing ye shall answer, or what ye shall say:

12 For the Holy Ghost (Holy Spirit is more correct) *shall teach you in the same hour what ye ought to say.'*

This is the true 'talking in tongues' of Acts 2, written about in the book of Joel, as Peter said in Acts 2:16-ff. It is not the 'babel' that they talk today in many churches, thinking it is 'talking in tongues'. The latter is a misunderstanding and a deception, and by the way, 'babel' means confusion, and that is what it sounds like.

For the elect to refuse to let the Holy Spirit talk through them at this time, which is when Satan is here 5 months playing Christ, is the only unforgivable sin. That is why it is written in the prior verse

10......: but unto him that blasphemeth against the Holy Ghost (Holy Spirit) it shall not be forgiven.

So the unforgivable sin can only be committed by the elect and only when antichrist is here.

The synagogues are the synagogues of Satan, of course, of Rev 2:9 and 3:9, 'they who say they are Jews, but are not' = the Kenites and their synagogues and churches.

Cp. Nethinims = given to service, the Kenites, not of Levi, Ezra 2:43, 61-62, which means, that when the tribes of Judah and Benjamin came back from the captivity in Babylon, there were no Livite priests left in the 'church', but only Nethinims, Ezra 8:15.

It is almost the same today, which Ezra is the type of. The Kenites have always slipped into the church. The Livite priests got lazy and hired people to shop wood, and over time they got lazy to prepare the preaching too, and the Kenites took over. King Solomon, 1 Kings 9:20-21, let the Kenites, 1 Chron 2:55, work in the temple for the priests, the Levites, and successively the Kenites took over the responsibility of the Levites. Cp. Ezra 2:58 also. It is difficult to discern who is a Christian, a Jew (of Israel or of Judah), or a Kenite, and that's the way it is supposed to be, cp. Mark 13:28, the parable of the fig tree, Jer 24, which is about Judah contra the Kenites today from the creation of the Israelic nation May 1948. There are many Kenites in the church today and there have always been, cp. Matt 13:28-30, 38-40.

Observe also what it is written in Luke 21:

15 For I will give you a mouth and wisdom, which all your adversaries shall not be able to gainsay nor resist.

Who is our chief adversary? Satan of course and his children. Satan can not gainsay nor resist the Word of the Holy Spirit, that is mouthed by the elect, the ships of Chittim, at the time he is here 5 months, the first tribulation.

Back to Dan 11:

41 He shall enter also into the glorious land, and many countries shall be overthrown: but these shall escape out of his hand, even Edom, and Moab, and the chief of the children of Ammon.

The glorious land is the Holy Land, Mount Zion, cp. Dan 11: 45, the glorious holy mountain. This is also written in 2 Thess 2:4.

We have to go to Ezekiel 38 an 39 to understand the rest. The chief prince of Meshech and Tubal, in 38:2 and 3, is Russia. 'Chief' is the Hebrew word 'rosh'. This word changed by the river 'russ' Volga, and then became Russia. Russia is Edom, another name for Esau and his descendants, according to Gen 36. Esau came out 'red' when he was born, Gen 25:25. Edom means red. Even the pottage Jacob sold for Esau's birth right was red. I don't think there is any doubt that Esau's descendants became the communistic government of Russia, the 'red' nation. The flag is red too. Everything is red there.

Moab, is the son between Lot and his eldest daughter. Ammon are the descendants of Ben-ammi, the son between Lot and his younger daughter.

All these peoples intermixed and migrated north. History tells so. They shall escape for they are already Satan's buddies.

We read in Ez 39:

11 And it shall come to pass in that day, that I will give unto Gog a place there of graves in Israel, the valley of the passengers on the east of the sea: and it shall stop the noses of the passengers: and there shall they bury Gog and all his multitude: and they shall call it the valley of Hamon-gog.

Hamon-gog means 'the multitude of Gog'. Gog means mountain, which means country.

USA bought Alaska from Russia for seven million dollars. This is the valley of Hamon-gog. It is east of the sea. Gog is the chief prince again, Russia.

Where are Israel? Everywhere the 10 northern tribes are. Where are they? They became the western Christian nations after God scattered them, 1 Kings 11:31, 12:19, Lev 26:33, and around there, and many other places.

So what is going to happen here according to the prophecy? There is going to be a war between Esau (Russia) and his allies, and Israel, which are the western Christian nations: Europe, USA, Canada, etc., and the battle field is a valley in Alaska. This war the Lord is going to win for Israel with overflowing rain, great (150 LB) hailstones, fire and brimstones, Ez 38:22, Cp. Joshua 10:11, which is a type, again. In prior verse it is written about the two brothers, Esau and Jacob.

Jacob is the natural seed of Israel, that is, all 12 tribes. See also Job 38:22-23, which is alluding to this war.

Back to Dan 11:

42 He shall stretch forth his hand also upon countries: and the land of Egypt shall not escape.

43 But he shall have power over the treasures of gold and of silver, and over all the precious things of Egypt: and the Libyans and the Ethiopians shall be his steps.

'Steps' means 'companion'. 'He' is 'Antichrist' = Satan, as in the prior verses. We see his power structure here.

All this happens in the 6th trumpet, Rev 9:13-21, the 5 months, the first tribulation

44 But the tidings out of the east and out of the north shall trouble him: therefore he shall go forth with great fury to destroy, and utterly to make away with many.

The tidings are the ships of Chittim again, the bruisers (cp. 'bruise' in Gen 3:15), the Holy Spirit talking through the elect, Mark 13:11, Luke 12:11-12, Matt 24:14, etc., see above.

45 And he shall plant the tabernacles of his palace between the seas in the glorious holy mountain; yet he shall come to his end, and none shall help him.

This is Satan's last 15 minutes of his 5 month's reign, the first tribulation.

Satan is going to 'plant' his churches in the Americas, which is between the Atlantic and the Pacific ocean.

Let's continue with Dan 7:

7 After this I saw in the night visions, and behold a fourth beast, dreadful and terrible, and strong exceedingly; and it had great iron teeth; it devoured and brake in pieces, and stamped the residue with the feet of it: and it was diverse from all the beasts that were before it; and it had ten horns.

These 10 horns are going to have 10 crowns on them, as in Rev 13:1.

The fourth beast is the 'one world order'. The residue is the deceived church.

8 I considered the horns, and, behold, there came up among them another little horn, before whom there were three of the first horns plucked up by the roots: and, behold, in this horn were eyes like the eyes of a man, and a mouth speaking great things.

10 horns – 3 horns = 7 horns, watch!

'The little horn' is Satan in the office of Antichrist. Satan is a man speaking great things.

9 I beheld till the thrones were cast down, and the Ancient of the days did sit, Whose garment was white as snow, and the hair of His head like the pure wool: His throne was like the fiery flame, and his wheels as burning fire.

'The Ancient of the days' is God. God is a consuming fire, Hebr 12:29.

10 A fiery stream issued and came forth from before Him: thousand thousands ministered unto Him, and ten thousand times ten thousand stood before him: the judgment was set, and the books were opened.

This is judgment day, which is after the millennium, Rev 20:11-15.

11 I beheld then because of the voice of the great words which the horn spake: I beheld even till the beast was slain, and his body destroyed, and given to the burning flame.

We can see in Rev 19:20, that Satan's office as false prophet, antichrist, shall not be any more. Its body is going to be destroyed. This means perish, be blotted out in the lake of fire, as never existed.

God is the consuming fire, 'the burning flame', as mentioned earlier.

12 As concerning the rest of the beasts, they had their dominion taken away: yet their lives were prolonged for a season and time.

The 'one world order', 'their dominion', the system, is taken away in the same way as the 'false prophet', 'Antichrist' above, Rev 19:20. Read it for yourself.

The peoples though, that practiced in the dominion of the beast, 'the one world order' are not destroyed but they shall live, in their celestial body, 1 Cor 15:51, through the millennium, Rev 20:5. They will be spiritually dead until after the millennium, when they can overcome, if they work for and make Jesus their Lord. They are judged according to their 'works', Rev 20:12-13, because they can see Christ. We are saved by faith now for we can not see Christ.

13 I saw in the night visions, and, behold, one like the Son of Man came with the clouds of heaven, and came to the Ancient of days, and they brought Him near before Him.

OK! This is Christ's return.

14 And there was given Him dominion, and glory, and a kingdom, that all people, nations, and languages, should serve Him: His dominion is an everlasting dominion, which shall not pass away, and His kingdom that which shall not be destroyed.

Pretty obvious!

Let's go now to Rev 17:

7 And the angel said unto me, "Wherefore didst thou marvel? I will tell the mystery of the woman, and of the beast that carrieth her, which hath the seven heads and ten horns.

8 The beast that thou sawest was, and is not; and shall ascend out of the bottomless pit, and go into perdition: and they that dwell on the earth shall wonder, whose names were not written in the book of life from the foundation of the world, when they behold the beast that was, and is not, and yet is.

'When they behold the beast that was' means, that the elect stood against Satan, with God, in the first earth age at the Katabole, when Satan was overthrown, Ez 28, at the foundation of this present earth age.

Only the elect, therefore, have their names written in the book of life, from the 'foundation of the world', the Katabole, the overthrow of Satan in the first earth age.

Other 'people' or 'souls', which is the same, do not have that.

9 And here is the mind which hath wisdom. The seven heads are seven mountains, on which the woman sitteth.

Mountains are countries or groups of countries.

10 And there are seven kings: five are fallen, and one is, and the other is not yet come; and when he cometh, he must continue a short space.

Satan has had five roles, names, five used up at this point = 'five are fallen'. The kings here are not the same as the 10 kings in verse 12, which is a political system, the hidden dynasty of politics.

'Continue a short space' is the same as in Rev 20:3, 'loosed a little season', meaning Satan's short time of deceiving, Rev 20:3,7 and 8. See next verse.

11 And the beast that was, and is not, even he is the eighth, and is of the seven, and goeth into perdition.

'Even he is the eighth' means Satan's role as deceiver after the millennium, the eighth dispensation, Rev 20:3 and 20:7-8. Eight means 'new beginning also', which is the case after the millennium, for we get a renewed earth and a renewed heaven then, Rev 21:1. That's how we know it's him here, and also because he is going into perdition, perish, be blotted out, Rev 20:10 and Ez 28:18-19, in the lake of fire, Hebr 12:29. Satan is the 'son of perdition', Apollyon, Rev 9:11 and 2 Thess 2:3. God is the consuming fire that blots the soul out. Remember, we are not talking fire here that burns flesh, but blots out souls.

12 And the ten horns which thou sawest are ten kings, which have received no kingdom as yet; but receive power as kings one hour with the beast.

The ten kings are a political system, see comment on verse 10, which of course is part of the 'one world order'.

The wound of Rev 13:3 is healed here by Satan as Antichrist = the beast.

'Hour' here is 'the hour of temptation', the 'first tribulation', see Mark 13:19, Matt 24:21, and many other places. This is Satan's literal reign here on earth, as Antichrist, five months, as you know now, 2 Thess 2:3-4, Mark 13:14 and Matt 24:15, Rev 9:5 and 10.

The ten kings receive power first when Antichrist is here.

13 These have one mind, and shall give their power and strength unto the beast.

They are going to support Satan, work with him. They have 'one mind' for they are 'the "one" world order'.

14 These shall make war with the Lamb, and the lamb shall overcome them: for He is Lord of lords, and King of kings: and they that are with Him are called, and chosen, and faithful.

The chosen are the elect = the 'zadok', the just, Rom 8:26-34, the souls that stood up against Satan in the first earth age.

15 And he saith unto me," The waters which thou sawest, where the whore sitteth, are peoples, and multitudes, and nations, and tongues.

The 'waters', or the 'sea' in other Scriptures, is the world population.

We know who the 'whore' is now, basically the 'rapture-Christians'.

16 And the ten horns which thou sawest upon the beast, these shall hate the whore, and shall make her desolate and naked, and shall eat her flesh, and burn her with fire.

The ten horns, that are the 'one world order', or 'new world order' if you wish, are the Kenites, the sons of Cain, who is the son of Satan. They are going to hate the deceived Christian church, the whore, and its members, and rip them off, spiritually, and/or financially, that will say with whatever chastisement God wants to send upon them, to get them to wake up to the truth. They can not touch the elect spiritually because of Rev 9:

4 And it was commanded them that they should not hurt......; but only those men which have not the seal of God in their foreheads.

'Seal', see Rev 7:3. To have the seal of God in your forehead is to know the truth, the Word of God. No one, including Satan, can deceive you, that is, 'hurt' you spiritually, once you know the truth. The opposite is to have the 'mark of the beast', Rev 13:16-17 and 19:20, that will say, to be deceived, not know the truth.

142

Back to Rev 17 and verse

17 For God hath put in their hearts to fulfill His will, and to agree, and give their kingdom unto the beast, until the words of God shall be fulfilled.

The Kenites are going to give the 'one world order' to Satan, and it is going to last until Christ returns. In Rev 19:20, we see where both the 'one world order' and Satan's 'office' as Antichrist are cast into the lake of fire, meaning that God is going to blot that power structure out.

18 And the woman which thou sawest is that great city, which reigneth over the kings of the earth.

The great city is Jerusalem, sister Babylon, when and where Antichrist, Satan, is going to have his reign, five months, 2 Thess 2.

In Rev 12:3 Satan's power structure has 7 crowns upon 7 heads. This is in the first earth age.

In Rev 17:12,16, Dan 7:7, Rev 13:1, Satan's power structure has 10 crowns upon 10 horns. This is in this earth age. The 10 horns in Dan 7:7 so have 10 crowns upon them, and therefore represent the ten kings, or rulers of the end time. That is now.

This means that Satan has a new plan for this earth age, and so we also understand that the Scriptures are talking about two different times here. We have a clear time element involved, that helps us to divide the Word.

Chapter X

The Beginning of this Earth Age, and Who were Adam and Eve, and the People of Nod from where Cain took his Wife, and Who was Cain?

I have written about the three earth ages in an other chapter, so I will not go in to that here specifically.

The Bible begins with, Gen 1:

1 In the beginning God created the heavens and the earth.

This was millions of years ago. In the next verse

2 And the earth was without form and void; and darkness was upon the face of the deep.

we are just finishing the first earth age, or we are beginning the second, if you will. The word 'was' shall be 'became'. Why? Because the Devil rebelled, and God overthrew him, which is called the 'katabole', and God also destroyed the first earth age, see Ez 28, 2 Pet 3, Is 45:18, Jer 4:18-ff, Matt 13:35. This happened about 14 thousand years ago. The creation of this earth age took 8 thousand years = 8 days, cp. 2 Pet 3, and we have been here, in this earth age, about 6000 years = 8+6=14.

In Isaiah 45:

18 For thus saith the Lord That created the heavens; God Himself That formed the earth and made it; He hath established it, He created it not in vain, he formed it to be inhabited: 'I am the Lord; and there is none else.

the word 'vain' is the same word 'tuhu', in the Hebrew, as the word 'without form' in Gen 1:2, and therefore it must have *become tuhu*: which is exactly what Gen 1:2 declares. The world was not created 'tuhu' = in vain, without form, *He created it not in vain.* In Gen 1:1 we have 'the world that then was, cp. 2 Pet 3:6, and in verse 2 we have the ruin into which it fell. We are not told how, when, or why, or how long it lasted. When geologists have settled how many years they require, they may place them between vv. 1 and 2 of Gen 1. In Gen 1:2-2:4, we have 'the heavens and the earth which are now' of 2 Pet 3:7. Both are set in contrast with the 'new heavens and the new earth' of 2 Pet 3:13.

I have explained most of this in the mentioned chapter about the three world ages.

Now let's go in to the subject of this chapter. Let's go to Gen 1:

26 And God said, 'Let Us make man in Our image, after Our likeness:......

'Us' is us=we, for our souls were created in the beginning, in Gen 1:1. We were not in flesh, but we were in our celestial body, 1 Cor 15:40. We were present when God created this earth age.

27 So God created man in His own image, in the image of God created He him; male and female created He them.

The word 'man' here is 'adam' in the Hebrew which means 'mankind', and it has no article in verse 26. It means that God created man with a flesh body. The body we have in this earth age.

Let's go to Gen 2:

7 And the Lord formed man of the dust of the ground and breathed into his nostrils the breath of life; and man became a living soul.

The word 'man' here is 'Adam' = 'eth-Ha adham' with article and particle, which is very emphatic, meaning 'the specific man Adam'. What specific Adam? The Adam from which lineage Christ would be born.

So what do we have here? The sixth day, Gen 1:26-27, God created the 'gentiles' = the nations = the heathen people – all people that are not Jews = are not from the 12 tribes (not only Judah) – are not the Hebrew people. In Gen 1:31 God said after He did that: *And God saw everything that He had made, and, behold, it was very good......*

The eighth day God created Adam from which lineage Christ would be born. Christ could not be born from the 'gentiles', the 'nations', for Christ would not be a perfect sacrifice for our sins that way, when He died on the cross. This is what the Bible much is about, to protect and keep this lineage 'clean'. This is not a racist statement but just the plain truth from the Word of God.

When Cain, Gen 4:16-17, took a wife from the land of Nod, she was from adam's seed, the Gentiles, not from Adam's, eth-Ha adham's, lineage.

Now let's see who Cain was. Let's go to Gen 3:

1 Now the serpent was more subtle than any other beast of the field, which the Lord God had made. And he said unto the woman, 'yea, hath God said, "Ye shall not eat of every tree of the garden"'?

The serpent is the Devil, Satan, the very shining beautiful cherub of Ez 28:

12......'Thou sealest up the sum, full of wisdom, and perfect beauty.

He looks like Jesus, almost.

The woman is Eve. Back to Gen 3:

2 And the woman said unto the serpent, 'We may eat of the fruit of the trees of the garden:

3 But of the fruit of the tree which is in the midst of the garden, God hath said, "Ye shall not eat of it, neither shall ye touch it, lest ye die." '

The word 'touch' here is 'naga' in the Hebrew, which means 'lie with a woman', when it is used in an euphemistic way, that will say a 'nicer' word is used instead of the actual word.

I think the Appendix in the Companion Bible summarizes Gen 3 and its consequences very elegantly:

The history of Gen 3 is intended to teach us the fact that Satan's sphere of activities is in the religious sphere, and not the spheres of crime or immorality; that his battlefield is not the sins arising from human depravity, but the unbelief of the human heart. We are not to look for Satan's activities today in the newspaper press, or the police courts; but in the pulpit, and in professors' chairs. Wherever the Word of God is called in question, there we see the trail of 'that old serpent, which is the devil, and Satan'. This is why anything against the true interest of the Word of God, as being such, finds a ready admission into the newspapers of the world, and is treated as 'general literature'. This is why anything in favor of its inspiration and Divine origin and its spiritual truth is rigidly excluded as being 'controversial'.

This is why Satan is quite content that the letter of Scripture should be accepted in Gen 3, as he himself accepted the letter of Ps. 91:11. He himself could say 'It is written', Matt 4:6, so long as the letter of what is 'written' could be put instead of the truth that is conveyed by it; and so long as it is misquoted or misapplied.

This is his object in perpetuating the traditions of the 'snake' and the 'apple', because it ministers to the acceptance of his lie, the hiding of God's truth, the support of tradition, the jeers of the infidel, the opposition of the critics, and the stumbling of the weak in faith.

End of quote.

Now we understand what really happened in the garden. There was no apple. There is no apple mentioned in the Bible here. When we read on in Gen 3 we also see that they, Adam and Eve made fig leaves for aprons, for they saw they were naked, after they had 'touched' the tree in the 'midst' of the garden, which was 'the tree of the knowledge of good and evil' = Satan, Gen 2:

17 But of the tree of the knowledge of good and evil, thou shalt not eat of it: for in the day that thou eatest thereof thou shalt surely die.'

'Tree' here is the Hebrew word 'ets' from 'atsah' = to close the eyes, related to the word 'atseh' = the spine, as giving firmness to the body, backbone. Cp. The tree of life, Gen 3:22,24, which is Jesus. So we see we have to do with a person.

Close your eyes here is of course meant spiritually, which was the case for Adam and Eve after they had touched the tree.

To 'die' here means that the flesh, our flesh body, became mortal, that will say it became liable to die, which we all know, Gen 2:17, 5:5, Adam died within 1000 years = one day = 'in the day'.

So what do we have now? Satan, who knew that Christ was going to be born from the lineage of Adam, eth-Haadham, tried to destroy that lineage. The result was Cain, the son of Satan and Eve. Abel was by Adam and Eve, Cain was not. Cain and Abel were two egg twins with different fathers. If we read on in Gen 3;

13 And the Lord God said unto the woman, 'What is this that thou hast done?' And the woman said, 'The serpent beguiled me, and I did eat.'

and 2 Cor 11:

3 But I fear, lest by any means, as the serpent beguiled Eve through his subtlety, so your minds should be corrupted from the simplicity that is in Christ.

148

we see that the word 'beguiled' is the Greek word 'exapataho' = wholly seduce. Wholly seduce can only mean one thing. What do you think?

Back to Gen 3:

14 And the Lord God said unto the serpent, 'Because thou hast done this, thou art cursed above all cattle, and above every beast of the field; upon thy belly shalt thou go, and dust shalt thou eat all the days of thy life:

15 And I will put enmity between thee and the woman, and between thy seed and her Seed; It shall bruise thy head, and thou shalt bruise His heal.'

To 'go upon thy belly' and 'eat dust' are figures of speech and mean to have a very low position, which Satan has.

The enmity is between Satan's seed, the Kenites, Cain's children, and Adam's children, the Hebrew people, the 12 tribes, through Lamech, Gen 5:28, Noah's father. The others were destroyed in the flood. Cain was not Adam's son. Remember? Satan would bruise Christ's heal on the Cross, but Christ is going to bruise Satan's head in the lake of fire, Rev 20. If the head is bruised you are finished.

Cain's children, the Kenites are ruling this world, with **'the four hidden dynasties: education, religion, politics and the economy.** Cain has his own genealogy, Gen 4:17-ff.

The Kenites are mentioned through the Word of God, and play a very important role in this earth age and in the Word of God. Ultimately they are the negative part of God's plan, that will say, God is letting them play their role as a test for us, to see if we choose Satan or God? We can make the correct choice, only if we study the Word enough to know the difference. That will say, if we love the truth enough, 2 Thess 2:10.

The Kenites are the great traders since the beginning, since the little 'rock' island, Tyre, or Tyrus, outside Zidon, on the Palestinian coast, a celebrated commercial city of Phoenicia, cp. Joel 3:4. Tyre means 'rock', and sometimes 'Satan' in the Scriptures, the false 'rock', see the Prince of Tyrus in Ez 28 for example, not the true Rock, Christ.

It is evident, that under Solomon there was a close alliance between the Hebrews and the Tyrians. Hiram, king of Tyre, supplied Solomon with cedar wood, for the Temple, precious metals and workmen, and gave him sailors for the voyage to Ophir and India, while on the other hand Solomon gave Hiram supplies of corn and oil, ceded to him some cities, and permitted him to make use of some havens on the Red Sea, 1 Kings 9:11-14, 26-28, 10:22.

Now the Kenites are operating from the World Trade Centers instead, and many other places.

Just to be sure you get the message I will explain a little more here.

Were the races, including the Kenites, destroyed in the flood? No! There were not. Let's read in Gen 6:

19 And of every living thing of all flesh, two of every sort shalt thou bring into the ark, to keep them alive with the; they shall be male and female.

What does 'all flesh' means? It means 'all flesh', which means 'all' of 'all' races of course, including the Gentiles, the Kenites and the Adamic. So there we see, that two of each race survived the flood.

Also there is a common misunderstanding of where the 'black' race comes from.

Traditions of men say that the black race comes from when Ham lay with his father's, Noah's wife, Gen 9:

22 And Ham, the father of Canaan, saw the nakedness of his father, and told his two brethren without.

'To see the nakedness' of his father means to lie with his father's wife, Lev 18:8, 20:11. The son from this relationship was Canaan. God is very natural, in fact he is 'super' natural, which means 'more' natural than we are. Canaan was not a black man, for from two

Adamic people, Ham and his father's wife, who also was Adamic, can not come a black man. It is scientifically impossible. God always works in a natural way.

We know from Gen 6:

9.......: Noah was a just man and perfect in his generations,......

that his family was straight Adamic, that will say not mixed with the Gentiles or the fallen angels. So Noah's wife was Adamic.

You may think this chapter sounds occult or something like that. Not so it is! It is the truth from the Scriptures. You see most Christians are Biblically illiterate. Most Christians have the mark of the beast, of Rev 13 and 19, which means they are deceived, they don't know the truth, but have listened to traditions of men, in the churches, rather than the word of God and have not studied the word themselves.

To have the mark of the beast in your right hand is to work for Satan, and to have the mark in your forehead = in your brain = thinking process is to be deceived by him and his children.

If you read Rev 13:

3.......: and all the world wondered after the beast.

you see that ALL the world = the majority of the world's population are going to worship the beast, which in this case is 'the one world order', which is set up and ruled by the Kenites, and ultimately is going to be turned over to Antichrist, Satan, when he appears here on earth for a period of five months, playing Christ, just before the true Christ returns, Rev 17:

13 These have one mind, and shall give their power and strength to the beast.

'These' are the Kenites and the 'beast' here is Satan in the role of Antichrist.

2 Thess 2:

1 Now we beseech you, brethren, by the coming of our Lord Jesus Christ, and by our gathering together unto Him,

2 That ye be not soon shaken in mind, or be troubled, neither by spirit, nor by word, nor by letter, as from us, as that the day of Christ is at hand.

3 Let no man deceive you by any means: for that day shall not come, except there come a falling away first, and that man of sin be revealed, the son of perdition,

Before Christ returns there shall be 'apostasy', which is the Greek word used here for 'falling away'.

The 'son of perdition' here is Satan's Greek name Apollyon, which you can read about in Rev 9:11.

4 Who opposeth and exalteth himself above all that is called God, or that is worshipped; so that he as God sitteth in the Temple of God, shewing himself that he is God.

Here we see Satan in the role of Antichrist 'playing' Christ.

Rev 9:

4 And it was commanded them that they should not hurt the grass of the earth, neither any green thing, neither any tree; but only those men which have not the seal of God in their foreheads.

We see here that 'they' are not locust but people, for they don't eat grass, etc. They are Satan's, Antichrist's buddies.
To have the 'seal of God' in your forehead is to know the truth.

5 And to them was given that they should not kill them, but that they should be tormented five months:......

"Tormented" here means in a spiritual sense = deceived.

10 And they had tails like unto scorpions, and there were stings in their tails: and their power was to hurt men five months.

The analogy with scorpions is of course a figure of speech, which tells how the deception shall be, digesting in the victim's body, in this case the spirit.

You see Satan's children are very active in these last days. They know they don't have long time left until they are blotted out in the lake of fire, Rev 20. They have a chance though to repent and change and become a child of God, if they so decide.

The Kenites have always been a pain to the Jews, for they call themselves Jews, but are not, Rev 2:9 and 3:9. The Jews have to take the blame for what the Kenites do, charging usury and other greediness. You know what I mean, the background for the world wars and all, and today's economy, for example the IMF, etc. There is much you could say about this.

I am going to give you another example from the Scriptures telling who the Kenites are. Let's go to Matt 13:

24 Another parable put He forth unto them, saying, 'The kingdom of heaven is likened unto a man which sowed good seed in his field:

The word for 'seed' here is 'sperma'= male sperm.

25 But while men slept, his enemy came and sowed tares among the wheat, and went his way.

This is what Satan did in the garden to Eve.

26 But when the blade was sprung up, and brought forth fruit, then appeared the tares also.

The Kenites appeared among the 'Jews' = in the meaning of all 12 tribes.

27 So the servants of the householder came and said unto him, 'Sir, didst not thou sow good seed in thy field? From whence then hath it tares?'

28 He said unto them, 'An enemy hath done this.' The servants said unto him, 'Wilt thou that we go and gather them up?'

29 But he said, 'Nay; lest while ye gather up the tares, ye root up also the wheat with them.

If we start sifting out Kenites among the worlds population, we are also going to take some Jews with us by mistake. So Jesus is saying, that we are not supposed to sift out Kenites in this earth age. Leave them alone. Let the angels sift in the end, at harvest time, see next verse.

30 Let both grow together until the harvest: and in the time of harvest I will say to the reapers, 'Gather ye together first the tares, and bind them in bundles to burn them: but gather the wheat into my barn.'

Let's jump in the same chapter to verse

34 All these things spake Jesus unto the multitude in parables; and without a parable spake He not unto them:

35 That it might be fulfilled which was spoken by the prophets, saying, 'I will open my mouth in parables; I will utter things which have been kept secret from the foundation of the world.'

36 Then Jesus sent the multitude away, and went into the house: and His disciples came unto Him saying, 'Declare unto us the parable of the tares of the field.'

Why is Jesus sending the multitude away? Because they are not supposed to know the secret about the Kenites. So is the case with most Christians today and have always so been. Let's look at this in Mark 4:

9 And He said unto them, 'He that hath ears to hear, let him hear.'

Jesus talks like this, when He talks to the elect.

10 And when He was alone, they that were about Him with the twelve asked of Him the parable.

11 And He said unto them, 'Unto you it is given to know the mystery of the kingdom of God: but unto them that are without, all these things are done in parables:

It is obviously not ment for everybody to know, understand, about the Kenites.

12 That seeing they may see, and not perceive; and hearing they may hear, and not understand; lest at any time they should be converted, and their sins should be forgiven them.'

This is a quote from Is 6:9-10. This has to do with what is explained in Rom 11:8 and that God is blinding some people from the truth. He does this to protect the weak minded to be responsible for their sins. It sounds strange, but it isn't. If you once know the truth, and sin, because you are deceived, receive the mark of the beast, that will say don't understand that Antichrist is Satan playing Christ, in the end, and therefore do not repent, because you think you are doing right, you are in bad shape before God. But if God puts a 'stupor' (katanuxis in the Greek, see Rom 11:8) on you, as he does in Rom 11, you are not responsible. That means that everybody is not supposed to understand the truth now. God is sparing them that, until the millennium teaching, Rev 20:6, when we do not have evil present, for Satan is locked in the pit, Rev 20:1-3.

13 And he said unto them, 'Know ye not this parable? And how then will ye know all parables?

If we don't understand about the Kenites, we don't understand the whole truth of the Word of God. If we don't, we are in the risk of being deceived.

Now back to Matt 13:

37 He answered and said unto them, 'He That soweth the good seed is the Son of man;

Remember that 'seed' still is the Greek word 'sperma' = male sperm.

The title 'The Son of man' when used of Christ, always has the Article; and the word for 'man' is the Greek word 'anthropos'. When used of a human being, as in Ez, it never has the Article. In this case it has the Article, so we know it is talking about Jesus here.

38 The field is the world; the good seed are the children of the kingdom; but the tares are the children of the wicked one;

Who is the wicked one? One guess! Satan of course, see next verse.

39 The enemy that sowed them is the devil; the harvest is the end of the world; and the reapers are the angels.

40 As therefore the tares are gathered and burned in the fire; so shall it be in the end of the world.

41 The son of man shall send forth His angels, and they shall gather out of His kingdom all things that offend, and them which do iniquity;

42 And shall cast them into a furnace of fire: there shall be wailing and gnashing of teeth.

'Furnace of fire' is of course the 'lake of fire', Rev 20.

43 Then shall the righteous shine forth as the sun in the kingdom of their Father. Who hath ears to hear, let him hear.

Talking to the elect again.

Let's go now to John 8:39-47. John 8:

39 They answered and said unto Him, 'Abraham is our father.' Jesus saith unto them, 'If ye were Abraham's children, ye would do the works of Abraham.

'They' are the Kenites. Their father is not Abraham, but Satan.

40 But now ye seek to kill Me, a Man That hath told you the truth, which I have heard of God: this did not Abraham.

41 Ye do the deeds of your father.' Then said they to Him, 'We be not born of fornication; we have one Father, even God.'

The fornication took place in the Garden, Gen 3.

42 Jesus said unto them, 'If God were your Father, ye would love Me: for I proceeded forth and came from God; neither came I of Myself, but he sent Me.

43 Why do ye not understand My speech? Even because ye cannot hear My word.

44 Ye are of your father the devil, and the lusts of your father ye will do. He was a murderer from the beginning, and abode not in the truth, because there is no truth in him. When he speaketh a lie, he speaketh of his own: for he is a liar, and the father of it.

Cain was the first murderer, and he was the son of the devil, Satan, not Adam, through fornication with Eve in the Garden, Gen 3. Satan wholly seduced Eve as Paul says in 2 Cor 11:

3 But I fear, lest by any means, as the serpent beguiled Eve through his subtlety, so your minds should be corrupted from the simplicity that is in Christ.

The word 'beguiled' here is the Greek word 'exapataho', which only means 'wholly seduced', including loss of virginity. Satan = 'the serpent' is very subtle. He is very beautiful also, see Ez 28.

Now back to John 8:

45 And because I tell you the truth, ye believe Me not.

46 Which of you convinceth Me of sin? And if I say the truth, why do ye not believe Me?

47 He that is of God heareth God's words: ye therefore hear them not, because ye are not of God.'

The Kenites are not of God, but of Satan. They are his children umbilicalcord to umbilicalcord. They can become children of God though, if they except Jesus Christ.

I hope this has cleared up some questions for you.

The Companion Bible, Appendix 146, has a good analyze of what the 'katabole' and the 'foundation of the world' are.

To arrive at the true meaning of the expression the 'foundation of the world', we must note that there are two words translated 'foundation' in the New Testament: (1) themelios, and (2) katabole.

The Noun, themelios, occurs, in Luke 6:48-49, 14:29, Acts 16:26, Rom 15:20, 1 Cor 3:10-12, Eph 2:20, 1 Tim 6:19, 2 Tim 2:19, Heb 6:1, 11:10, Rev 21:14,19. It is never used of the world (kosmos) or the earth (ge). The corresponding Verb (themelioo) occurs in Matt 7:25,

Luke 6:48, Eph 3:17, Col 1:23, Heb 1:10 and 1 Pet 5:10. The verb is only once used of the earth (ge), Heb 1:10.

A comparison of all these passages will show that these are proper and regular terms for the English words 'to found', and 'foundation'.

The Noun, katabole, cocurs in Matt 13:35, 25:34, Luke 11:50, John 17:24, Eph 1:4, Heb 4:3, 9:26, 11:11, 1 pet 1:20, Rev 13:8, 17:8, and the corresponding Verb (kataballo) occurs in 2 Cor 4:9, Heb 6:1, and Rev 12:10.

A comparison of all these passages (especially 2 Cor 4:9, and Rev 12:10) will show that kataballo and katabole are not the proper terms for founding and foundation, but the correct meaning is casting down, or overthrow.

Consistency, therefore, calls for the same translation in Heb 6:1, where, instead of 'not laying again', the rendering should be 'not casting down'. That is to say, the foundation already laid, of repentance, &c., was not to be cast down or overthrown, but was to be left—and progress made unto the perfection.

Accordingly, the Noun katabole, derived from, and cognate with the Verb, ought to be translated 'disruption', or 'ruin'.

The remarkable thing is that in all occurrences (except Heb 11:11) the word is connected with 'the world' (Gr. Kosmos), and therefore the expression should be rendered 'the disruption or ruin of the world', clearly referring to the condition indicated in Gen 1:2, and described in 2 Pet 3:5-6. For the earth was not created tohu (Is 45:18), but became so, as stated in the Hebrew of Gen 1:2 and confirmed by 2 Pet 3:6, where 'the world that then was by the word of God', Gen 1:1, perished, and 'the heavens and the earth which are now, by the same word' were created, Gen 2:4, and are 'kept in store, reserved unto fire against the day of judgment', 2 Pet 3:7, which shall usher in the 'new heavens and the new earth' of 2 Pet 3:13.

'The disruption of the world' is an event forming a great dividing line in the dispensations of the ages. In Gen 1:1 we have the 'foundation' of the world, Heb 1:10 = themelioo, but in Gen 1:2 we have its overthrow.

This is confirmed by a further remarkable fact, that the phrase, which occurs ten times, is associated with the Preposition 'apo' = 'from' seven times, and with 'pro' = 'before' three times. The former refers to the kingdom, and is connected with the 'counsels' of God; the latter refers to the Mystery or Secret and is connected with the 'purpose' of God, see John 17:24, Eph 1:4, 1 Pet 1:20.

Ample New Testament testimony is thus given to the profoundly significant fact recorded in Gen 1:2, that 'the earth became tohu and bohu, i.e. waste and desolate; and darkness was on the face of the deep', before the creation of 'the heavens and the earth which are now', 2 Pet 3:7.

In other words, after Satan rebelled in the first earth age, Ez 28, God destroyed the first earth age, and then he created the present earth age, Gen 1:3-ff. So when the Bible says 'before the foundation of the world', for example in Eph 1:4, it means 'before the foundation of the present earth age', which is just after Satan rebelled and God destroyed the first earth age.

Chapter XI

The Relationship Between Jews and Christians

I am here going to give a little more background that might help to tackle the problem with the relationship between "Jews" and Christians. Not many will accept it of course, for it's the root to the truth and truth is not popular.

Who is a Jew? A Jew can be several kinds of people actually. A Jew can be a resident of Judaea. That includes every person living in Judaea, Judah tribe's territory. The New Testament uses the Greek word 'Ioudaios', which means a resident of Judaea, in the sense of a country. We easy understand what it is to be of the tribe of Judah, but when we get to those who are not of the tribe of Judah, but live in Judaea, we can include many other peoples. Among those different peoples are the Kenites (sons of Cain), for example. So when the Bible is using the word Jew, it can mean peoples of the tribe of Judah, or Kenites, or any other person of any other race, or tribe living in Judaea. When we commonly use the term Jew I don't think we are really aware of who we are talking about. We commonly think of Jews as God's people of the Bible, but we don't define it closer than that.

Now we have another problem, for Judah is only one of the 12 tribes. Where do we have the rest of Jacob's sons, which is the natural seed of Israel, the whole nation today as it has always been. As we know God changed Jacob's name to Israel. OK! Israel is the name of the whole nation, all 12 tribes, at least up to a point. It changes in 1 Kings 11 and 12.

Here we see that Israel is split up in two parts. One part is called Israel, which are the ten northern tribes, and the other part is called Judah, which are the two southern tribes, Judah and Benjamin. They all will be joined back together again first at Christ's return Ez 37:16-22. Cp. also Zech 11:14.

The ten northern tribes, sometimes also called Joseph, as well as Israel, taken captive by Assyria, 2 Kings 15:29, 17:6, 21, 23, 18:11 (also documented in The Assyrian Tablets in The British Museum. The Assyrian is a type of Antichrist, which is Satan's office for the end times), about 200 years before Judah and Benjamin were taken captive into Babylon (Babylon means confusion, and is a type for the confused world in the end times, Rev 18:2, 10, cp. with Antichrist above, and Is 14, where also the king of Babylon is a type of Antichrist, cp. Lucifer, Is 14:12, who both are Satan), 2 Kings 23:27, 25:1ff., were later scattered all over the world. Of Judah only about 40000 returned from Babylon to the Holy Land, Ezra 2:64.

The rest stayed, and are now scattered all over the world also. Judah and Benjamin were probably a nation of about 1.5 million people at this point. So what do we have here? We have a nation scattered all over the world, who was to become many nations and kings, Gen 17:6, and a people as many as the stars of the heaven, and as the sand of the sea shore, Gen 22:17. That's a lot of people. Where are they now?

They became the western Christian nations of Europe and America, mixing into and taking over in part the heathen, Gentile, nations they entered. So there are more "Jews" than we normally think of, if we call all peoples from the 12 tribes Jews. When we talk about persecution, Jews have persecuted Jews (each other) a lot and have behaved unwisely from the beginning, for they also successively forgot who they were.

Most people from the 12 tribes don't know they are 'Jews', and many who think they are, are not. Jews started warring each other all ready in 1 Kings 12:19, 14:30, 15:6, 15:16, and have done it up to this day. It's all recorded in the Old Testament, the books of the Kings, the Chronicles and the prophets etc., and also historically in the Assyrian Tablets in the British Museum, and Josephus's Antiquities.

I would like to mention briefly in this context that the prophet Jeremiah brought Zedekiah's daughters to the British Isles at the time of the Babylonian captivity, and they became the mothers of the European king houses. The head of the British empire is of the tribe of Judah, the Jewish king line, mixed with the house of Israel. The

King James Bible translation was initiated by this house through King James I.

Jeremiah brought with him also the Stone of Scone, also called the Stone of Destiny, which is Jacob's pillows and pillar in Gen 28. This stone ('coronation stone') is still under the coronation throne in the Westminster Abbey in London, and the monarchs are crowned over it, saying they are the protector of the faith. It has been carried from and to Scotland and back, so now it is broken into two pieces. It weighs 400 pounds by the way. Interesting? I think so. It has been written about in the British newspapers not long ago.

We have more problems, cp. Matt 13:24-43. Do you have ears to hear? The Kenites who call themselves Jews but are not, Rev 2:9 and 3:9. King Solomon, 1 Kings 9:20-21, let the Kenites, 1 Chr 2:55, work in the temple for the priests, the Levites, and the Kenites slowly took over the whole church, so in Ezra 8:15 there are no Levite priests left, cp. Ezra 2:58. We still have Kenites today in the synagogues and in the Christian churches, so they are out there calling themselves Jews and Christians and put the true Jews and Christians in a lot of trouble, mildly said. It is done through deception through the Four Hidden Dynasties.

The Kenites are in fact ruling this world, with God's permission, with the Four Hidden Dynasties: the economy, politics, education and religion. When you control all that, you can deceive a whole world, which is exactly what they do and always done. And they are good at it.

This is completely obvious from the Word of God, The Bible, and historical facts. It started with trade on the island Tyrus, which prince is a type of Antichrist, who is Satan, who is the son of perdition, who is Apollyon, Ez 28:2, 16, Rev 9:11, 2 Thess 2:3, John 17:12.

Today the Kenites are creating "the one world order" which is the first beast in Rev 13. The second is Satan himself. In Dan 11:23, for example, the Kenites are called "a small people." The "one world order" is the fourth beast in Dan 7:7. In Dan 8:23 we have both the "one world order" and Satan, and in Dan 8:22 the "four hidden dynasties." This is just a few examples of many occurrences in the Bible.

To explain this further will take a separate study which is too much to go into here and now. It is nevertheless true.

The Kenites are used as the negative part of God's plan. We are here in this earth age (Gr. kosmos), in this race as Paul said, to make a choice between God and Satan. The Kenites are Satan's sons umbilical cord to umbilical cord. They are very loyal to their father but can of course be saved too if they turn to Christ. Caiaphas was most likely a Kenite, appointed by the Roman Government, not by God. The Kenites were the ones that cried, "crucify Him," to stir up the crowd, not the Jews from the 12 tribes. So the Jews did not crucify Jesus.

See here also the Parable of the Fig Tree, Mark 13:28 and Jer 24, which concerns the restoration of the Jewish nation May 1948, and the Jews, not all the 12 tribes but only Judah, contra the Kenites.

See E. Raymond Capt's 'Abrahamic Covenant' (Artisan Publishers), which is an excellent study over the 12 'Jewish' tribes scattering all over the world, on how they became Vikings, Germans, Celts, Anglo-Saxons, and became the modern western Christian countries. Saxon comes from Isaac, for example, and means 'sons of Isaac'. 'Caucasian', what the white races (they are two) are called, is from that the tribes went over the Caucasus mountains. It's not quite correct to call all white people Caucasians though, for one part is not. Only the 10 northern tribes are rightly Caucasians. A special study for another time.

It's interesting that Hitler, who was himself half Jewish, wanted to get rid of the 'Jews', basically Judah tribe, his own people, to create a 'pure' white race, out of his own people (again!?) which logically would be the 12 tribes, which includes Judah and the 10 northern tribes, and also the white race created the sixth day, Gen 1:26 (a subject for another time), together the large part of the German population and other 'western' country's. I call this total confusion, and if Hitler was not ignorant about these relations, he was more evil than we ever thought of. Few others seemed to know either. It's the same today. Total confusion, that will say Babylon.

We see what ignorance creates. Here we have Jews fighting against Jews. The deliberation of Europe by the allies in the W.W.II was also in part Jews fighting against Jews, that will say civil war.

How can that happen? They don't know who they are. They forgot, and the Bible says they would, and with God's help, because of their disobedience to God. 1 Kings 11:33, Jer 9:16, 13:24, 18:17, Ez 12:15, 20:23 are just a few references about this of many. It is all for their own hurt, and for their own best, as a result in the end, Ez 22:15, Zech 10, and many other addresses.

What I mean with this document is to emphasize that you need to have a solid background knowledge, before you make your mind up how you shall tackle the issue concerning the relationship Jews-Christians.

Chapter XII

Easter
and Passover

Acts 12:4 has a mistranslation in the King James Bible. 'Pascha' in the Greek text is translated□ Easter instead of Passover. This mistranslation of Passover is only one time, in the King James, and here in Acts.

Pascha in the Greek, or Pecach from Pacach in the Chaldee is the Passover, the meal, the day, the festival, or the special sacrifice connected with it. Pecach, a pretermission, i.e. exemption, used only of the Jewish Passover, the festival or the victim, Passover offering. Pacach, a primitive root, to hop, i.e. figuratively to skip over, or spare, by implication to hesitate, pass over. See Ex 11:1-14:31 where Passover started and 1 Cor 5:7-8 declaring that Jesus is our Passover. If we believe of course, upon Him, not otherwise.

Easter is a heathen term derived from the Saxon goddess Eastre, the same as Astarte, the Syrian Venus, called Ashtoreth in the Old Testament, which has to do with fertility rites and sexual orgies in the woods, and therefore are eggs, rabbits and quick like a bunny associated with it. It is the special evil of the Canaanite nations. The name is derived from the Asherah. The Asherah was idolatry of the most revolting form of immorality under the guise of religion. All virtue surrendered. 'The going of whoring' is more than a figure of speech. Asherah, is the Phallus image of Is 57:8 and 'the image of the male,' Ez 16:17. I can tell more about it, but I suggest you to make your own study on the subject.

Places to study in the Bible could be 1 Ki 11:5, 33, 2 Ki 23:13, cp. Judg 2:13, 1 Sam 7:3, 12:10, 31:10, Deut 1:4, Josh 9:10, 12:4, 13:12, 31, Judg 10:6, 1 Sam 7:4.

Easter ought to have nothing to do with, or be mixed with, Passover used from Ex 12:11 to Heb 11:28 in the correct way in the King James Bible, 77 times except one, Acts 12:4.

166

So, dear churches of the world, sharpen up and know what you are doing when you celebrate Passover and call it Easter.

Some newer translations, or variations, of the Bible have 'corrected' this mistranslation, for example The Amplified Bible, and have the correct word Passover instead of Easter. Some Bibles in other languages, for example the Swedish Bible, have the correct translation, but Swedish people still eat and paint eggs at Passover. The Swedish Bible uses the word 'Pask' which is very close to the Greek word Pascha, as you can see. It is certainly not Easter.

The French Bible has 'Paque', which is also close to Pascha. The German Bible just says 'Fest' of the people, which means Festival, as you most likely can see for yourself.

Whoever put Easter into the King James Bible must have been a 'false' scribe who wanted to confuse the church, and he succeeded very well, for most English speaking churches in the world wrongly use the word Easter instead of Passover, which naturally is an abomination before God, mixing sexual orgies with the celebration of Christ's death and resurrection. Most likely was this scribe a Kenite. So, you see the Kenites are still in the religious sector to try to confuse people just like their father, Satan, does.

Further more you can see what God thinks about this in Ez 8:

6 He said furthermore unto me, 'Son of man, seest thou what they do? even the great abomination that the house of Israel committeth here, that I should go far off from My sanctuary? but turn thee yet again, and thou shalt see greater abominations.'

The house of Israel is of course the ten northern tribes that were scattered, the Western Christian nations.

7 And He brought me to the door of the court; and when I looked, behold a hole in the wall.

8 Then said He unto me, 'Son of man, dig now in the wall:' and when I had digged in the wall, behold a door.

They hide their abominations, and there are so many that there is even a door into the hiding place.

9 And He said unto me, 'Go in, and behold the wicked abominations that they do here.'

10 So I went in and saw; and behold every form of creeping things, and abominable beasts, and all the idols of the house of Israel, pourtrayed upon the wall round about.

11 And there stood before them seventy men of the ancients of the house of Israel, and in the midst of them stood Jaazaniah, the son of Shaphan, with every man his censer in his hand; and a thick cloud of incense went up.

'The ancients' is the priesthood. Jaazaniah means 'heard from YHVH' = a priesthood that says, yes even thinks, it heard from God, but it is not from God at all. There are lots of them around in church today. Shaphan is the 'Easter rabbit'.

12 Then said He unto me, 'Son of man, hast thou seen what the ancients of the house of Israel do in the dark, every man in the chambers of his imagery? for they say, 'The Lord seeth us not; the Lord hath forsaken the earth.'

13 He said also unto me, 'Turn thee yet again, and thou shalt see greater abominations that they do.'

14 Then he brought me to the door of the gate of the Lord's house which was toward the north; and behold, there sat women weeping for Tammuz.

Tammuz is 'the Easter egg queen, the sprout of life in the sexual orgies.'

Chapter XIII

The Parable of the Tares

In Mark 4:13 Jesus is saying: *'Know ye not this parable? And how then will ye know all parables.'*

What does this mean? Exactly what Jesus says. If we do not understand the parable of the sower we can not understand God's Word.

Observe what Jesus is saying in Mark 4:9, *'He that hath ears to hear, let him hear.'* He is talking to the elect, the Zedek = the just = the souls that stood up for God in the first earth age, when the Devil rebelled against God, which led to the katabole = the overthrow of Satan, Ez 28. Observe in Matt 13:36 that Jesus sent the multitude away and explained the parable for the disciples only. Jesus always spoke in parables to the multitude without explaining it to them. Why? Read Mark 4:11, *'Unto you it is given to know the mystery of the kingdom of God: but unto them that are without, all these things are done in parables:......*

Let us now start reading Matt 13:

24 Another parable put He forth unto them, saying, 'The kingdom of heaven is likened unto a man which sowed good seed in his field:

25 But while men slept, his enemy came and sowed tares among the wheat, and went his way.

The word translated 'seed' here is 'sperma' = male sperm in the Greek. The word 'tares' is the Greek word 'zizania', not 'darnel', but known as 'zewan' today in Palestine. While growing it looks like wheat, but when full grown the ears are long and the grains almost black. Each grain of zewan must be removed before grinding wheat, or the bread is bitter and poisonous. Wheat is golden, but tares show there true color when they ripen.

26 But when the blade was sprung up, and brought forth fruit, then appeared the tares also.

27 So the servants of the householder came and said unto him, 'Sir, didst not thou sow good seed in thy field? from whence hath it tares?'

28 He said unto them. 'An enemy, hath done this.' The servants said unto him, 'Wilt thou then that we go and gather them up?'

29 But he said, 'Nay; lest while ye gather up the tares, ye root up also the wheat with it.'

30 Let both grow together until the harvest; and in the time of harvest I will say to the reapers, 'Gather ye together first the tares, and bind them in bundles to burn them; but gather the wheat unto my barn.'

Then Jesus spoke a couple of other parables. We continue with verse 34 in the same chapter.

34 All these things spake Jesus unto the multitude in parables; and without a parable spake He not unto them;

35 That it might be fulfilled which was spoken by the prophet, saying, 'I will open my mouth in parables; I will utter things which have been kept secret from the foundation of the world.'

'From the foundation of the world' should be correctly translated: 'from the overthrow of Satan' by God in the first earth age = katabole, Ez 28.

World is the Greek word 'kosmos' = the world as created, ordered, and arranged. It denotes the opposite of what man has called 'chaos', which God never created, see Is 45:18. 'Vain' in this verse is 'tuhu'; the same word as in Gen 1:2, 'without form'. In 2 Pet 3 Peter is explaining about the three earth ages. When the devil rebelled in the first earth age, God overthrew him, which is the 'katabole', see Rev

12:4, Ez 28, and Jer 4. Observe in Jer 4:25, that *'there was <u>no</u> man, and all the birds of the heavens were fled.'* We this way understand, that this is not the flood of Noa, for at Noa's flood there was a man, in fact several, and even women, Noa and his family, and all the races, two of all flesh, Gen 6:19. They were all on the ark, and in the second earth age. There were birds also, see Gen 8:7-12.

The first earth age God destroyed completely, but why? He didn't want to destroy the third of the stars, his souls, his children, that He had created in the beginning, that then followed Satan at his rebellion, Rev 12:4. To destroy your own children is not easy, so God created this second earth age, so every soul, except the fallen angels = souls, Gen 6:2 and Jude 6, and Satan, would have a fresh chance, in this second earth age, to be born innocent by woman, through the water in her womb, to make their mind up to love God or Satan. To be born innocent means to have the memory of the first earth age erased. This is so everybody has an equal fair chance. God is fair. This is what really 'born again' is about, but it is misunderstood, for the Greek is 'born from 'above' = the Greek 'anothen',' John 3:3.

36 Then Jesus sent the multitude away, and went into the house: and His disciples came unto Him, saying, 'Declare unto us the parable of the tares of the field.'

Why did Jesus sent the multitude away? Because it was only meant for the disciples to understand it.

37 He answered and said unto them, 'He that soweth the good seed is the Son of man;

The word for 'man' here is the Greek 'anthropos'. This title when used for Christ always has the Article.

38 The field is the world; the good seed are the children of the kingdom; but the tares are the children of the wicked one;

The children of the wicked one are the Kenites. The situation we are talking about here is when Satan beguiled Eve in the garden of

Eden. To understand 'beguiled' see 2 Cor 11:3, where it is the Greek word 'exapataho' = 'wholly seduce', including loss of virginity. This is the only meaning this word can have in the Greek. 'The serpent' and 'the tree of the knowledge of good and evil' in the garden was Satan. The word 'touch' in Gen 3:3 is 'naga', which is used for 'lie with a women' when it is used euphemistically. So, we are here talking not about a spiritual seed, but a literal seed, male sperm.

39 The enemy that sowed them is the devil; the harvest is the end of the world; and the reapers are the angels.

The end of the world = the end of this earth age.

40 As therefore the tares are gathered and burned in the fire; so shall it be in the end of this world.

See here Rev 20:10 and 15, the lake of fire. See also Hebr 12:29 *'For our God is a consuming fire.'* = the lake of fire, which is a blotting out process, see Ez 28:18-19.

41 The Son of man shall send forth His angels and they shall gather out of His kingdom all things that offend, and them which do iniquity;

42 And shall cast them into a furnace of fire: there shall be wailing and gnashing of teeth.

43 Then shall the righteous shine forth as the sun in the kingdom of their Father. Who hath ears to hear, let him hear.

When, as I said, Jesus says, *'Who has ears to hear,'* he is talking to His elect.

Then Jesus is telling a couple of other parables. We continue in verse

51 Jesus saith unto them, 'Have ye understood all these things?' They say unto Him, 'Yea, Lord.'

52 Then said He unto them, 'Therefore every scribe which is instructed unto the kingdom of heaven is like unto a man that is an householder, which bringeth forth out of his treasure things new and old.

New here is the Greek word 'kainos' = new in character, not 'neos' = new in time.

53 And it came to pass, that when Jesus had finished these parables, He departed thence.

Finished marking the end of this special collocation of parables, showing them to be one whole.

Here are some references you should study: St. john 8:42-47, Rev 3:9, St. John 18:36-37. Observe that 'Jew' in St. John 18:36 is the Greek word 'ioudaios = be of the tribe of Judah, or a resident of Judaea. This word means in the sense of a country, and its residents, more than being of the tribe of Judah. It means it is talking about the Kenites. The Jews didn't crucify Christ, the Kenites did, stirring up the crowd crying, 'Crucify, Crucify', Luke 23:21.

Chapter XIV

The Number of the Beast and the Mark of the Beast

In Rev 13:18 we read: *Let him that hath understanding count the number of the beast: for it is the number of a man; and his number is Six hundred threescore and six.*

That is 666.

The word 'count' here is very interesting. It is the Greek word 'psephizo' from 'psephos', which is from 'pselaphao', from the base 'psallo'; cp. psocho. That looks very complicated. I will explain. Summarizing this means: to use pebbles in enumeration, i.e. (that is) to compute; a pebble is worn smooth by handling, by impl. of use as a counter of ballot, a verdict of acquittal or ticket of admission, a vote: - stone, voice, (cp. stone = Tyre = false rock, long time ago): to manipulate, verify by contact; fig. to search for; -feel after, handle, touch; strengthened from 'psao', to rub or touch the surface; to triturate, i.e. (by analogy) to rub out (kernels from husks with the fingers or hand): -rub, cp. Luke 14:28

'Count' here means to calculate from the beginning, the first earth age, and all the way to present time, through knowledge and insight, understanding of the Word of God, who the beast is, and he is Satan, the Devil, the serpent, little horn, Dan 7:8, the dragon etc., see Rev 12:9. The number 666 means that he appears in the 6th seal, the 6th trump and the 6th plague or vial filled with plague. There are seven of them, all three. Read Rev 15:1-8 and 21:9, for example.

You can read about the seals in Rev 5:1-2, 5, 9, 6:1-12, 7:2, 8:1, and the trumpets, or trumps, in Rev 8:2-6, 1 Cor 15:52, Rev 9:14, 1 Thess 4:16.

Seals are to be unveiled, because they contain the truth. They are unveiled one after another, but not in chronological order. Trumpets are actions, and they are in chronological order. It starts in Rev 5:1.

666 is not a bar-code, or a chip, that is going to be placed on, or under, or in the skin in our forehead. The 'mark' of the beast, Rev 13:

16 And he causeth all, both small and great, rich and poor, free and bond, to receive a mark in their hand, or in their foreheads:

17 And that no man might buy or sell, save he that had the mark, or the name of the beast, or the number of his name.

is in the brain, that will say in the thinking process, and it means that if we believe Satan's lies we are deceived, we have the 'mark'. It is a Hebrew idiom. The lie, or the deception is, that people are not taught, that Satan comes as Antichrist before Christ, 2 Thess 2, that Satan is going to be here 5 months, Rev 9:5, 10, playing Christ in the house of God, prior to Christ's return. If you do not know that, you have the 'mark' of the beast in your forehead, in your brain, in your thinking process. The 'mark' in the right hand is to do Satan's work, work for Satan, and you will, if you don't know he is coming first. You are going to think Satan is Christ.

There will be some difficulties to buy and sell for the people who know the truth, that will say do not have the mark of the beast. God takes care of that though for us. That's His promise in Rev 9:4.

The 'rapture' theory is involved in this deception, see Ez 13:20.

Satan can tattoo people from toe to head. That will not change their believes. Or what do you think? Will it yours? I think not. Satan is more intelligent than that.

The 'seal' of God, which is the knowledge of the truth, Rev 7:3, and protects you from being deceived by Satan's deception, flood of lies in Rev 12:15-16, is the opposite of the 'mark' of the beast, naturally.

Chapter XV

The Only Two Churches
That Teach the Truth

In Rev 2:8-11 and 3:7-13 we read about the only two churches, out of seven, that Christ is satisfied with, Smyrna and Philadelphia. They existed but are also types of churches that exist now.

The Greek word used for Jews here is Ioudaios = resident of Judaea or of the tribe of Judah, which means you do not have to be of the tribe, be a real Jew, a Hebrew, but just a resident in the country, to call yourself a Jew.

I think it's in its place to explain why some writing is in past tense and some in future tense in the book of Revelation. The reason is that John was taken to the Lord's day, Rev 1:10, to view the revelation he received from the Lord, from that day. The Lord's day is when He returns.

What do these two churches teach? Rev 2:

9......the blasphemy of them that say they are Jews and are not, but the synagogue of Satan.

Rev 3:

7......He that hath the key of David, He that openeth, and no man shutteth, and shutteth, and no man openeth;

To have the 'key of David' is, in part, to know the lineage from where Christ was born, see Is 22:22.

8......thou......hast kept My word, and hast not denied My name.

9......them of the synagogue of Satan, which say they are Jews, and are not, but do lie;......

10 Because thou hast kept the word of My patience,......

They teach the truth including the Kenites, who say they are Jews but are not, but the are the seed = sperma = sons of Cain = sons of Satan and Eve from the garden of Eden, Gen 3.

If you go to a church today and ask who the Kenites are, and they do not know, that church is dangerous. It does not know the truth, the Word. They do not know the Scriptures and they are going to be deceived by the instead of Christ, which is the Devil, Satan, the son of perdition, Apollyon, Rev 9:11, Antichrist, when he comes to earth playing Christ = playing Jesus in the house of God, 2 Thess 2, Rev 12:9. If you do not know or understand who the Kenites are, you can not understand the rest of the Scriptures, the parable of the sower, Matt 13:24-43, for example. The tares are the children, the Kenites, of the wicked one = Satan, in the garden of Eden.

So only two out of seven churches today teach the truth? If you listen to them, it sounds like it.

They who have no chance now, here in this dispensation, are going to get their first chance after Christ returns. Believe the Scripture on this point, Rev 20:6. Christ and His elect, the Zadok (from tsadaq = right = righteous = just = the souls that stood up for God in the first earth age, when the Devil rebelled, and are already judged by God, Rom 8:26-33, and therefore participate in the first resurrection, Rev 20:6), are going to teach during the millennium, Rev 20:6, thousand years, to give them a chance who never had a chance now, with the lack of true teaching of the Word, in today's churches. That's the whole point with the millennium, and why Satan is loosed in the end of the millennium to test these new Christians, Rev 20:6-8. Even their saved relatives can help them during this time, Ez 44:25.

God, our Father, loves His children and would never send anyone to the lake of fire, 'hell' if you wish, that will say blot anyone out, never to be remembered, as never existed, Rev 20:15, before He has given them a fair chance first to understand the Word, know the truth about Him. He, in fact, even gives some of His children the spirit of 'slumber', in the Greek 'katanuxis = 'stupor', today to protect them from being accountable if they go wrong, Rom 11:8, *eyes that they should not see, and ears that they should not hear.* He blinds them,

Rom 11:7, from the truth. If God himself puts a blinder on people, He is not going to blot them out at the judgment day in the end of the millennium, Rev 20:15, without giving them a fair chance first to learn the truth. See also Matt 13:10-11, for example.

Watch for the coming revival, the greatest ever, in your flesh, in your terrestrial body, 1 Cor 15:40. It is Satan's revival, the first tribulation.

Christ's revival, the second tribulation, is going to be in your celestial, heavenly or spiritual, body, and after Satan has had his revival, 2 Thess 2, Rev 12:9, to test us 5 months, Rev 9:4-5, 10, Mark 13:20, Matt 24:21-22, Luke 21. The first tribulation is only going to effect the elect 10 days, Rev 2:10.

Before Satan comes to earth, Rev 12:9, there shall come, or actually there is already now, we are there, 'a falling away first' = 'apostasia' in the Greek text = desertion of faith = changing of religion, 2 Thess 2:3. Be careful!

Remember Luke 13:24-28 and Matt 7:15-23. Matt 7:

22-23 Many will say to Me in that day (when Christ has returned), *Lord, Lord, have we not prophesied in Thy name? and in Thy name have we cast out devils? and in Thy name done wonderful works? And then will I profess unto them, 'I never knew you: depart from Me, ye that work iniquity'.*

Se also Matt 23 for example.

Watch therefore, learn the truth, study the Bible, do not read so many books (Eccl 12:12) about the Bible, unless it's teaching you how to understand the Bible for yourself. Ask God for help. Study for yourself if you can not find a good teacher that is teaching chapter by chapter, verse by verse, precept on precept, line by line. Do not listen to men and their traditions. The worst deception is in the churches. It is sad but true, and a very Biblical statement.

A good summary of the problem, you can find in the Appendix of the Companion Bible:

The history of Gen 3 is intended to teach us the fact that Satan's sphere of activities is in the religious sphere and not the sphere of crime or immorality; that his battlefield is not the sins arising from human depravity, but unbelief of the human heart (mind). We are not to look for Satan's activities today in the newspaper press, or the police courts, but in the pulpit and professor's chairs. Wherever the Word of God is called in question, there we see the trail of 'that old serpent, which is the Devil, and Satan,' Rev 12:9. This is why anything against the true interest of the Word of God (as being such) finds a ready admission into the newspapers of the world, and is treated as 'general literature'. This is why anything in favor of its inspiration and Divine origin and its spiritual truth is rigidly excluded as being controversial.

This is why Satan is quite content that the letter of Scripture should be accepted in Gen 3, as he himself accepted the letter of Ps 91:11. He himself could say when he tried to tempt Christ in the wilderness: 'It is written', Matt 2:6, so long as the letter of what is 'written' could be put instead of the truth that is conveyed by it; and so long as it is misquoted or misapplied.

This is his object in perpetuating the traditions of the 'snake' and the 'apple', because it ministers to the acceptance of his lie, the hiding of God's truth, the support of tradition, the jeers of the infidel, the opposition of the critics, and the stumbling of the weak in faith.

End of quote.

You see there is only one true church, the people who know the truth and accept it, now or in the millennium. Now it is them that have the seal of God in their forehead = brain, Rev 7:3, 9:4, the Bride and the Wife of Christ, Rev 19:7, and not the mark (the lies; the rapture doctrine for example, see Ez 13:20) of the beast = Satan, Rev 13:16 = believe that Satan is Jesus, 2 Thess 2:3-4, and work for Satan = have his mark in their right hand. The false bride, the 'whore' of Rev 17, are 'they that are with child and they that give suck,' Mark 13:17, because they have jumped in bed with Satan, spiritually, thinking he is Christ. Satan could deceive them for they did not know the truth. They did not know the Bible, the Scriptures, the Word of God. We who know the truth will 'stand against the wiles of the Devil', Eph 6:11.

We thank You Father that you have foretold us all things, Mark 13:23, and we ask You to help them that want to receive the love of the truth, 2 Thess 2:10, so that they might be saved now or in the millennium.

Chapter XVI

Talking In Tongues

Talking in tongues is quite a different thing from what is commonly taught.

Let us see what God's Word says about it.

The place to start looking is Acts 2 and then 1 Cor 12 and 14. Acts 2:

1 And when the day of Pentecost was fully come, they were all with one accord in the place.

Fifty days, or on the fiftieth day after Christ had resurrected the disciples were assembled together in Jerusalem, as Christ had commanded in Acts 1:4.

2 And suddenly there came a sound from heaven as of a rushing mighty wind, and it filled all the house where they were sitting.

3 And there appeared unto them cloven tongues like as fire, and it sat upon each of them.

4 And they were filled with the Holy Spirit, and began to speak with other tongues, as the Spirit gave them utterance.

'Tongues' here is the Greek 'glossa' = language, specifically one naturally unacquired, not gained = your mother tongue. 'Other' is the Greek 'heteros' = another of a different kind, usually denoting generic distinction.

5 And there were dwelling at Jerusalem Jews, devout men, out of every nation under heaven.

6 Now when this was noised abroad, the multitude came together, and were confounded, because that every man heard them speak in his own language.

Language here is the Greek 'dialectos' = dialect, so people heard and understood what they said in their own home dialect. They did not hear anything that had to be interpreted by somebody as in 1 Cor 14:27, where it is talking about translation of a foreign language. Mark that the word unknown in every verse in chapter 14 is in Italics which means it is not in the Manuscripts, that will say the original Greek text, but added by the translators of the King James. I will go through chapter 14 in 1 Cor later on. We will also go into what they said, which is very important.

7 And they were all amazed and marveled, saying one to another, 'Behold, are not all these which speak Galileans?

8 And how hear we every man in our own tongue, wherein we were born?

'Tongue' here is the same 'dialectos' in Greek as in verse 6 where it is translated 'language.'
Verses 9-15 you can read from your own Bible.
Peter is then saying in verse

16 But this is that which was spoken by the prophet Joel; (Joel 2:28-31)

17 'And it shall come to pass in the last days,' saith God, 'I will pour out of My Spirit upon all flesh: and your sons and your daughters shall prophesy, and your young men shall see visions, and your old men shall dream dreams:

18 And on My servants and My handmaidens I will pour out in those days of My Spirit; and they shall prophecy:

In verse 18 we see what is talked about in, for example, Mark 13:9-11, specifically in verse 11. Same thing is talked about in Luke 12:10-12. It means that the elect, the justified, the already judged, because they stood up for God in the first earth age, when the Devil rebelled, Ez 28, which is called the 'katabole', see Rev 20:6, where these therefore participate in the first resurrection, shall be brought up in the synagogue of Satan to witness against him, with the truth, as they did in the first earth age, see Rev 2:9 and 3:9. The Holy Spirit shall talk through them exactly the same way it happened at Pentecost in Acts 2, above. The content of what they say may not necessarily be the same though. This is when Satan is here 5 months, see Rev 9:5, 10, Matt 24:15 and Mark 13:20, just before Christ returns, see 2 Thess 2 = the first tribulation, Satan playing Christ as Spurious Messiah or Antichrist. 'Son of perdition' is 'Apollyon' in the Greek in 2 Thess 2:3, which is one of Satan's names, see Rev. 9:11, which proves it. The whole world is going to understand what the elect are saying, in everybody's own home dialect, no interpretation necessary.

Do you start to understand now what it is all about, and how deception has crept in about 'talking in tongues.' Real 'tongue talking' has not happened yet in these end times, because Satan is not here yet. The so called 'talking in tongues' that is done today is fake and a misunderstanding of the Scripture. It is 'babel', which means 'confusion' in the Hebrew tongue, and it sounds just like it. I am going to show later on that 1 Cor 14 does not agree with the present 'tongue talking' either.

Acts 2:19-21 you can read from your Bible.

So there we have it.

I want to make one comment here.

Remember that evil spirits can fake 'talking in tongues', so a person who have never talked a foreign language, for example, can by an evil spirit do so. But remember that every body listening must hear it in his own home dialect, if it is the Holy Spirit talking through the person. That is the evidence of the presence of the Holy Spirit, and no one can fake that, not even evil spirits. So, if you hear somebody say, that he heard somebody speak in tongues, because that person talked in a language they are not able to speak, it is most likely an evil spirit talking through them, or simply, they are faking it by having learned a phrase just to impress. You never know what people can do. Stick to the Word of God, not traditions of men.

Remember again, that everybody listening must hear the True Tongue in their own home dialect simultaneously. Not just one language or dialect at a time is distributed. The Holy Spirit matches every listeners home dialect simultaneously. The listener only hears the Holy Spirit in his own dialect, not the other's. You see, there is no confusion, and all understand loud and clear what is said, no interpreter needed, just like at Pentecost in Acts 2. That is the evidence of the presence of the Holy Spirit. Unfakable.

Be careful when you read the Bible in modern languages. King James and other translations are not perfect. You have to brake it back to the original text, the Manuscripts. With a King James Bible and a Strong's Exhaustive Concordance you can do that.

When studying the Old Testament, you may also check things out in the Massorah, if you can get hold of one. Some knowledge about this can be gathered from Neh 8:8, see Ezra 7:6, 11.

You also have to get rid of the traditions of men, that have slipped into your mind from the teachings in churches you have attended earlier, most likely most of them. Most church people, including pastors, doctors etc., don't know the Word. The Bible says so. Why would otherwise *'all' the world wonder after the beast* in Rev 13:3, which is 'the one world order', which is the 'one world political and economical system', that we have today. Education and religion may be included too, so we have all 'the four hidden dynasties', led by the Kenites.

'All' the world worship Satan's system? Yes! How many are 'all'? The absolute majority of the population of the world, including the church. Only a remnant will not worship the beast, and they are the elect, the seven thousand of Rom 11:4.

This last information for you to be careful not to believe everything you hear and read, just because it is from the church. Stick with the Word itself, not peoples words.

Christ has foretold us all things according to Mark 13:23, not the church or people.

Now let's see what is said about 'tongues' in 1 Cor 12:

10 To another the working of miracles; to another prophecy; to another discerning of spirits; to another divers kinds of tongues; to another the interpretation of tongues:

Now let's brake this down to be able to rightly understand it. 'Divers' is in Italics, which means it is not in the Manuscripts. 'Kind' is the Greek word 'genos' as in 1 Cor 14:10, which means 'kin', which means 'generation, kindred, nation' etc. The verse is talking about a gift of talking several foreign languages. Simple. It is not talking about some 'unknown' tongues, for the word 'unknown' is not in the manuscripts, as said above.

Let's skip on to 1 Cor 14:

1 Follow after charity, and desire spiritual gifts, but rather that ye may prophesy.

2 For he that speaketh in an unknown tongue speaketh not unto men, but unto God: for no man understandeth him; howbeit in the spirit he speaketh mysteries.

Now we have to brake this down to understanding. 'Unknown' is in Italics, which means the word is not in the Manuscripts, but is added by the translators of the King James Bible. See then how it says that 'no man understandeth'. The word 'tongue' is the Greek word 'glossa', see above under Acts 2:4, which means the mother tongue. I don't understand how your mother tongue can be unknown, which the translators implicate. They apparently did not understand what they tried to translate. It has nothing to do with the Greek word 'dialectos', which is the English word 'dialect', either, which it should if it is related to Acts 2, because everybody is to understand it in their own home dialect. I think the evidence is enough already here, that the so called 'talking in tongues' is fake and a misunderstanding of the Bible, and is more an emotional flop as many other church flops, as for example many of the healings are emotional and psychological experiences more than real healings by our Lord Jesus Christ. I mention that here for I think it belongs to each other. That is why Jesus said in Matt 7:23, **'I never knew you: depart from Me, ye that work iniquity'.** Read the verses before this verse for full understanding and context. 'Gifts' is in Italics too. What it really says is, that if I speak Swedish preaching in a church in Italy, with people who don't know Swedish, they can't understand anything of what I am saying. Let's skip on to 1 Cor 14:

3 But he that prophesieth speaketh unto men to edification, and comfort.

We shall take a look, in this context, at Is 28:

11 For with stammering lips and another tongue will He speak to this People.

First! Who is speaking? He, with capital 'H'. It is God. What does this mean? 'Stammering' here is 'jabbering' from the Hebrew word 'la'eg' that comes from 'la'ag' which means to deride; as if imitating a foreigner or to speak unintelligibly, laugh to scorn, mock, a buffoon, a mocker. 'Another' = 'foreign' refers to the Assyrian language they were soon to hear in captivity. The Assyrian is a type of Antichrist, see Is 33:19 and Deut 28:49. This has clearly nothing to do with The Holy Spirit talking through people, specifically the elect. The word 'tongue' here is the Hebrew word 'lashon' which means 'babbler' or 'evil speaker', for example; it comes from the word 'lashan', that means 'to wag the tongue, accuse, slander.' This is what it means.

4 He that speaketh in an unknown tongue edifieth himself; but he that prophesieth edifieth the church.

Prophesy here is the Greek word 'propheteuo' = speak under inspiration = teach the word of God with the help of the Holy Spirit, basically. The prophet or the teacher talks in a language that people can understand without need of an interpreter or translator. As we already know, 'unknown' is not in the Manuscripts.

5 I would that ye all spake in tongues, but rather that ye prophesied: for greater is he that prophesieth than he that speaketh with tongues, except he interpret, that the church may receive edifying.

This simply means that greater is he that teaches the Word than he that speaks a foreign language. It means speak so people understand; speak the same language as the listeners.

6 Now, brethren, if I come unto you speaking with tongues, what shall I profit you, except I shall speak to you either by revelation, or by knowledge, or prophesying, or by doctrine?

What does this mean? Simply that if Paul does not teach in a language that the listener understands, the listener has no profit of it, waste of time in other words.

Read 'by' = in the Greek 'en' as within and continuance in time, in union and fellowship. 'Knowledge' here is the Greek 'gnosis' = knowledge acquired by learning, effort, or experience. This is important to note because 'tongue talkers' claim it is the Holy Spirit talking through them or inspiring them, that will say, it is not learned by effort, but simply received from the Holy Spirit. This has nothing to do with that, at all. This is also explained above.

7 And even things without life giving sounds, whether pipe or harp, except they give a distinction in the sounds, how shall it be known what is piped or harped.?

8 For if a trumpet give an uncertain sound, who shall prepare himself to the battle?

9 So likewise ye, except ye utter by the tongue words easy to be understood, how shall it be known what is spoken? For ye shall speak into the air.

This means that if you talk a language, foreign, that people don't understand, like above the Swedish Bible teacher speaking Swedish for Italians, no one understands what you are saying. The word 'air' here is 'spirit' = 'aemi' in the Greek = to breathe unconsciously, respire, same as in 1 Thess 4:17, not 'auranos' in Greek, which is 'sky' in the English.

10 There are, it may be, so many kinds of voices in the world, and none of them is without signification.

11 Therefore if I know not the meaning of the voice, I shall be unto him that speaketh a barbarian, and he that speaketh shall be a barbarian unto me.

Obvious!

12 Even so ye, for as much as ye are zealous of spiritual gifts, seek that ye excel to the edifying of the church.

Does it need to be explained? I don't think so.

13 Wherefore let him that speaketh in an unknown tongue pray that he may interpret.

As before 'unknown' is not in the Manuscripts, but added by the translators. It means simply 'he that speaks a foreign language, let him pray that he translates,' or have a translator, interpreter, with him.

14 For if I pray in an unknown tongue, my spirit prayeth, but my understanding is unfruitful.

This means that I think best in my mother tongue and not so well in the tongues or languages, foreign, that I have learned, at school if you wish, or by my self, or living in a foreign country.

15 What is it then? I will pray with the spirit, and I will pray with the understanding also: I will sing with the spirit, and I will sing with my understanding also.

This has to do with the same as verse 14.

16 Else when thou shalt bless with the spirit, how shall he that occupieth the room of the unlearned say 'Amen' at thy giving of thanks, seeing he understandeth not what thou sayest?

In other words, if people don't understand what you are talking about, how do they know when they shall say 'Amen', if you are teaching in a foreign language.

Take for example, to really emphasize what the Word is saying, a person talking in so called 'tongues', which is a lie, we know that now, don't we?: everybody is supposed to understand what the person is saying in their own home dialect, and here nobody understands. If we relate to Acts 2 something is wrong, and that is exactly what it is. 'Tongue talking' does not exist again until Antichrist = Satan sits in the Holy Place in Jerusalem and plays Christ, see 2 Thess 2:2-4 and Luke 12:10-12.

17 For thou verily givest thanks well, but the other is not edified.

Only God understands you, He understands all languages, He created them, but the people don't understand you, if you talk in a foreign language for them.

18 I thank God, I speak with tongues more than ye all:

19 Yet in the church I had rather speak five words with my understanding, that by my voice I might teach others also, than ten thousand words in an unknown tongue.

Again, 'unknown' is not in the Manuscripts. (Unknown) tongue means simply foreign language. Paul was a brilliant Hebrew scholar, a linguist. He studied under Gamaliel, who was a leading scholar at that time. Paul also spoke 'street' Greek, Latin etc. He was a Roman citizen.

What Paul is saying is, that he rather speak in a language that his audience understand than talk Latin to Hebrew people, for example.

20 Brethren, be not children in understanding: howbeit in malice be ye children, but in understanding be men.

Malice means ignorance.

21 In the law it is written, 'With men of other tongues and other lips will I speak unto this people; and yet for all that will they not hear Me, saith the Lord.'

In fact, here is the evidence. This verse Paul has inserted to tell us, that he is talking about foreign languages in this chapter. Quoted from Is 28:8-11 and mentioned above. This has nothing to do with the Holy Spirit talking through people. This has to do with the Assyrian tongue Israel was going to hear, when they became captives of the Assyrian.

Also, everybody must understand it in their own home dialect. In this verse it says, that they will not even hear God.

'Tongue' here is the Greek word 'heteroglossos', so it means man of another tongue, a foreigner, stranger.

That this has nothing to do with the Holy Spirit can we see also if we look at Luke 21:12-15 and 12:10-12.

Luke 21:

15 For I will give you a mouth and wisdom, which all your adversaries shall not be able to gainsay nor resist.

This is when the elect are brought up in the synagogues of Satan to witness about God, when Satan is here 5 months as Antichrist.

If the adversaries shall not be able to gainsay nor resist the mouth of wisdom God is giving the elect, it must be more than 'heteroglossos'. It must be the Holy Spirit instead. Which or Who it naturally is. It is Jesus talking, God our Father, The Living God.

Now back to 1 Cor 14:

22 Wherefore tongues are for a sign, not to them that believe, but to them that believe not: but prophesying serveth not for them that believe not, but for them which believe.

Here we are talking about the tongue of Pentecost, Acts 2, not foreign languages. 'Tongue' here is 'glossa' = mother tongue.

23 If therefore the whole church be come together in one place, and all speak with tongues, and there come in those that are unlearned, or unbelievers, will they not say that ye are mad?

24 But if all prophesy, and there come in one that believeth not, or one unlearned, he is convinced of all, he is judged of all:

Paul is saying that the Pentecostal tongue is for a sign. Of course it is, for everybody understands it in his own mother dialect. That is startling for the unbeliever, in fact for everybody, to hear a person, who can not talk a certain language, talking in your own dialect.

If we look in Luke 12:9-12 and 21:12-15 we see, that if the elect do not let the Holy Spirit talk through them, they commit the unforgivable sin. There is only one unforgivable sin. This one. All other sins are forgivable. Here in Luke we also see that at the same occasion, when the elect are brought up in the synagogue of Satan, and talk in the Pentecostal tongue, not even their adversaries shall be able to gainsay nor resist their witness. Why? Because God is speaking. Through them.

The Pentecostal tongue is the Holy Spirit talking through the elect when Satan is here playing Christ, 2 Thess 2, as we know by now.

Then in verse 23, Paul is saying that if everybody is talking in a foreign language when the church gets together, it is going to be a little confusing. The evidence that Paul is talking about languages here and not about the Pentecostal tongue is, that the Pentecostal tongue is not confusing, because everybody hears it in his own mother dialect. We don't hear it in more than our own mother dialect, not the other's. That is not confusing at all, but loud and clear.

If everybody talks in different foreign languages at the same time, it is confusing.

25 And thus are the secrets of his heart made manifest; and so falling down on his face he will worship God, and report that God is in you of a truth.

26 How is it then, brethren? When ye come together, every one of you hath a psalm, hath a doctrine, hath a tongue, hath a revelation, hath an interpretation.
Let all things be done unto edifying.

'Tongue' here is 'glossa' = mother tongue, see above.

27 If any man speak in an unknown tongue, let it be by two, or at the most by three, and that by course; and let one interpret.

What Paul is saying is that if you have people teaching in foreign languages in the church, let not more than two or three foreigners speak and have everything properly translated. If too many foreigners are talking in different languages, it is going to be confusing. Most of you have probably not experienced this in reality. It is very confusing, and at Paul's time there were many nationalities present in the church at the same time. I wonder what a pastor would say today if Spanish, Swedish, English, Serbo-Croatian, German, and Italian preachers started preaching in his church at the same time without interpreter.

'Unknown' is, as you know by now, not in the Manuscripts, but added by the translators. Paul is also saying that one person shall interpret everything.

28 But if there be no interpreter, let him keep silence in the church; and let him speak to himself, and to God.

We see here again, as above, that we are talking about languages, not the Pentecostal tongue, because the Pentecostal tongue needs no interpretation.

29 Let the prophets speak two or three, and let the other judge.

30 If any thing be revealed to another that sitteth by, let the first hold his peace.

31 For ye may all prophesy one by one, that all may learn, and all may be comforted.

32 And the spirit of the prophets are subject to the prophets.

33 For God is not the author of confusion, but of peace, as in all churches of the saints.

When people talk, or 'babel', in the 'false tongue', as I call it, it really is confusing. It doesn't mean anything. Also, if the Pentecostal tongue is for a sign for the unbelievers, why do people only talk it in their church, when they get together with their fellow believers and don't talk it out in the streets of the world to the unbelievers, which it is a sign for? The True Pentecostal Tongue should of course work here, everybody listening hearing it in his own home dialect, but not the 'babel' the believers create today, that no one understands. It is sad how easy deceived people are, to 'babel', and believe it is the Holy Spirit. Come on! Get a life! Wake up!

Let's skip on to verse

39 Wherefore, brethren, covet to prophesy, and forbid not to speak with tongues.

By the way, Acts 10:46 and 11:15-17 are talking about the True Pentecostal Tongue, cp. Acts 2:4 and John 1:1. It did't happen in the end times though, see Acts 2:17.

There we have it. Believe it or not. It is entirely up to you.

Thank You Father for having foretold us all things, Mark 13:23.

I would be happy if somebody could prove me wrong on this subject. Write me a letter in that case.

God Bless You!

Chapter XVII

This Is That, Act 2:16

What did they say at Pentecost? Let's go to Joel 2:

28 And it shall come to pass afterward that I will pour out My spirit upon all flesh; and your sons and your daughters shall prophesy, your old men shall dream dreams, your young men shall see visions:

29 And also upon the servants and upon the handmaidens in those days will I pour out My spirit.

30 And I will shew wonders in the heavens and in the earth, blood, and fire, and pillars of smoke.

31 The sun shall be turned into darkness, and the moon into blood, before the great terrible day of the Lord come.

32 And it shall come to pass, that whosoever shall call on the name of the Lord shall be delivered: for in mount Zion and in Jerusalem shall be deliverance, as the Lord hath said, and in the remnant whom the Lord shall call.

The remnant is the elect, the souls that stood up for God in the first earth age, at the 'katabole' = when the Devil rebelled and was cast out of the mountain of God, Ez 28:16.

I do not know! Are you called? If you have ears to hear and eyes to see you are. You are one of the elect.

What does 'afterward' mean? 'After' what? The answer is 'after' the temporal blessings of verses 23-27. In verse 23 it says 'the first month', which is the first of the five months when Apollyon, Satan, the Spurious Messiah, Antichrist, the son of perdition, the abomination of desolation, the desolator, is here playing Christ just before Jesus returns, the True Christ, Rev 9:11, 2 Thess 2, Mark

13:14, Daniel 9:27, 12:11, Matt 24:22, 12:7-9, Rev 9:4-5. The elect are going to receive blessings in this first month. Temporal is pertaining to the present life, this earth age, dispensation. 'Afterward', 'after' this blessing, God's Spirit, which is the Holy Spirit, shall be poured out on <u>all</u> flesh. Has that happened yet? Of course not. The structure shows us that the whole subject of 2:18-3:21 is evil removed from the Land and the People, and blessing bestowed on both. That has certainly not happened yet.

The prophecy of Joel 2:28-32 links up with the last clause of the 'song of Moses' in Deut 32:43, see Rev 15:3.

The Hebrew word used here is not the simple word 'ahar' = after, but the compound 'aharey-ken' = after that, as in Gen 6:4.

At Pentecost the Holy Spirit was not poured out on all flesh; only on some of those present. None of the great signs had been shown. No deliverance took place in Jerusalem: both land and people were still under Roman yoke. So, from a careful study of the two passages, it will be seen that there is a wide divergence between the statements of apostle and prophet on the one hand, and the general belief of Christendom, which the majority hold so tenaciously, that 'the church' was formed at Pentecost, on the other.

Because of the word used for 'after' it is certain that the word 'this' in Acts 2:16 refers to what follows, and not to what precedes; to the future events predicted by Joel, and not to those then taking place in Jerusalem.

None of the things detailed in verses 17 and 19 came to pass. 'This' therefore could not be the fulfillment of Joel's prediction, as the 'pouring out' was only on the apostles and those associated with them.

In Acts 2:11 we see that they spoke in 'tongues' 'the wonderful works of God' = 'great things' = the Greek 'megaleios', here and Luke 1:49, only.

What wonderful works? It does not say that in the Scriptures specifically, but Peter recognized Joel's prophecy, so they most likely spoke some of the contents of the book of Joel, for example the judgment removed mentioned above, Joel 2:18-3:21.

Chapter XVIII

Health God's Way

Genesis 1:

29 And God said, 'Behold, I have given you every herb bearing seed, which is upon the face of all the earth, and every tree, in the which is the fruit of a tree yielding seed; to you it shall be for meat.

No flesh food till after the flood.

Genesis 9:

3 Every moving thing that liveth shall be meat for you; even as the green herb have I given you all things.

4 But flesh with the life thereof, which is the blood thereof, shall ye not eat.

This is after the flood, and flesh becomes food for us, but you shall not eat blood.

You have to observe the food laws in Leviticus 11 though. You can not eat all animals. Some of them are unclean for food. Swine, crayfish, lobster, for example, you are not supposed to eat, just to take some examples of 'foods' that are commonly consumed in today's society. They are very dangerous to eat and create lots of common diseases.

Daniel 1:

12 Prove thy servants, I beseech thee, ten days; and let them give us pulse to eat, and water to drink.

Daniel wanted vegetable food instead of meat. The main reason for this was that the Babylonians did not bleed their animals, and they also ate scavengers. Do not eat blood. They were heathens and ate animals, scavengers, that were not healthy to eat according to The Law, mainly Leviticus 11. Also observe that Daniel asked for water to drink. They mostly drank wine in those days. It contains alcohol though. Wine is not healthy in larger amounts than may be a glass a day. That's not enough liquid. We see later in verse 15 that Daniel's and his friends' *countenances appeared fairer and fatter in flesh than all the children which did eat the portion of the king's meat.*

Ecclesiastes 12:

11 The words of the wise are as goads, and as nails fastened by the masters of assemblies, which are given from one shepherd.

12 And further, by these, my son, be admonished: of making many books there is no end; and much study is a weariness of the flesh.

13 Let us hear the conclusion of the whole matter: Fear God, and keep His commandments: for this is the whole duty of man.

14 For God shall bring every work into judgment, with every secret thing, whether it be good, or whether it be evil.

All wisdom comes from God. Most of it is in the word of God, the Bible, the Scriptures. If you start with knowing, understanding, the word of God, you will always go right there-after what ever science you study or what ever you do.

Deuteronomy 29:

29 The secret things belong unto the Lord our God: but those things which are revealed belong unto us and to our children for ever.

Do not cast pearls for swine. That is, do not try to convince people if you see they are not interested. Do not waste your time. God is in control and knows all, so He takes care of them, when it is their time.

John 14:

6 Jesus saith unto him, 'I am the way, the truth, and the life: no man cometh unto the Father, but by me.

You will not have eternal life, or learn the truth, through any one else, but Christ.

John 17:

17 Sanctify them through Thy truth: Thy word is truth.

God's word, the Bible, the Scriptures, is the truth.

Psalms 119:

159 Consider how I love Thy precepts: Quicken me, O Lord, according to Thy lovingkindness.

160 Thy word is true from the beginning: And every one of Thy righteous judgments endureth for ever.

God created us, so when He gave the prophets the Scriptures, as we read them now in the Bible, about what to eat for example, we can trust it. It is scientifically proved today, that God's 'food laws' in the Bible are accurate.

Luke 4:

4 And Jesus answered him, saying, 'It is written, That man shall not live by bread alone, but by every word of God.'

The word of God gives you peace, naturally, for when you know the truth, the only way to peace, you have peace. Confusion, through many books for example, Ecclesiastes 12:12 above, makes you worry, and to live in stress, which is unhealthy. I am not saying that you should not study books at all, educate yourself, but start with the word of God. This way you will not be deceived, for there is a lot of deception out there, not least in the church and the education system.

2 Timothy 2:

15 Study to shew thyself approved unto God, a workman that needeth not to be ashamed, rightly dividing the word of truth.

You must study with understanding. Ask God for help and use available tools like Strong's Concordance, the Companion Bible, for example, or ask God to find a good scholar that can help you. We all, most likely, need a teacher in the beginning into self study, and it all starts with loving the truth, 2 Thessalonians 2:10-11, having that true desire to find it.

Colossians 2:

14 Blotting out the handwriting of ordinances that was against us, which was contrary to us, and took it out of the way, nailing it to His cross;

When Christ was crucified, the blood ordinances were nailed to the cross. They have no value any more. But the law is still in effect, even the food laws. Jesus is saying that in Matthew 5:

17 Think not that I am come to destroy the law, or the prophets: I am not come to destroy, but to fulfill.

18 For verily I say unto you, Till heaven and earth pass, one jot or tittle shall in no wise pass from the law, till all be fulfilled.

The body has not changed. It is the same as it was when God gave the Scriptures to the prophets.

Malachi 3:

6 For I am the Lord, I change not; therefore ye sons of Jacob are not consumed.

God is keeping His covenant with Jacob, Gen 28:13-15.

Leviticus 3:

16 And the priest shall burn them upon the altar: it is the food of the offering made by fire for a sweet savour: all the fat is the Lord's.

The fat is the Lord's?! Look and learn! and do not eat fat that is visible on animals.

17 It shall be a perpetual statute for your generations throughout all your dwellings, that ye eat neither fat nor blood.'

There it is! Don't eat fat or blood. Animal fat is the most dangerous fat of all. You shall eat fat of growing plants instead, see Genesis 1:29. It is much healthier, and eat it in its natural state, not concentrated. You may also eat some animal's flesh, see Genesis 9:3-4 (before the law was given) and Leviticus 11, but do not eat the visible fat.

Leviticus 7:

23 'Speak unto the children of Israel, saying, 'Ye shall eat no manner of fat, of ox, or of sheep, or of goat.

What is the Scriptures saying to us? Eat as little fat as possible. Period! The processed foods we have today have an 'unnatural' amount of fat in it. It is put there by man. Only God knows how much fat we need, and therefore knows how much fat He shall put in our food; invisible fat in animal meat for example.

1 Timothy 4:

3 Forbidding to marry, and commanding to abstain from meats, which God hath created to be received with thanksgiving of them which believe and know the truth.

This doesn't mean that all foods, including scavengers, have become healthy just of a sudden, but that we shall eat only what ***God has created to be received*** according to the food Law in Lev 11, that will say what the food Law permits, and we shall leave the scavengers alone. It's the same with fat. God said, 'Ye shall eat no manner of fat......

8 For bodily exercise profiteth little, but godliness is profitable unto all things, having promise of the life that now is, and of that which is to come.

This doesn't mean that you should not exercise, but be obedient to God and put His word first in your life.

2 Corinthians 11:

3 But I fear, lest by any means, as the serpent beguiled Eve through his subtlety, so your minds should be corrupted from the simplicity that is in Christ.

Don't be deceived. The Kenites, Satan's children are ruling this world with 'the four hidden dynasties', education, religion, politics and the economy. If you are not grounded in the word of God, you are in bad shape. In Revelation 13:3 it says......***and all the world wondered after the beast.*** The 'beast' here is 'the one world order', which is part of 'the four hidden dynasties'. How many is 'all'? It is all, the majority of the world's population. Are you going to be among them? I hope not.

Leviticus 3:

3 And he shall offer of the sacrifice of the peace offering an offering made by fire unto the Lord; the fat that covereth the inwards, and all the fat that is upon the inwards,

Don't eat visible fat of animals. The whole world, all the world, does it, because it is deceived by the 'four hidden dynasties'.

4 And the two kidneys, and the fat that is on them, which is by the flanks, and the caul above the liver, with the kidneys, it shall he take away.

Don't eat the inward organs of animals.

5 And Aaron's sons shall burn it on the altar upon the burnt sacrifice, which is upon the wood that is on the fire: it is an offering made by fire, of a sweet savour unto the Lord.

Animal fat was for offerings to God, not for food.

6 And if his offering for a sacrifice of peace offering unto the Lord be of the flock; male or female, he shall offer it without blemish.

7 If he offer a lamb for his offering, then shall he offer it before the Lord.

8 And he shall lay his hand upon the head of the offering, and kill it before the tabernacle of the congregation: and Aaron's sons shall sprinkle the blood thereof round about upon the altar.

Don't eat blood. It was also for offerings to God. It is not any more though, because Christ nailed all ordinances, that has to do with burnt offerings and blood, to the cross, Colossians 2:14 mentioned above.

9 And he shall offer of the sacrifice of the peace offering an offering made by fire unto the Lord; the fat thereof, and the whole rump, it shall he take off hard by the backbone; and the fat that covereth the inwards, and all the fat that is upon the inwards,

Don't eat visible animal fat.

Leviticus 11 you can read out of your Bible. Here you can read about what you should and should not eat. Don't eat swine for example. Swine is a scavenger. It is created by God to clean the earth. And it does. It eats everything from the ground, rats, and so on, and the poison it eats is stored in the flesh, the fat mostly.

Do you eat snakes? I hope not. They are also scavengers, just like swine.

You can also read in Leviticus 11, that you are not supposed, it is unhealthy, to eat crayfish and lobster. They are also scavengers. They clean the bottom of lakes and the sea, from poisons, and store it in their flesh.

Many years ago before I knew the word of God, I thought that Jews didn't eat swine, just for 'some kind of' religious reason. Now I know it is for health reasons. It is also scientifically proved that swine is unhealthy to eat. The first the doctor tells you not to eat, when you are sick, is swine.

I think the rest of Leviticus 11 will be a good, healthy Bible study for yourself.

Deuteronomy 7:

15 And the Lord will take away from thee all sickness, and will put none of the evil diseases of Egypt, which thou knowest, upon thee; but will lay them upon all them that hate thee.

If you don't love the truth = God, He will send you strong delusion, send you false teachers, etc., 2 Thessalonians 2:10-11. I think that's fair.

If you don't know the word of God, you are going to be deceived and eat the wrong thing.

203

Deuteronomy 23:

12 Thou shalt have a place also without the camp, whither thou shalt go forth abroad:

13 And thou shalt have a paddle upon thy weapon; and it shall be, when thou wilt ease thyself abroad, thou shalt dig therewith, and shalt turn back and cover that which cometh from thee:

I included this, just to show that God's word is complete. Water closet is not a good thing. It poisons the lakes and seas. Even if you purify the waste water, you still produce sludge. New York, for example, transported its sludge out into the Atlantic ocean and dumped it there from 1938 until 1992. Now it's used as fertilizer, which is good. So it ended up in the water any way. We are not supposed to have big cities either, see Isaiah 5:8 *Woe unto them that join house to house,......*

Leviticus 13 you may also read from your Bible.

Isaiah 65:

3 A people that provoketh Me to anger continually to My face; that sacrificeth in gardens, and burneth incense upon altars of brick;

4 Which remain among the grave, and lodge in the monuments, which eat swine's flesh, and broth of abominable things is in their vessels;

Here is swine's flesh again. The twelve tribes are rebellious, and they eat swine's flesh. The whole western 'Christian' world does, except they who know they are 'Jewish'. The ten northern tribes do not know they are 'Jewish' = from Jacob. They were scattered by God, see 1 Kings 11:28-32, 12:19, 2 Kings 15:29, 17:6, 23, 19:32-34. They have lost knowledge of who they are.

5 Which say, 'Stand by thyself, come not near to me; for I am holier than thou.' 'These are a smoke in My nose, a fire that burneth all the day.

Here it is talking about the priest, that thinks he is holier than the lay-man.

Acts 10:

9 On the morrow, as they went on their journey, and drew nigh unto the city, Peter went up upon the housetop to pray about the sixth hour:

10 And he became very hungry, and would have eaten: but while they made ready, he fell into a trance,

11 And saw heaven opened, and a certain vessel descending unto him, as it had been a great sheet knit at the four corners, and let down to the earth:

12 Wherein were all manner of fourfooted beasts of the earth, and wild beasts, and creeping things, and fowls of the air.

13 And there came a voice to him, 'Rise, Peter; kill, and eat.'

14 But Peter said, 'Not so. Lord; for I have never eaten any thing that is common or unclean.'

15 And the voice spake unto him again the second time, 'What God hath cleansed, that call not thou common.'

16 This was done thrice: and the vessel was received up again into heaven.

17 Now while Peter doubted in himself what this vision which he had seen should mean, behold, the men which were sent from

Cornelius had made inquiry for Simon's house, and stood before the gate,

18 And called, and asked whether Simon, which was surnamed Peter, were lodged there.

19 While Peter thought on the vision, the Spirit said unto him, 'Behold three men seek thee.

20 Arise therefore, and get thee down, and go with them, doubting nothing: for I have sent them.'

21 Then Peter went down to the men which were sent unto him from Cornelius; and said, 'Behold, I am he whom ye seek: what is the cause wherefore ye are come?'

22 And they said, 'Cornelius the centurion, a just man, and one that feareth God, and of good report among all the nation of the Jews, was warned from God by an holy angel to send for thee into his house, and to hear words of thee.'

23 Then called he them in, and lodged them. And on the morrow Peter went away with them, and certain brethren from Joppa accompanied him.

24 And the morrow after they entered into Caesarea. And Cornelius waited for them, and had called together his kinsmen and near friends.

25 And as Peter was coming in, Cornelius met him, and fell down at his feet, and worshipped him.

26 But Peter took him up, saying, 'Stand up; I myself also am a man.'

27 And as he talked with him, he went in, and found many that were come together.

28 And he said unto them. 'Ye know how that it is an unlawful thing for a man that is a Jew to keep company, or come unto one of another nation; but God hath shewed me that I should not call any man common or unclean.

34 Then Peter opened his mouth, and said, 'Of a truth I perceive that God is no respecter of persons:

35 But in every nation he that feareth Him, and worketh righteousness, is accepted with Him.

36 The word which God sent unto the children of Israel, preaching peace by Jesus Christ: (He is Lord of all:)

This passage in the Scriptures has been misunderstood by many. The misunderstanding is, that people think this passage means we can eat everything. Not so! People do not read the whole passage. As you read the whole passage, you see that this Scripture means that even the Gentiles = the 'nations' = the 'ethnos' in the Greek = people that are not of the Jewish family can be 'saved'. So this scripture has nothing to do with food.

1 Timothy 4:

1 Now the Spirit speaketh expressly, that in the latter times some shall depart from the faith, giving heed to seducing spirits, and doctrines of devils;

Don't listen to any man, including this man, without checking him out, for yourself, in the word of God.

2 Speaking lies in hypocrisy; having their conscience seared with a hot iron;

'It is difficult to teach people that are 'seared' with Satan's lies, for 'scared' tissue have numb nerves', is what this means.

As you see, I did not intend to make a nutritional expert chapter out of this, for there are many good, honest, nutritionists out there. Go to any library and pick a good book about nutrition, and read and learn about what is healthy to eat, respectively what is unhealthy to eat.

Generally said, you shall eat food that is as close to its natural state as possible, that is, as little processed as possible.

Modern nutrition science can be summarized with this simple statement: ***The worst health risk is to eat too much fat. The second is lack of exercise. The third is smoking.*** If you stay away from these three risks, you have excluded 80% of the risk to get cancer, heart disease, etc.

It is important to eat fiber.

Only eat cold press olive oil. All other oils are destroyed at the manufacturer, for they are all heated up when they extract them.

Never eat hydrogenated oils.

Eat lots of vitamins and minerals. You have to, for the agricultural ground is destroyed by pesticides, and is 'over used', and it never rests, see Lev 25:3-5.

Try to eat as much of your food as you can organically grown. This way you avoid pesticides, etc.

Drink a lot of pure plain water like Daniel did.

In Leviticus 11 you can read which meats are clean and unclean for food.

In the old days exercise was no issue, for most people walked or rode all the time. People exercised 'naturally' so to say. Today we sit in a car.

There is another problem today with food. The food processing industry, where the nutrients get destroyed. We don't need this industry. It is created solely to canalize peoples interest to certain products, to make a profit. If we eat food that is 'natural', that will say not processed, that will say in its natural state, we are eating right. Fruit, meat, eggs, vegetables, fish, beans, juice, water, etc., are all foods in their natural state. We don't need the processed food. The little processing that is necessary we can do at home.

Remember there is a lot of deception going on out there. AMA, The American Medical Association, for example, is lying about how much fat we shall eat. AMA say we shall eat less than 30% fat, when the real truth is less than 10%. Why do they lie? If they said 10%, they would be out of work, for 80% of all diseases would be gone, if we in addition exercise and don't smoke. No patients no work for doctors. It is so simple when you think about it.

Live on the country, but if you have to live in a big city, try to arrange so you can go by public transportation (if there is a good one), and use enough time for it, so you don't have to stress. Most of Europe and several USA cities are well arranged here. Try to live where it is silent, no traffic noise, or other noise.

It is your life, and no one, I said NO ONE, should be able to control you. Not even Mr. Money.

Is 5:

8 Woe unto them that join house to house, that lay field to field, till there be no place, that they may be placed alone in the midst of the earth!

Chapter XIX

Have We Existed
In Another Life?

Ephesians 1:

4 According as He hath chosen us in Him before the foundation of the world, that we should be holy and without blame before Him in love:

'The foundation of the world' here means 'the foundation of this earth age'. There are two words translated 'foundation' in the New Testament: *themelios* and *katabole*.

In this instance it is 'katabole'. This is not a proper word to transfer into 'foundation' in the English. The proper meaning of the Greek word 'katabole' is 'casting down' or 'overthrow.' What is it talking about? It is talking about the 'overthrow' of Satan, Ezekiel 28, when Satan rebelled against God, in the first earth age, and was condemned by God to perish, be blotted out and never exist any more. Satan is going to be blotted out after the millennium, see Revelation 20.

Some people stood up for God against Satan in the first earth age. They are called the elect, see Romans 11:4......*'I have reserved to Myself seven thousand men, who have not bowed the knee to the image of Baal.'*

Baal represents Satan. Check it out for yourself.

The elect were therefore 'chosen before the foundation of the world', which must be right after the 'katabole'. This is the reason Genesis 1:2 is saying...*the earth was without form, and void;* which should be *'became'* without form, and void = *tohu va bohu* in the Hebrew. It must because God did not create the earth tuhu = in vain, see Isaiah 45:18......*He created it not in vain = tuhu.* It became vain because God destroyed the first earth age and created the present earth age, for He did not want to destroy the souls that followed Satan in his rebellion, the third of all the souls that God had created, Revelation 12:4 *And his tail drew the third part of the stars of heaven, and did cast them to the earth:*

God wanted to give his children a fair chance to understand Him. It is not all done in this earth age either, with all the deception going on, for the coming millennium is also there to help everybody to be informed about the kingdom of God, see Revelation 20:6......, *but they shall be priests of God and of Christ, and shall reign with Him a thousand years.* What do priests do? They teach the word of God. 'They' are the 'elect'.

Read my chapter about the three world ages.

Now back to Ephesians 1:

5 Having predestinated us unto the adoption of children by Jesus Christ to Himself, according to the good pleasure of His will,

Predestinated the elect as mentioned above.

6 To the praise of the glory of His grace, wherein he hath made us accepted in the Beloved:

7 In Whom we have redemption through His blood, the forgiveness of sins, according to the riches of His grace,

8 Wherein He hath abounded toward us in all wisdom and prudence;

9 Having made known unto the mystery of His will, according to His good pleasure which He hath purposed in Himself;

God has revealed the mystery for His elect, see Matthew 13:34-37 and Mark 4:10-13.

10 That in the dispensation of the fullness of times he might gather together in one all things in Christ, both which are in heaven, and which are on earth; even in Him:

'The dispensation of fullness' is first after the millennium, Revelation 21.

11 In Whom also we have obtained an inheritance, being predestinated according to the purpose of Him Who worketh all things after the counsel of His own will:

Proverbs 8:

1 Doth not wisdom cry? And understanding put forth her voice?

2 She standeth in the top of high places, By the way in the places of the paths.

3 She crieth at the gates, at the entry of the city, at the coming in at the doors.

22 The Lord possessed me in the beginning of His way, Before His works of old.

Wisdom was with God when he created the first earth age.

23 I was set up from everlasting, from the beginning, Or ever the earth was.

24 When there were no depths, I was brought forth; When there were no fountains abounding with water.

25 Before the mountains were settled, Before the hills was I brought forth:

26 While as yet He had not made the earth, nor the fields, Nor the highest part of the dust of the world.

Here we have the 'atom'.

27 When He prepared the heavens, I was there: When He set a compass upon the face of the depth:

28 When He established the clouds above: When He strengthened the fountains of the deep:

29 When He gave to the sea His decree, That the waters should not pass His commandment: When he appointed the foundations of the earth:

30 Then I was by Him, as one brought up with Him: And I was daily His delight, Rejoicing always before Him;

31 Rejoicing in the habitable part of His earth; And my delights were with the sons of men.

Here we see that 'the sons of men' = 'we' existed with 'wisdom' in the very beginning, in the first earth age.

32 Now therefore hearken unto me, O ye children: For blessed are they that keep my ways.

33 Hear instruction, and be wise, And refuse it not.

34 Blessed is the man that heareth me, Watching daily at my gates, Waiting at the posts of my doors.

35 For who so findeth me findeth life, And shall obtain favour of the Lord.

36 But he that sinneth against me wrongeth his own soul: All they that hate me love death.

Now to Job 1:

6 Now there was a day when the sons of God came to present themselves before the Lord, and Satan came also among them.

7 And the Lord said unto Satan, 'Whence comest thou?' Then Satan answered the Lord, and said, 'From going to and fro in the earth, and from walking up and down in it.'

This is not now in this earth age, for Satan is not here now. He is in heaven with Michael, see Revelation 12:7 and 2 Thessalonians 2:6.

Job 38:

1 Then the Lord answered Job out of the whirlwind, and said,

God answers Job after he has been poorly advised by his 'friends', to no good, for about 36 chapters.

2 'Who is this that darkeneth counsel by words without knowledge?

3 Gird up now thy loins like a man; for I will demand of thee, and answer thou Me.

4 Where wast thou when I laid the foundations of the earth? declare, if thou hast understanding.

5 Who hath laid the measures thereof, if thou knowest? or who hath stretched the line upon it?

6 Whereupon are the foundations thereof fastened? or who laid the corner stone thereof;

7 When the morning stars sang together, and all the sons of God shouted for joy?

8 Or who shut up the sea with doors, when it brake forth, as if it had issued out of the womb?

9 When I made the cloud the garment thereof, and thick darkness a swaddlingband for it,

10 And brake up for it My decreed place, and set bars and doors,

11 And said, 'Hitherto shalt thou come, but no further: and here shall thy proud waves be stayed'?

12 Hast thou commanded the morning since thy days; and caused the dayspring to know his place;

13 That it might take hold of the ends of the earth, that the wicked might be shaken out of it?

14 It is turned as clay to the seal; and they stand as a garment.

15 And from the wicked their light is withholden, and the high arm shall be broken.

23 Which I have reserved against the time of trouble, against the day of battle and war?

Verse 23 has to do with Ezekiel 38 and 39, and Revelation 16, the battles of Hamon-gog and Armageddon.

2 Peter 3:

1 This second epistle, beloved, I now write unto you: in both which I stir up your pure minds by way of remembrance;

Remembrance from the first earth age.

2 That ye may be mindful of the words which were spoken before by the holy prophets, and of the commandment of us the apostles of the Lord and Saviour:

3 Knowing this first, that there shall come in the last days scoffers, walking after their own lusts,

4 And saying, 'Where is the promise of His coming? for since the fathers fell asleep, all things continue as they were from the beginning of the creation.'

5 For this they willingly are ignorant of, that by the word of God the heavens were of old, and the earth standing out of the water and in the water:

6 Whereby the world that then was, being overflowed with water, perished:

The first earth age perished. This is not Noah's flood, for the the earth did not perish at Noah's flood. The dove in Genesis 8:10-11, which is Noah's flood, came back with an olive leaf in its mouth. The earth could not have perished at Noah's flood, if there were still olive trees. An olive tree takes a long time to develop, and that kind of time was not available, for the dove was sent out and came back directly when the waters of Noah's flood were abated.

The destruction of the first earth age is recorded in Jeremiah 4:23-27. Jeremiah 4:

23 I beheld the earth, and, lo, it was without form, and void; and the heavens, and they had no light.

The earth was not without form and void after Noah's flood, and there was light also of course. Noah could see the dove and everything else.

24 I beheld the mountains, and, lo, they trembled, and all the hills moved lightly.

There was no trembling and moving of mountains and hills at Noah's flood.

25 I beheld, and, lo, there was no man, and all the birds of the heavens were fled.

Noah and his people and all the races were still there after his flood. That was the whole point of the flood. And the dove was there and picked the olive leaf and brought it back to Noah. It didn't escape somewhere.

26 I beheld, and, lo, the fruitful place was a wilderness, and all the cities thereof were broken down at the presence of the Lord, and by His fierce anger.

Yes, there were cities in the first earth age, and they were broken down at the 'katabole', we are talking about in these verses, by the fierce anger of the Lord. Why was the Lord angry? Satan had rebelled, Ezekiel 28, and drawn the third part of the stars = souls, with him, Rev 12:4.

27 For thus hath the Lord said, 'The whole land shall be desolate; yet will I not make a full end.

Now back to 2 Peter 3:

7 But the heavens and the earth which are now, by the same word are kept in store, reserved unto fire against the day of judgment and perdition of ungodly men.

We are now talking about this present earth age and its destiny, with rejuvenation and blotting out of all evil, see the rest of 2 Peter 3.

8 But, beloved, be not ignorant of this one thing, that one day is with the Lord as a thousand years, and a thousand years as one day.

9 The lord is not slack concerning His promise, as some men count slackness; but is long-suffering to us-ward, not willing that any should perish, but that all should come to repentance.

John 17:

6 I have manifested Thy name unto the men which Thou gavest Me out of the world: Thine they were, and Thou gavest them Me; and they have kept Thy word.

We are talking here about the elect chosen at the 'katabole' in the first earth age.

'Men' are both men and women, no gender of course. We are talking about souls.

7 Now they have known that all things whatsoever Thou hast given Me are of Thee.

8 For I have given unto them the words which Thou gavest Me; and they have received them, and have known surely that I came out from Thee, and they have believed that Thou didst send Me.

9 I pray for them: I pray not for the world, but for them which Thou hast given Me; for they are Thine.

10 And all Mine are Thine, and Thine are Mine; and I am glorified in them.

11 And now I am no more in the world, but these are in the world, and I come to Thee. Holy Father, keep through Thine own name those whom Thou hast given Me, that they may be one, as We are.

12 While I was with them in the world, I kept them in Thy name: those that Thou gavest Me I have kept, and none of them is lost, but the son of perdition; that the scripture might be fulfilled.

'The son of perdition' = Satan was, in the first earth age, judged to perish, Ezekiel 28.

13 And now come I to Thee; and these things I speak in the world, that they might have My joy fulfilled in themselves.

14 I have given them Thy word; and the world hath hated them, because they are not of the world, even as I am not of the world.

Most people don't like you when you teach the real truth from God's word. Christian and other religious traditions they might like, but not the real truth.

15 I pray not that Thou shouldest take them out of the world, but that Thou shouldest keep them from the evil.

16 They are not of the world, even as I am not of the world.

Have you ever felt, that you do not belong to this world? If you have, you might be one of God's elect.

17 Sanctify them through Thy truth: Thy word is truth.

18 As Thou hast sent Me into the world, even so have I also sent them into the world.

19 And for their sakes I sanctify Myself, that they also might be sanctified through the truth.

20 Neither pray I for these alone, but for them also which shall believe on Me through their word,

The Lord is praying for them that believe what the elect say.

Now let's go to Romans 8:

22 For we know that the whole creation groaneth and travaileth in pain together until now.

23 And not only they, but ourselves also, which have the firstfruits of the Spirit, even we ourselves groan within ourselves, waiting for the adoption, to wit, the redemption of our body.

The elect have the firstfruits of the Spirit.

24 For we are saved by hope: but hope that is seen is not hope: for what a man seeth, why doth he yet hope for?

25 But if we hope for that we see not, then do we with patience wait for it.

26 Likewise the Spirit also helpeth our infirmities: for we know not what we should pray for as we ought: but the Spirit Itself maketh intercession for us with groanings which cannot be uttered.

This is not about talking in 'tongues' as many believe; see the two chapters about this for an in depth study of what 'tongues' really are.

This is simply about what it says. We don't know what to pray for, so the Holy Spirit helps us.

27 And He That searcheth the hearts knoweth what is the mind of the Spirit, because He maketh intercession for the saints according to the will of God.

28 And we know that all things work together for good to them that love God, to them who are the called according to His purpose.

Called, chosen, at the 'katabole'.

29 For whom He did foreknow, He also did predestinate to be conformed to the image of His Son, that He might be the firstborn among many brethren.

30 Moreover whom He did predestinate, them He also called: and whom He called, them He also justified: and whom He justified, them He also glorified.

To be justified is to be judged. The elect have already been judged. That is why they participate in the first resurrection, Revelation 20:

6 Blessed and holy is he that hath part in the first resurrection: on such the second death hath no power,......

Back to Romans 8:

31 What shall we then say to these things? If god be for us, who can be against us?

32 He that spared not His own Son, but delivered Him up for us all, how shall he not with Him also freely give us all things?

33 Who shall lay any thing to the charge of God's elect? It is God That justifieth;

Romans 9:

11 (For the children being not yet born, neither having done any good or evil, that the purpose of God according to election might stand, not of works, but of Him That calleth;)

13 As it is written, 'Jacob have I loved, but Esau have I hated.'

How could God hate Esau and love Jacob, even before they were born, and still in the womb. Because of what they did in the first earth age. I don't see any other fair explanation for it. Do you? It also says, *that the purpose of God according to election might stand,......*There we have it. There was an earth age before the present, and there was a choosing of souls there.

We see the same thing in Jeremiah 1:

4 Then the word of the Lord came unto me, saying,

5 'Before I formed thee in the belly I knew thee; and before thou camest forth out of the womb I sanctified thee, and I ordained thee a prophet unto the nations.'

How could God knew Jeremiah before he was formed in the belly? God knew him from the first earth age, and knew He could trust him, because of what Jeremiah did.

'Nations' here are the 'Gentiles' = all peoples except the twelve Hebrew tribes.

6 Then said I, 'Ah, Lord God! behold, I cannot speak: for I am a child.'

'Child' here is better translated 'youth'.

7 But the Lord said unto me, 'Say not, 'I am a child:' for thou shalt go to all that I shall send thee, and whatsoever I command thee thou shalt speak.

8 Be not afraid of their faces: for I am with thee to deliver thee, saith the Lord.

I think its fascinating.

Now to Matthew 13:

10 And the disciples came, and said unto Him, 'Why speakest Thou unto them in parables?'

11 He answered and said unto them, 'Because it is given unto you to know the mysteries of the kingdom of heaven, but to them it is not given.

It is not meant for everybody to understand the mysteries of the kingdom of heaven, obviously.

34 All these things spake Jesus unto the multitude in parables; and without a parable spake He not unto them:

35 That it might be fulfilled which was spoken by the prophet, saying, 'I will open my mouth in parables; I will utter things which have been kept secret from the foundation of the world.'

Here we have 'the foundation of the world' again = the katabole = the overthrow of Satan in the first earth age, after his rebellion, Ezekiel 28.

36 Then Jesus sent the multitude away, and went into the house: and His disciples came unto Him, saying, 'Declare unto us the parable of the tares of the field.'

37 He answered and said unto them,……

And Jesus explained the parable for the disciples. Not for the multitude.

Conclusion

We have existed in another life, and here on earth, in the first earth age, but not in flesh. We had a spiritual body, or celestial, as Paul is teaching in 1 Corinthians 15:

40 There are also celestial bodies, and bodies terrestrial:......

So, we are not talking about 'reincarnation', at all. We only live in the flesh once.

Our soul has always existed, from the beginning, Genesis 1:1. We just put on other bodies, celestial, terrestrial, and celestial again. To have eternal life means to exist from the beginning without ceasing. No soul has ceased yet, not even Satan's, but his and some are going to in the lake of fire, Revelation 20:15, which is a 'blotting out process' for all evil things by God's shekinah glory = God is a consuming fire, Hebrews 12:29. For the righteous this fire feels like warming comfort. Remember also that we are not in a flesh body when this happens.

Chapter XX

Elect

Is 65:

1 I am sought of them that asked not for Me; I am found of them that sought Me not: I said, 'Behold Me, behold Me,' unto a nation that was not called by My name.

2 I have spread out My hands all the day unto a rebellious People, which walketh in a way that was not good, after their own thoughts;

This is quoted in Rom 10:20-21.

3 A People that provoketh Me to anger continually to My face; that sacrificeth in gardens, and burneth incense upon altars of brick;

Sacrifices in gardens is 'grove worship', which is sexual orgies, Ashteroth or Asherah from where **Easter** is derived. 'An Ashera' is 'a grove'. 'Asherah' is from the root 'ashar', to be straight, erect, or upright. The Asherah, the grove, was so called because it was something set upright or erect in the ground, and worshipped. It is often coupled with 'mazzevoth', or stone 'pillars' connected with Baal-worship. So with the 'Asherah', originally a tree, symbolical of 'the tree of life', it was an object of reverence and veneration. Then came the perversion of the earlier idea which simply honored the origin of life; and it was corrupted and debased into the organ of procreation, which was symbolized by the form and shape given to the Asherah. It was the Phallus image of Is 57:8, and 'the image of the male', Ez 16:17. These symbols, in turn, became the incentive to all forms of impurity which were part of its libidinous worship, with the swarms of devotees involved in its obscene orgies. The serpent was involved also.

'Brick' in stead of 'golden' altars. 'Provoketh' is better translated 'insult'.

4 Which remain among the graves, and lodge in the monuments, which eat swine's flesh, and broth of abominable things is in their vessels;

They don't even know the health laws. We are not supposed to eat swine, Lev 11. Strange that people still do, and mostly the Christian western countries, that absolutely should know better. They don't know better for they are Biblically illiterate. It is sad.

5 Which say, 'Stand by thyself, come not near to me; for I am holier than thou.' 'These are a smoke in My nose, a fire that burneth all the day.

A priest that think he is holier than other people is a good example, or other religious upmanship competition among the clergy. They are trying to compete about who has heard from God the most when it was not even God that spoke to them, but there own flesh, because they had a sour pickle, or maybe even an evil spirit talked to them. They don't know the difference any way.

6 Behold, it is written before Me: I will not keep silence, but will recompense, even recompense into their bosom.

7 Your iniquities, and the iniquities of your fathers together,' saith the Lord, 'which have burned incense upon the mountains, and blasphemed Me upon the hills: therefore will I measure their former work into their homes.'

8 Thus saith the lord, 'As the new wine is found in the cluster, and one saith, 'Destroy it not; for a blessing is in it: 'so will I do for My servants' sakes, that I may not destroy them all.

'The new wine' are the elect.

9 And I will bring forth a seed out of Jacob, and out of Judah an inheritor of My mountains: and Mine elect shall inherit it, and My servants shall dwell there.

A seed out of Jacob are all tribes but Judah. The word 'elect' is translated from the Hebrew word 'bachiyr' = select, which is from the word 'bachar' = to try.

10 And Sharon shall be a fold of flocks, and the valley of Achor a place for the herds to lie down in, for My People that have sought Me.

'Sharon' means 'fruitful place' = place for the best production. 'Achor' means 'trouble'

11 But ye are they that forsake the Lord, that forget My holy mountain, that prepare a table for that troop, and that furnish the drink offering unto that number.

'That troop' is 'Gad' = a Babylonian deity, the god of luck, fortune teller. 'Number' is 'Meniy' = fate as an idol.

12 Therefore will I number you to the sword, and ye shall all bow down to the slaughter: because when I called, ye did not answer; when I spake, ye did not hear; but did evil before Mine eyes, and did choose that wherein I delighted not.'

Who is God, through Isaiah, talking to here? The twelve tribes, Jacob, or Israel in the sense of all twelve tribes, not Israel in the sense of the scattered northern ten tribes.

Bow down to the slaughter means bow down to the false Christ, bow down to Satan, that is Antichrist.

Leif Werner

John 15:

15 Henceforth I call you not servants; for the servant knoweth not what his lord doeth: but I have called you friends; for all things that I have heard of My Father I have made known unto you.

Christ talking to the elect. If you are an elect, you are not only a servant, but you are a friend, for you know what your Lord does, for your Lord has explained everything for you, so you can understand. That's why Christ sent away the crowd, before he explained the parables for the disciples, Matt 13:

36 Then Jesus sent the multitude away, and went into the house: and his disciples came unto Him, saying, 'Declare unto us the parable of the tares of the field.'

37 He answered and said unto them, 'He That......

To understand this even better we have to go to Matt 13:

9 Who hath ears to hear, let him hear.'

10 And the disciples came, and said unto Him, 'Why speakest Thou unto them in parables?'

11 He answered them and said unto them, 'Because it is given unto you to know the mysteries of the kingdom of heaven, but to them it is not given.

12 For whosoever hath, to him shall be given, and he shall have more abundance: but whosoever hath not, from him shall be taken away even that he hath.

13 Therefore speak I to them in parables: because they seeing see not; and hearing they hear not, neither do they understand.

14 And in them is fulfilled the prophecy of Esaias, which saith, 'By hearing ye shall hear, and shall not understand; and seeing ye shall see, and shall not perceive:

15 For this people's heart is waxed gross, and their ears are dull of hearing, and their eyes they have closed; lest at any time they should see with their eyes, and hear with their ears, and should understand with their heart, and should be converted, and I should heal them.'

16 But blessed are your eyes, for they see: and your ears, for they hear.

17 For verily I say unto you, That many prophets and righteous men have desired to see those things which ye see, and have not seen them; and to hear those things which ye hear, and have not heard them.

18 Hear ye therefore the parable of the sower.

Now back to John 15:

16 Ye have not chosen Me, but I have chosen you, and ordained you, that ye should go and bring forth fruit, and that your fruit should remain: that whatsoever ye shall ask of the Father in My name, He may give it you.

Here we see that the elect have not chosen Christ, but Christ has chosen them, because of what they did in the first earth age. They made a stand against Satan, for God, at the katabole, when he rebelled, Ez 28, and the earth became (= hayah) 'tohu va bohu' = without form and void, Gen 1:2. The world was not created 'tohu', for in Is 45:18 it is written about the earth:......*He created it not in vain*......The word 'vain' here is the same word 'tohu' used in Gen 1:2. You don't have contradictions in the Scriptures. If you think there is, you have misunderstood. God created the earth perfect and not in chaos, or 'tohu'. It became 'tohu', when He destroyed the first earth age. He did that for he didn't want to blot out, destroy, a third of His children, the stars, Rev 12:4, that followed Satan at his rebellion. Then God created this earth age to start over again, to let everybody be born through women, innocent, which means the memory from the first earth age erased, to make a choice between God and Satan. In Gen 1:28 we see that the Hebrew comes through even in the English:...... *'Be fruitful, and multiply, and replenish the earth, and subdue it:......'*'Replenish' for we lived here before, but not in flesh, but in our celestial, heavenly, body. So from Gen 1:3 it is talking about creation of this, the second, earth age, not the first earth age.

Now back to the elect. They are not volunteers in this second earth age. Remember how Christ struck Paul down on the way to Damascus. He didn't get right with Christ voluntarily. He is one of the elect, chosen at, or before, the foundation of the world, this earth age, which was just after the 'katabole', Satan's fall. Paul had no free will when he walked to Damascus, because he was justified, judged, and glorified in the first earth age, because he stood against Satan.

So the elect are therefore 'ordained' by Christ in the first earth age.

When it comes to receive every thing we ask for, this only applies to things that is necessary for us to accomplish the work we are doing for God. Not a Cadillac, if it is not absolutely necessary. It could be, but not just because we ask for it.

1 Pet 2:

6 Wherefore also it is contained in the Scripture, 'Behold, I lay in Sion a chief corner stone, elect, precious: and he that believeth on Him shall not be confounded.'

7 Unto you therefore which believe He is precious: but unto them which be disobedient, the Stone Which the builders disallowed, the same is made the head of the corner.

'Disobedient' includes, that they don't study and learn the Word, the Scriptures.

8 And a Stone of stumbling, and a Rock of offense, even to them which stumble at the word, being disobedient: whereunto also they were appointed.

Christ is going to be a stumbling block for them, they who do not study and learn the truth, for they are not going to see the difference between Antichrist and the True Christ. They don't know that Antichrist, Satan, is coming, and will be here five months, Rev 9:5,10, just before Christ returns, 2 Thess 2. They are going to worship Antichrist believing it is Christ. They don't even know that Antichrist is Satan, 'the son of perdition' = Apollyon, Rev 9:11. Look it up for yourself in Strong's Concordance. They think Antichrist is a person living in flesh, a human being, which is wrong of course, not Biblical.

1 Pet 1:

2 Elect, according to the foreknowledge of God the Father, through sanctification of the Spirit, unto obedience and sprinkling of the blood of Jesus Christ: Grace unto you, and peace, be multiplied.

The elect are the souls that stood up for God, against Satan, in the first earth age, when Satan rebelled and fell, the katabole, called also 'the foundation of the world' in the English translations; see my newsletter Sealing. That's why it says 'foreknowledge' in this verse. There is written more about the elect, sanctification for example, in Rom 8, see below.

Jer 1:

4 Then the word of the Lord came unto me, saying,

5 'Before I formed thee in the belly I knew thee; and before thou camest forth out of the womb I sanctified thee, and I ordained thee a prophet unto the nations.'

Here we see that God knew Jeremiah before he was 'formed' in the 'belly'. This is because God knew him from the first earth age, and what he did there, stood up against Satan. That's why God can trust Jeremiah and He can use him in this second earth age. Jeremiah was sanctified, judged, and even ordained prophet in the first earth age. He is one of the elect.

6 Then said I, 'Ah, Lord God! Behold, I cannot speak: for I am a child.'

'Child' is better translated 'youth'.

7 But the Lord said unto me, 'Say not, 'I am a child:' for thou shalt go to all that I shall send thee, and whatsoever I command thee thou shalt speak.

Jeremiah is a true 'apostle' = 'a sent one' by God.

Because Jeremiah was judged, God could use him for what He wanted. Jeremiah did not have free will any more. If God gives you eternal life, judges you, He can use you for what ever purpose He wants. Remember how Christ struck Paul (Saul) down on the way to Damascus. Paul didn't volunteer to become a Christian. God opened his eyes, so he could, correctly, understand the Word, he had studied so carefully before this happened. God knew him from the first earth age, and decided it was time to use Paul. Paul was already judged in the first earth age. Paul wrote half of the New Testament, and probably from memory, because he was in prison a large part of his life. He didn't walk around with a scroll under his arm. Paul was (is in fact) a brilliant Old Testament scholar, and quoted, from memory, many Old Testament Scriptures and his entire writings was built on the Old Testament. Paul had studied with, Gamaliel, one of the absolute best scholars of the time, see Acts 5:34, 22:3.

8 Be not afraid of their faces: for I am with thee to deliver thee, saith the Lord.

9 Then the Lord put forth His hand, and touched my mouth. And the Lord said unto me, 'Behold, I have put My words in thy mouth.

10 See, I have this day set thee over the nations and over the kingdoms, to root out, and to pull down, and to destroy, and to throw down, to build, and to plant.'

Rom 8:

26 Likewise the Spirit also helpeth our infirmities: for we know not what we should pray for as we ought: but the Spirit Itself maketh intercession for us with groanings which cannot be uttered.

This has not to do with 'talking in tongues', of Acts 2, as many think. A subject for an other time, see my chapter about this subject with that name.

27 And He That searcheth the hearts knoweth what is the mind of the Spirit, because He maketh intercession for the saints according to the will of God.

'Hearts' is better translated 'mind', most times. The Holy Spirit makes intercession.

28 And we know that all things work together for good to them that love God, to them who are the called according to His purpose.

The elect have a purpose for God, because of there actions in the first earth age. As long as you have not made up your mind, that you shall follow God and not Satan, God has no plan for you; you have no destiny. You are wondering in the wilderness.

29 For whom he did foreknow, he also did predestinate to be conformed to the image of His Son, that he might be the firstborn among many brethren.

Predestinated, chosen, in the first earth age, because of work for God, against Satan. See called below also.

30 Moreover whom he did predestinate, them he also called: and whom he called, them He also justified: and whom He justified, them He also glorified.

'Justified' is the same as 'judged'. 'Glorified' is to participate in the first resurrection, Rev 20:6, to have your soul made immortal by God; see 1 Cor 15 below. The elect receive eternal life already before the millennium, the rest after the millennium, if they make it, overcome, after the teaching in the millennium.

31 What shall we then say to these things? If God be for us, who can be against us?

32 He that spared not His own Son, but delivered Him up for us all, how shall He not with Him also freely give us all things?

All things we need to accomplish the work for God; for His plan, not everything we 'want'.

33 Who shall lay any thing to the charge of God's elect? It is God That justifieth;

God is the Judge. There is no other.

34 Who is he that condemneth? It is Christ That died, yea, rather, That is risen again, Who is even at the right hand of God, Who also maketh intercession for us.

Rom 9:

11 (For the children being not yet born, neither having done any good or evil, that the purpose of God according to election might stand, not of works, but of Him That calleth;)

God knows us, from how we behaved in the first earth age.

12 It was said unto her, 'The elder shall serve the younger.'

Quoted from Gen 25:23.

13 As it is written, 'Jacob have I loved, but Esau have I hated.'

Quoted from Mal 1:2-3. If God loved one and hated the other even before they were born into flesh, it must be for something they did in the first earth age; and that's how it is. God is always fair. He is not just picking a soul, here and there, and blessing it, or cursing it, for no reason.

14 What shall we say then? Is there unrighteousness with God? God forbid.

That's right.

15 For He saith to Moses, 'I will have mercy on whom I will have mercy, and I will have compassion on whom I will have compassion.'

According to how we have behaved. The blessing or cursings always come after the work, Rev 14:13.

16 So then it is not of him that willeth, nor of him that runneth, but of God That sheweth mercy.

17 For the Scripture saith unto Pharaoh, 'Even for this same purpose have I raised thee up, that I might shew My power in thee, and that My name might be declared throughout all the earth.'

Pharaoh is one of the elect; believe it or not. God used him, as it says here. Not many think about that.

18 Therefore hath he mercy on whom He will have mercy, and whom He will He hardeneth.

God hardened Pharaoh's heart, mind, to accomplish His plan.

19 Thou wilt say then unto me, 'Why doth He yet find fault? For who hath resisted His will?'

20 Nay but, O man, who art thou that repliest against God? 'Shall the formed say to him that formed it 'Why hast thou made me thus?"

21 Has not the potter power over the clay, of the same lump to make one vessel unto honour, and another unto dishonour?

The potter can do what ever He likes with the clay. The clay can not do anything about that.

22 What if God, willing to shew His wrath, and to make His power known, endured with much longsuffering the vessels of wrath fitted to destruction:

23 And that He might make known the riches of His glory on the vessels of mercy, which He afore prepared unto glory,

24 Even us, whom he hath called, not of the Jews only, but of the Gentiles?

25 As he saith also in Osee, 'I will call them My people, which were not My people; and her beloved, which was not My beloved.

'Osee' is Hosea, the prophet.

26 And it shall come to pass, that in the place where it was said unto them, 'Ye are not My people;' there shall they be called the children of the living God.'

27 Esaias also crieth concerning Israel, 'Though the number of the children of Israel be as the sand of the sea, a remnant shall be saved:

28 For he will finish the work, and cut it short in righteousness: because a short work will the Lord make upon the earth.'

29 And as Esaias said before, 'Except the Lord of Sabbath had left us a seed, we had been as Sodom, and been made like unto Gomorrha.'

30 What shall we say then? That the Gentiles which followed not after righteousness, have attained to righteousness, even the righteousness which is of faith.

31 But Israel, which followed after the law of righteousness, hath not attained to the law of righteousness.

32 Wherefore? Because they sought it not by faith, but as it were by the works of the law. For they stumbled at that stumblingstone;

33 As it is written, 'Behold, I lay in Sion a stumblingstone and rock of offense: and whosoever believeth on Him shall not be ashamed.'

Rom 11:

1 I say then, hath God cast away His people? God forbid. For I also am an Israelite, of the seed of Abraham, of the tribe of Benjamin.

'Seed' here is 'sperma', so it is a literal biological seed it is talking about.

2 God hath not cast away his people which He foreknew. Wot ye not what the Scripture saith of Elias? how he maketh intercession to God against Israel, saying,

'Foreknow' from the first earth age, the elect.

3 'Lord, they have killed Thy prophets, and digged down Thine altars; and I am left alone, and they seek my life.'

Israel is a very rebellious people. Israel is basically the western Christian nations. I have explained that before. I don't want to go in to that here. It is too much digressing.

4 But what saith the answer of God unto him? 'I have reserved to Myself seven thousand men, who have not bowed the knee to the image of Baal.'

'Seven thousand men' are 'the elect'. Baal represents Satan. This is future. It's going to happen when Satan is here as Antichrist, the five months, just before Christ returns. Baal is a Phoenician deity used here as a symbol of idolatry.

5 Even so then at this present time also there is a remnant according to the election of grace.

The remnant are the elect.

6 And if by grace, then is it no more of works: otherwise grace is no more grace. But if it be of works, then is it no more grace: otherwise work is no more work.

7 What then? Israel hath not obtained that which he seeketh for; but the election hath obtained it, and the rest were blinded

8 (According as it is written, 'God hath given them the spirit of slumber, eyes that they should not see, and ears that they should not hear';) unto this day.

'Slumber' is the Greek word 'katanuxis' = stupor. Why is God stupefying people. Because they are too weak-minded to stand against Antichrist. Remember Jesus talking in Matt 13:11 and 15. If they understand the truth and fall away when Antichrist is here, they are responsible for there actions. If God has put a stupor on them, they are not responsible, and God can not judge them negatively. Those people are 'saved' for the millennium teaching, Rev 20:6, which is a better spiritual environment for them, and can be saved then, if they so choose.

9 And David saith, 'Let their table be made a snare, and a trap, and a stumblingblock, and a recompense unto them:

They think Antichrist is Christ, during the five months he is here.

Eph 1:

4 According as He hath chosen us in Him before the foundation of the world, that we should be holy and without blame before Him in love:

Here we are looking back again to the first earth age, and how He has chosen the elect.

5 Having predestinated us unto the adoption of children by Jesus Christ to Himself, according to the good pleasure of his will,

6 To the praise of the glory of His grace, wherein He hath made us accepted in the Beloved:

7 In Whom we have redemption through His blood, the forgiveness of sins, according to the riches of His grace,

8 Wherein He hath abounded toward us in all wisdom and prudence;

9 Having made known unto us the mystery of His will, according to His good pleasure which He hath purposed in Himself;

10 That in the dispensation of the fullness of times He might gather together in one all things in Christ, both which are in heaven and which are on earth; even in Him:

'The dispensation of the fullness of times' is the third world age, Rev 21.

11 In Whom also we have obtained an inheritance, being predestinated according to the purpose of Him Who worketh all things after the counsel of His own will:

12 That we should be to the praise of His glory, who first trusted in Christ.

'First' trusted in Christ, because the elect trusted Him already in the 'first' earth age.

Eph 3:

1 For this cause I Paul, the prisoner of Jesus Christ for you Gentiles,

Gentiles are all nations, peoples, except the twelve Hebrew tribes.

2 If ye have heard of the dispensation of the grace of God which is given me to you-ward:

3 How that by revelation He made known unto me the mystery; (as I wrote afore in few words,

Remember Matt 13:11,.......*it is given unto you to know the mysteries of the kingdom of heaven, but to them it is not given.*

Back to Eph 3:

4 Whereby, when ye read, ye may understand my knowledge in the mystery of Christ)

5 Which in other ages was not made known unto the sons of men, as it is now revealed unto His holy apostles and prophets by the Spirit;

Here we have 'other ages' written directly in the Word, and in the first earth age we were not told about God's plan, like we are now from the Word.

6 That the Gentiles should be fellowheirs, and of the same body, and partakers of His promise in Christ by the gospel:

2 Pet 3:

1 This second epistle, beloved, I now write unto you; in both which I stir up your pure minds by way of remembrance;

Remembrance of the first earth age for the elect.

2 That ye may be mindful of the words which were spoken before by the holy prophets, and of the commandments of the apostles of the Lord and Saviour:

3 Knowing this first, that there shall come in the last days scoffers, walking after their own lusts,

4 And saying, 'Where is the promise of His coming? for since the fathers fell asleep, all things continue as they were from the beginning of the creation.'

5 For this they willingly are ignorant of, that by the word of God the heavens were of old, and the earth standing out of the water and in the water:

Talking about the first earth age.

6 Whereby the world that then was, being overflowed with water, perished:

Still talking about the first earth age.

7 But the heavens and the earth which are now, by the same word are kept in store, reserved unto fire against the day of judgment and perdition of ungodly men.

Now we are talking about the second earth age, the present one.

8 But, beloved, be not ignorant of this one thing, that one day is with the Lord as a thousand years, and a thousand years as one day.

9 The Lord is not slack concerning His promise, as some men count slackness; but is longsuffering to us-ward, not willing that any should perish, but that all should come to repentance.

10 But the day of the Lord will come as a thief in the night; in the which the heavens shall pass away with a great noise, and the elements shall melt with fervent heat, the earth also and the works that are therein shall be burned up.

The word 'element' is the Greek word 'stoicheion' = rudiment, which means the evil things. The earth is not going to be destroyed, but it's going to be cleansed from all evil, and be restored. There is not going to be a nuclear war or destruction of the earth. It is not mentioned anywhere in the Scriptures.

Look at Matt 13:41......*His angels, and they shall gather out of His kingdom all things that offend, and them that do iniquity;*

Back to 2 Pet 3:

11 Seeing then that all these things shall be dissolved, what manner of persons ought ye to be in all holy conversation and godliness,

12 Looking for and hasting unto the coming of the day of God, wherein the heavens being on fire shall be dissolved, and the elements shall melt with fervent heat?

Cp. Hebr 12:

25 See that ye refuse not Him That speaketh. For if they escaped not who refused Him That spake on earth, much more shall not we escape, if we turn away from Him That speaketh from heaven:

26 Whose voice then shook the earth: but now He hath promised, saying, "yet once more I shake not the earth only, but also heaven."

27 And this word, 'Yet once more,' signifieth the removing of those things that are shaken, as of things that are made, that those things which cannot be shaken may remain.

We see here that the unshakable things remain. Only the evil things, the rudiments, will be blotted out.

28 Wherefore we receiving a kingdom which cannot be moved, let us have grace, whereby we may serve God acceptably with reverence and godly fear:

29 For our God is a consuming fire.

God's 'Shekinah' Glory will comfort, respectively blot out.

Back to 2 Pet 3:

13 Nevertheless we, according to His promise, look for new heavens and a new earth, wherein dwelleth righteousness.

'New' is renewed.

14 Wherefore, beloved, seeing that ye look for such things, be diligent that ye may be found of Him in peace, without spot, and blameless.

15 And account that the longsuffering of our Lord is salvation; even as our beloved brother Paul also, according to the wisdom given unto him, hath written unto you;

Peter here giving Paul credentials.

16 As also in all his epistles, speaking in them of these things; in which are some things hard to be understood, which they that are unlearned and unstable wrest, as they do also the other Scriptures, unto their own destruction.

'Unlearned and unstable', biblically illiterate Christians. Therefore they are unstable.

Matt 19:

30 But many that are first shall be last; and the last shall be first.

The elect are born last in this earth age. Why? Because they have to be here witnessing, when Antichrist is here.

Matt 20:

1 For the kingdom of heaven is like unto a man that is an householder, which went early in the morning to hire labourers into his vineyard.

2 And when he had agreed with the labourers for a penny a day, he sent them into his vineyard.

3 And he went out about the third hour, and saw others standing idle in the marketplace,

4 And said unto them; 'Go ye also into the vineyard, and whatsoever is right I will give you.' And they went their way.

5 Again he went out about the sixth and ninth hour, and did likewise.

6 And about the eleventh hour he went out, and found others standing idle, and saith unto them, 'Why stand ye here all the day idle?

7 They say unto him, 'Because no man hath hired us.' He saith unto them, 'Go ye also into the vineyard; and whatsoever is right, that shall ye receive.'

8 So when even was come, the lord of the vineyard saith unto his steward, 'Call the labourers, and give them their hire, beginning from the last unto the first.'

9 And when they came that were hired about the eleventh hour, they received every man a penny.

10 But when the first came, they supposed that they should have received more; and they likewise received every man a penny.

11 And when they had received it, they murmured against the goodman of the house,

12 Saying, 'These last have wrought but one hour, and thou hast made them equal unto us, which have borne the burden and heat of the day.'

13 But he answered one of them, and said, 'Friend, I do thee no wrong: didst not thou agreed with me for a penny?

14 Take that thine is, and go thy way: I will give unto this last, even as unto thee.

15 Is it not lawful for me to do what I will with mine own? Is thine eye evil, because I am good?

16 So the last shall be first, and the first last: for many be called, but few chosen.'

I don't think this need much explanation.

Let's go to Ez 48:

11 It shall be for the priests that are sanctified of the sons of Zadok; which have kept My charge, which went not astray when the children of Israel went astray, as the Levites went astray.

This is in the millennium, looking back to the time, when Israel bowed down to Antichrist, Satan, during the first tribulation. Zadok are the elect. Zadok means 'the just'.

And to Ez 44:

15 But the priests the Levites, the sons of Zadok, that kept the charge of My sanctuary when the children of Israel went astray from me, they shall come near to Me to minister unto Me, and they shall stand before me to offer unto Me the fat and the blood, saith the Lord God.

We are in the millennium here also. It might be surprising for some, but only the elect can come close to Christ in the millennium. The rest have to stay in the utter court. They can not enter into the inner court or the sanctuary.

16 They shall enter into My sanctuary, and they shall come near to My table, to minister unto Me, and they shall keep My charge.

17 And it shall come to pass, that when they enter in to the gates of the inner court, they shall be clothed with linen garments; and no wool shall come upon them, whiles they minister in the gates of the inner court, and within.

18 They shall have linen bonnets upon their heads, and shall have linen breeches upon their loins; they shall not gird themselves with any thing that causeth sweat.

19 And when they go forth into the utter court, even into the utter court to the People, they shall put off their garments wherein they ministered, and lay them in the holy chambers, and they shall put on other garments; and they shall not sanctify the People with their garments.

20 Neither shall they shave their heads, nor suffer locks to grow long; they shall only poll their heads.

21 Neither shall any priest drink wine, when they enter into the inner court.

22 Neither shall they take for their wives a widow, nor her that is put away: but they shall take maidens of the seed of the house of Israel, or a widow that had a priest before.

We have to think spiritually here, for it is not marriage in the flesh it is talking about, but it is talking about *preparing wives for Christ.* We are not in flesh at this time, for we are in the millennium. In the millennium we are in our celestial, heavenly, body, 1 Cor 15. Cp., here and for the following verses, Deut 30:

4 If any of thine be driven out unto the outmost parts of heaven, from thence will the Lord thy God gather thee, and from thence will He fetch thee:

Back to Ez 44:

23 And they shall teach My people the difference between the holy and profane, and cause them to discern between the unclean and the clean.

24 And in controversy they shall stand in judgment; and they shall judge it according to My judgments: and they shall keep My laws and My statutes in all Mine assemblies; and they shall hallow My sabbaths.

25 And they shall come at no dead person to defile themselves: but for father, or for mother, or for son, or for daughter, for brother, or for sister that had no husband, they may defile themselves.

This means, that the elect, in the millennium, can go over to the other side of the 'gulf' Luke is talking about in his gospel, Luke 16:21, and give their family members, who didn't make it, a 'disciplined Bible lecture in love', to pull them over to the other side of the gulf, for eternal life.

26 And after he is cleansed, they shall reckon unto him seven days.

When we have pulled a family member over to the 'right' side of the gulf, we have to wait seven days.

27 And in the day that he goeth into the sanctuary, unto the inner court, to minister in the sanctuary, he shall offer his sin offering saith the Lord God.

28 And it shall be unto them for an inheritance: I am their inheritance: and ye shall give them no possession in Israel: I am their possession.

The elect's inheritance is God Himself.

29 They shall eat the meat offering, and the sin offering, and the trespass offering; and every dedicated thing in Israel shall be theirs.

Chapter XXI

The Parable of The Fig Tree

Matthew 7:

15 Beware of false prophets, which come to you in sheep's clothing, but inwardly they are ravening wolves.

16 Ye shall know them by their fruits. Do men gather grapes of thorns, or figs of thistles?

Thorns are in the Bible symbolic of Satan.

17 Even so every good tree bringeth forth good fruit; but a corrupt tree bringeth forth evil fruit.

18 A good tree can not bring forth evil fruit, neither can a corrupt tree bring forth good fruit.

What fruit? Basically this is talking about what the prophet teaches. If it is not the Word of God, he is a false prophet, he is bearing evil fruit.

Many people think this is talking about if the prophet smokes for example, just to be trivial, or what car he has, or if he is rich, or if he is kind all the time. A prophet can be very stern some times. Be very careful, for Satan, as Antichrist, and his children, the Kenites, are 'entering peaceably, and obtaining the kingdom by flatteries', Daniel 21, 24, 32, 34. Remember that Satan is going to play Christ according to 2 Thess 2, so he must act lovingly, and what comes with it, to be convincing.

It is about what the prophet teaches that counts.

Always check the prophet out in the Word; what he/she teaches, not so much how the person teaches and the behavior, necessarily, although, of course, a man, or woman, of God most likely don't smoke or drink, and most likely have a gentle and peaceful behavior. You can fake behavior, but not what you teach.

19 Every tree that bringeth not forth good fruit is hewn down, and cast into the fire.

Ultimately this is the lake of fire of Rev 20. God is the consuming fire, Hebrews 12:29.

20 Wherefore by their fruits ye shall know them.

21 Not every one that saith unto Me, 'Lord, Lord,' shall enter into the kingdom of heaven; but he that doeth the will of My Father Which is in heaven.

22 Many will say to Me in that day, 'Lord, Lord, have we not prophesied in Thy name? and in Thy name have cast outdevils? and in Thy name done many wonderful works?'

23 And then will I profess unto them, 'I never knew you: depart from Me, ye that work iniquity.'

You see, if you are teaching your church to believe on the 'rapture', for example, the Lord will say as in verse 23 to you, when He returns.

Mark 13:

28 Now learn a parable of the fig tree; When her branch is yet tender, and putteth forth leaves, ye know that summer is near:

Jesus is saying this very emphatically. The Lord is telling us to learn 'the parable of the fig tree.' So let's do it. Observe that it says leaves, not fruit.

29 So ye in like manner, when ye shall see these things come to pass, know that it is nigh, even at the doors.

Jesus is referring to what He has taught in Mark 13.

30 Verily I say unto you, that this generation shall not pass, till all these things be done.

'This generation' is of course 'the generation of the fig tree'. Which one is that? Let's check it out.

Mark 11:

11 And Jesus entered into Jerusalem, and into the temple: and when He had looked round about upon all things, and now the eventide was come, He went out unto Bethany with the twelve.

12 And on the morrow, when they were come from Bethany, He was hungry:

13 And seeing a fig tree afar off having leaves, he came, if haply He might find any thing thereon: (and when He came to it, He found nothing but leaves); for the time of figs was not yet.

Jesus knew of course that it was not harvest time.

14 And Jesus answered and said unto it, "No man eat fruit of thee hereafter for ever." And His disciples heard it.

Jesus is doing this for a purpose

15 And they come to Jerusalem: and Jesus went into the temple, and began to cast out them that sold and bought in the temple, and overthrew the tables of the moneychangers, and the seats of them that sold doves;

16 And would not suffer that any man should carry any vessel through the temple.

17 And he taught, saying unto them, 'Is it not written, 'My house shall be called of all nations the house of prayer? But ye have made it a den of thieves.'

18 And the scribes and chief priests heard it, and sought how they might destroy Him: for they feared Him because all the people was astonished at His doctrine.

Nice religious people trying to kill Jesus. It is the same today and in the church, if you try to teach the Truth.

19 And when even was come, he went out of the city.

20 And in the morning, as they passed by, they saw the fig tree dried up from the roots.

21 And Peter called to remembrance saith unto Him, 'Master, behold, the fig tree which Thou cursedst is withered away.'

Jesus had cursed the Kenites, the bad figs.

22 And Jesus answering saith unto them, 'Have faith in God.

23 For verily I say unto you, That whosoever shall say unto this mountain, 'Be thou removed, and be thou cast into the sea; and shall not doubt in his heart, but shall believe that those things which he saith shall come to pass; he shall have whatsoever he saith.

Observe that it says 'this mountain', for it is not talking about a literal mountain but a nation, and the nation of the Kenites, the sons of Cain, 'the bad figs', which ultimately are the sons of Satan. I explain later.

24 Therefore I say unto you, What things soever ye desire, when ye pray, believe that ye receive them, and ye shall have them.

This is not if I desire a Cadillac or alike, but resources I desire for being able to spread the Word.

Now the explanation of 'the bad figs'. Jeremiah 24:

1 The Lord shewed me, and, behold, two baskets of figs were set before the temple of the Lord, after that Nebuchadrezzar king of Babylon had carried away captive Jeconiah the son of Jehoiakim king of Judah, and the princes of Judah, with the carpenters and smiths, from Jerusalem, and had brought them to Babylon.

2 One basket had very good figs, even like the figs that are first ripe: and the other basket had very naughty figs, which could not be eaten, they were so bad.

Here we have the 'bad figs', and the 'good figs' also. The good figs are Judah.

3 Then said the Lord unto me, 'What seest thou, Jeremiah?' And I said, 'Figs; the good figs, very good; and the evil, very evil, that cannot be eaten, they are so evil.'

4 Again the word of the Lord came unto me, saying,

5 'Thus saith the Lord, the God of Israel; 'Like these good figs, so will I acknowledge them that are carried away captive of Judah, whom I have sent out of this place into the land of the Chaldeans for their good.

Judah and Benjamin, here called just Judah, the two southern tribes, were taken captive by the Babylonians, which are the Chaldeans, 200 years after Israel, the ten northern tribes, were taken captive by the Assyrian. You can read about this in 1 Kings 11:31, 12:19, and 2 Kings 15:29, 17:6, 23, 19:32. Judah and Israel, still split, are going to join again first when Christ returns, Ez 37:16-28.

After the Assyrian captivity of the 10 northern tribes, the tribes walked over the Caucasus mountains, therefore called Caucasians today, and spread all over Europe. They Became Vikings, Germans, Anglo-Saxons (Saxons means sons of Isaac), and Celts. They later emigrated to the Americas, and USA is basically Israel today.

6 For I will set Mine eyes upon them for good, and I will bring them again to this land: and I will build them, and not pull them down; and I will plant them, and not pluck them up.

Judah became a nation again May 1948, the nation of Israel. They who move to Israel, or back if you wish, are mostly Judah with Kenites mixed in among them of course.

7 And I will give them an heart to know Me, that I am the Lord: and they shall be My People, and I will be their God: for they shall return unto Me with their whole heart.

This has not happened yet. It is going to happen in the millennium, Rev 20. Christ is back then.

8 And as the evil figs, which cannot be eaten, they are so evil; surely thus saith the Lord, So will I give Zedekiah the king of Judah, and his princes, and the residue of Jerusalem, that remain in this land, and them that dwell in the land of Egypt:

'Residue' means 'resident'.

9 And I will deliver them to be removed into all the kingdoms of the earth for their hurt, to be a reproach and a proverb, a taunt and a curse, in all places whither I shall drive them.

'Them' are the Kenites, the 'bad figs', see Amos 6:14 and 1 Chr 2:55.

10 And I will send the sword, the famine, and the pestilence, among them, till they be consumed from off the land that I gave unto them and to their fathers."

So what is the 'parable of the fig tree'? What does it mean? It is talking about that Christ is coming back in the generation from when Israel became a nation, Mark 13:30. That is within the generation that was born 1948. That is maximum 120 years from 1948, which is 2068. See chapter 1 also.

Isaiah 34:

1 Come near, ye nations, to hear; and hearken, ye people: let the earth hear, and all that is therein; the world, and all things that come forth of it.

'Ye nations' is the Kenites' 'one world system or order'. 'All things' are all the races.

2 For the indignation of the Lord is upon all nations, and His fury upon all their armies: He hath utterly destroyed them, He hath delivered them to the slaughter.

The slaughter is the deception by Antichrist and his children in the end times, a divine ban.

3 Their slain also shall be cast out, and their stink shall come up out of their carcasses, and the mountains shall be melted with their blood.

This is just before and at the 7th Trump, Christ's return, when we are changed into our spiritual, celestial, body, and flesh is gone, 1 Cor 15:52 and 1 Thess 4:17.

4 And all the host of heaven shall be dissolved, and the heavens shall be rolled together as a scroll: and all their host shall fall down, as the leaf falleth off from the vine, and as a falling fig from the fig tree.

Cp. Rev 6.

5 For My sword shall be bathed in heaven: behold, it shall come down upon Idumea, and upon the people of My curse, to judgment.

Idumea is Russia. 'Bathed in heaven' means 'make some cleansing'.

6 The sword of the Lord is filled with blood, it is made fat with fatness, and with the blood of lambs and goats, with the fat of the kidneys of rams: for the Lord hath a sacrifice in Bozrah, and a great slaughter in the land of Idumea.

'Made fat' means 'it is plenty to do'. 'Bozrah' is 'fortress' of Edom, which is Alaska, where the battle of Hamon-god is going to take place, between Israel = USA and allies, and Russia with its allies. God is going to win the battle for Israel with the help of a hail storm, see Ez 38 and 39.

7 And the unicorns shall come down with them, and the bullocks with the bulls; and their land shall be soaked with blood, and their dust made fat with fatness.

Unicorn is wild ox.

8 For it is the day of the Lord's vengeance, and the year of recompenses for the controversy of Zion.

This is the last day of this dispensation.

Rev 6:

13 And the stars of heaven fell unto the earth, even as a fig tree casteth her untimely figs, when she is shaken of a mighty wind.

Antichrist and his angels, Gen 6, Jude 6, Rev 12:9 are cast into the earth, untimely for it is the false Christ, it is Satan.

14 And the heaven departed as a scroll when it is rolled together; and every mountain and island were moved out of their places.

'Mountains' are 'nations', and 'islands' are 'small nations'.

15 And the kings of the earth, and the great men, and the rich men, and the chief captains, and the mighty men, and every bondsman, and every free man, hid themselves in the dens and in the rocks of the mountains;

16 And said to the mountains and rocks, "Fall on us, and hide us from the face of Him That sitteth on the throne, and from the wrath of the Lamb:

This is what the false teachers, among others, are going to say when Christ returns, for they thought Antichrist was the true Christ. They had not studied the Word enough, that will say loved the truth, 2 Thess 2:10-12, enough, to learn the difference between them.

17 For the great day of His wrath is come; and who shall be able to stand?"

They who know, and knew, the truth will stand, naturally, with the armor on, Eph 6:10-17.

Gen 3:

6 And when the woman saw that the tree was good for food, and that it was pleasant to the eyes, and a tree to be desired to make one wise, she took of the fruit thereof, and did eat, and gave also unto her husband with her; and he did eat.

The Kenites come from this relationship. The word 'touch' in Gen 3:3 is 'naga' which means 'lie with a women', when it is used euphemistically. In 2 Cor 11:3, where 'beguiled' is 'exapataho' in the

Greek text, which can only mean 'wholly seduced', we see that Eve's virginity was taken by Satan in the Garden.

7 And the eyes of them both were opened, and they knew that they were naked and they sewed fig leaves together, and made themselves aprons.

These fig leaves belong to the 'parable of the fig tree' too, because of the Kenites that came from this occasion.

8 And they heard the voice of the Lord God walking in the garden in the cool of the day: and Adam and his wife hid themselves from the presence of the Lord God amongst the trees of the garden.

9 And the Lord God called unto Adam, and said unto him, "Where art thou?"

10 And he said, "I heard Thy voice in the garden and I was afraid, because I was naked; and I hid myself."

11 And He said, "Who told thee that thou wast naked? Hast thou eaten of the tree, whereof I commanded thee that thou shouldest not eat?"

12 And the man said, "The woman whom Thou gavest to be with me, she gave me of the tree, and I did eat."

13 And the Lord God said unto the woman, "What is this that thou hast done?" And the women said, "The serpent beguiled me, and I did eat."

14 And the Lord God said unto the serpent, 'Because thou hast done this, thou art cursed above all cattle, and above every beast of the field; upon thy belly shalt thou go, and dust shalt thou eat all the days of thy life:

15 And I will put enmity between thee and the woman, and between thy seed and her Seed; It shall bruise thy head, and thou shalt bruise His heel.'

Satan bruised Christ's heel on the cross and Christ shall bruise Satan's head, when He blots him out in the lake of fire, Rev 20:10 and Ez 28:18-19.

There is and has always been a conspiracy from the Kenites against the Adamic race. Satan, their father, wanted, and tried from the beginning, to destroy the seed from the lineage from which Christ was going to be born. That lineage was Adam and Eve, which is the Adamic race, which is the Hebrew people.

Chapter XXII

UFOs in the Bible!?

Are there UFOs in the Bible? or as I call them IFOs, for they are 'identified' not 'unidentified.' Let's see.

Ezekiel 1:

3 The word of the Lord came expressly unto Ezekiel the priest, the son of Buzi, in the land of the Chaldeans by the river Chebar; and the hand of the Lord was there upon him.

4 And I looked, and, behold, a whirlwind came out of the north, a great cloud, and a fire infolding itself, and a brightness was about it, and out of the midst thereof as the colour of amber, out of the midst of the fire.

Cp. 2 Kings 2:11.
Ezekiel is doing a pretty good job here trying to describe an UFO, or as I call them IFO.
First, 'whirlwind' is of course the Hebrew 'ruach', which means spirit, the spirit of God.
Second, 'colour' is the Hebrew word for 'eye'. Third, 'amber', which is the Hebrew word 'chashmal', means 'highly polished bronze.'
Ezekiel is seeing a metal object obviously, and out of the midst of the fire, which is God's Shekinah Glory, for our God is a consuming fire, Hebrews 12:29.
'Cloud' is one of the symbols of YHVH's Glory. The other two are storm and fire.

5 Also out of the midst thereof came likeness of four living creatures. And this was their appearance; they had the likeness of a man.

The four living creatures are the 'zoa' of Revelation 4:6. They are the protectors of God's throne. They have not free will. Satan, also a cherubim, was the protector of the mercy seat one time, in the first earth age, Ezekiel 28, but he had free will, and he rebelled, so God is cautious about protecting His throne since.

'Zoa' or 'zoon' are cherubim, cp. Genesis 3:24, are distinguished from angels, and look like men, or angels, it seems from this verse, cp. Genesis 1:26,......***Let Us make man in Our image, after Our likeness:***......, where 'us' is 'God and the angels,' or 'we', for we are like the angels too.

6 And every one had four faces, and every one had four wings.

The 'zoon' appeared having four faces, for they were full of eyes before and behind, Revelation 4:6. The wings were the landing gears on the IFO, the carrier they were inside of, 'the flying saucer' if you wish.

7 And their feet were straight feet; and the sole of their feet was like the sole of a calf's foot: and they sparkled like the colour of burnished brass.

Here we clearer see that the wings were landing gears. We also see the color of them, same as the carrier, so the material was the same probably.

8 And they had the hands of a man under their wings on their four sides; and they four had their faces and their wings.

9 Their wings were joined one to another; they turned not when they went; they went every one straight forward.

Here we see that the carriers, or vehicles, were like saucers, round, for they didn't turn when they went. A round vehicle doesn't turn when it changes direction, like an ox cart does, necessarily.

10 As for the likeness of their faces, they four had the face of a man, and the face of a lion, on the right side: and they four had the face of an ox on the left side; they four also had the face of an eagle.

These are the standard symbols of Israel, see Nu 2.

11 Thus were their faces: and their wings were stretched upward; two wings of every one were joined one to another, and two covered their bodies.

12 And they went every one straight forward: whither the spirit was to go, they went; and they turned not when they went.

13 As for the likeness of the living creatures, their appearance was like burning coals of fire, and like the appearance of lamps: it went up and down among the living creatures; and the fire was bright, and out of the fire went forth lightning.

Ezekiel is describing the windows, lamps, of the vehicle here, while it is flying up and down in the Shekinah Glory of God.

14 And the living creatures ran and returned as the appearance of a flash of lightning.

The vehicles moved fast, faster then Ezekiel ever seen before. He was used to ox carts.

15 Now as I beheld the living creatures, behold one wheel upon the earth by the living creatures, with his four faces.

One landed.

16 The appearance of the wheels and their work was like unto the colour of beryl: and they four had one likeness: and their appearance and their work was as it were a wheel in the middle of a wheel.

We see the color described here again, yellow sapphire. There were four vehicles present, and they looked the same.

17 When they went, they went upon their four sides: and they turned not when they went.

Ezekiel was used to vertical wheels, on a cart, standing on the ground, not horizontal wheels flying around, so he does his best to describe it. We see here again that they didn't turn when they went. They were round, they were wheels for Ezekiel, so it seemed like they didn't turn, the way Ezekiel was used to, as an ox cart.

18 As for their rings, they were so high that they were dreadful; and their rings were full of eyes round about them four.

The 'eyes' are the windows of the vehicles.

19 And when the living creatures went, the wheels went by them: and when the living creatures were lifted up from the earth, the wheels were lifted up.

We see here that the living creatures were inside the vehicles, for they went when the vehicles went.

20 Whithersoever the spirit was to go, they went, thither was their spirit to go; and the wheels were lifted up over against them: for the spirit of the living creatures was in the wheels.

Here is the evidence. The spirit of the living creatures was inside the wheels.

21 When those went, these went; and when those stood, these stood; and when those were lifted up from the earth, the wheels were lifted up over against them: for the spirit of the living creatures was in the wheels.

Here we have it again.

22 And the likeness of the firmament upon the heads of the living creature was as the colour of the terrible crystal, stretched forth over their heads above.

'Terrible' is better translated 'awesome'.

23 And under the firmament were their wings straight, the one toward the other: every one had two, which covered on this side, and every one had two, which covered on that side, their bodies.

24 And when they went, I heard the noise of their wings, like the noise of great waters, as the voice of THE ALMIGHTY, the voice of speech, as the noise of an host: when they stood, they let down their wings.

Ezekiel hears God from the vehicles, and they are landing, letting down their landing gears.

25 And there was a voice from the firmament that was over their heads, when they stood, and had let down their wings.

26 And above the firmament that was over their heads was the likeness of a throne, as the appearance of a sapphire stone: and upon the likeness of the throne was the likeness as the appearance of a man above upon it.

Ezekiel sees God and His Throne.

27 And I saw as the colour of amber, as the appearance of fire round about within it, from the appearance of his loins even upward, and from the appearance of his loins even downward, I saw as it were the appearance of fire, and it had brightness round about.

Ezekiel sees God with His Shekinah Glory. Shekinah means 'God is there'.

28 As the appearance of the bow that is in the cloud in the day of rain, so was the appearance of the brightness round about.

This was the appearance of the likeness of the glory of the Lord. And when I saw it, I fell upon my face, and I heard a voice of One That spake.

Ezekiel sees the rain bow around God's Throne, which is the symbol of God's promise to never send another flood over the earth, like in the first earth age, and Noah's flood, Genesis 9:16.

God is here visiting Ezekiel in Person. I think this chapter is marvelous, and it's almost never taught!? God is leaving the same way in chapter 10.

Chapter XXIII

Can You Perform?

Exodus 4:

1 And Moses answered and said, "But, behold, they will not believe me, nor hearken unto my voice: for they will say, 'The Lord hath not appeared unto thee.'"

2 And the Lord said unto him, "What is that in thine hand?" And he said, "A rod."

3 And He said, "Cast it on the ground." And he cast it on the ground, and it became a serpent; and Moses fled from before it.

4 And the Lord said unto Moses, "Put forth thine hand, and take it by the tail." And he put forth his hand, and caught it, and it became a rod in his hand:

5 "That they may believe that the Lord God of their fathers, the God of Abraham, the God of Isaac, and the God of Jacob, hath appeared unto thee."

6 And the Lord said furthermore unto him, "Put now thine hand into thy bosom." And he put his hand into his bosom: and when he took it out, behold, his hand was leprous as snow.

7 And He said, "Put thine hand into thy bosom again." And he put his hand into his bosom again; and plucked it out of his bosom, and, behold, it was turned again as his other flesh.

8 And it shall come to pass, if they will not believe thee, neither hearken to the voice of the first sign, that they will believe the voice of the latter sign.

9 And it shall come to pass, if they will not believe also these two signs, neither hearken unto thy voice, that thou shalt take of the water of the river, and pour it upon the dry land: and the water which thou takest out of the river shall become blood upon the dry land.

10 And Moses said unto the Lord, "I am not eloquent, neither heretofore, nor since Thou hast spoken unto Thy servant: but I am slow of speech, and of a slow tongue."

11 And the Lord said unto him, 'Who hath made man's mouth? Or Who maketh the dumb, or deaf, or the seeing, or the blind? Have not I the Lord?

12 Now therefore go, and I will be with thy mouth, and teach thee what thou shalt say."

God will teach us what to say, cp. Luke 21:12-15.

13 And he said, 'O my Lord, send, I pray Thee, by the hand of Him Whom Thou wilt send."

14 And the anger of the Lord was kindled against Moses, and He said, 'Is not Aaron the Levite thy brother? I know that he can speak well. And also, behold, he cometh forth to meet thee: and when he seeth thee, he will be glad in his heart.

What do we see here? We see that Moses didn't act exactly like a hero. No! He was just like we are, fearful and doubting.

But God showed him that he could trust in Him, for success in his ministry. Moses still didn't trust God fully though.

Moses was a human being just like we are, and this is what God wants us to see with this Scripture.

We just need to be obedient to God to have success.

Judges 6:

11 And there came an Angel of the Lord, and sat under an oak which was in Ophrah, that pertained unto Joash the Abi-ezrite: and his son Gideon threshed wheat by the winepress, to hide it from the Midianites.

'An' Angel is better translated 'the' Angel, for it means 'the presence of the Lord'.
'Gideon' means 'cutter down'.

12 And the Angel of the Lord appeared unto him, and said unto him, "The Lord is with thee, thou mighty man of valour.'

'Thou' is better translated 'a'. Observe that God is calling Gideon 'a mighty man of valour.' Was he? Think for a moment.

13 And Gideon said unto Him, 'Oh my Lord, if the Lord be with us, why then is all this befallen us? And where be all his miracles which our fathers told us of, saying, 'Did not the Lord bring us up from Egypt?' but now the Lord hath forsaken us, and delivered us into the hands of the Medianites.'

14 And the Lord looked upon him, and said, 'Go in this thy might, and thou shalt save Israel from the hand of the Midianites: have not I sent thee?'

God is telling Gideon to go in 'thy might'. Did Gideon have any might? No! It was God that accomplished the victory.

15 And he said unto Him, 'Oh my Lord, wherewith shall I save Israel? behold, my family is poor in Manasseh, and I am the least in my father's house.'
Gideon has no confidence in himself, at all.

16 And the Lord said unto him, 'Surely I will be with thee, and thou shalt smite the Midianites as one man.'

The Lord is assuring Gideon of victory,

17 And he said unto Him, 'If now I have found grace in Thy sight, then shew me a sign that Thou talkest with me.

but he still wants a sign from God to be sure.

18 Depart not hence, I pray Thee, until I come unto Thee, and bring forth my present, and set it before Thee.' And He said, 'I will tarry until thou come again.'

19 And Gideon went in, and made ready a kid, and unleavened cakes of an ephah of flour: the flesh he put in a basket, and he put the broth in a pot, and brought it out unto Him under the oak, and presented it.

20 And the Angel of God said unto him, 'Take the flesh and the unleavened cakes, and lay them upon this rock, and pour out the broth.' And he did so.

21 Then the Angel of the Lord put forth the end of the staff that was in His hand, and touched the flesh and the unleavened cakes; and there rose up fire out of the rock, and consumed the flesh and the unleavened cakes. Then the Angel of the Lord departed out of his sight.

God excepted the offer.

22 And when Gideon perceived that he was an (the) Angel of the Lord, Gideon said, 'Alas, O Lord God! for because I have seen an (the) Angel of the Lord face to face.'

Now Gideon was convinced!?

23 And the Lord said unto him, 'Peace be unto thee; fear not: thou shalt not die.'

24 Then Gideon built an altar there unto the Lord, and called it Jehovah-shalom: unto this day it is yet in Ophrah of the Abi-ezrites.

'Jehovah' is a contaminated name for God. It is not correct at all, and it should be 'Yahaveh', YHVH, which is the correct name of God.

In Psalm 96:11 God's sacred name is spelled out with an acrostic. The initials of the four Hebrew words <u>*Y*</u>*ismehu* <u>*H*</u>*ashshamayim* <u>*V*</u>*ethagel* <u>*H*</u>*a'arez* making up the sentence *Let the heavens rejoice, and let the earth be glad* form the acrostic. The Massorah has a special rubric calling attention to the acrostic. There are a few other places too in the Bible where God's sacred named is spelled out like this.

25 And it came to pass the same night, that the Lord said unto him, 'Take thy father's young bullock, even the second bullock of seven years old, and throw down the altar of Baal that thy father hath, and cut down the grove that is by it:

Baal represents Satan worship of course, including burning children as sacrifice. The 'grove' is where sexual orgies worship took place, the 'asherah', from where Easter comes. Today churches celebrate Easter in stead of Passover, because of one mistranslation of 'Passover' in the King James Bible, in Acts.

26 And build an altar unto the Lord thy God upon the top of this rock, in the ordered place, and take the second bullock, and offer a burnt sacrifice with the wood of the grove which thou shalt cut down.'

27 Then Gideon took ten men of his servants, and did as the Lord had said unto him: and so it was, because he feared his father's household, and the men of the city, that he could not do it by day, that he did it by night.

28 And when the men of the city arose early in the morning, behold, the altar of Baal was cast down, and the grove was cut down that was by it, and the second bullock was offered upon the altar that was built.

29 And they said one to another, 'Who hath done this thing?' And when they inquired and asked, they said, 'Gideon the son of Joash hath done this thing.'

One of the ten servants must have leaked.

30 Then the men of the city said unto Joash, 'Bring out thy son, that he may die: because he hath cast down the altar of Baal, and because he hath cut down the grove that was by it.'

31 And Joash said unto all that stood against him, 'Will ye plead for Baal? will ye save him? he that will plead for him, let him be put to death whilst it is yet morning: if he be a god, let him plead for himself, because one hath cast down his altar.'

32 Therefore on that day he called him Jerubbaal, saying, 'Let Baal plead against him, because he hath thrown down his altar.'

'Jerubbaal' means 'Let Baal plead'.

So what do we see here? What is this an example of, to learn from? God is the One That accomplish things, not we, really. We do not have the wisdom without God's.

Let's go now to Judges 4:

4 And Deborah, a prophetess, the wife of Lapidoth, she judged Israel at that time.

Here we have a woman who is a prophet and a judge, so women are also used by God, and very much indeed. There are lots of women used by God in the Scriptures. Men, especially of the cloth, don't want to admit that, as we know from history. The reason is obvious. Men might loose power admitting women of God.

8 And Barak said unto her, 'If thou wilt go with me, then I will go: but if thou not go with me, then I will not go.

Barak had no guts. He had to ask a woman to go with him to battle.

9 And she said, 'I will surely go with thee: notwithstanding the journey that thou takest shall not be for thine honour; for the Lord shall sell Sisera into the hand of a woman.'

18 And Jael went out to meet Sisera, and said unto him, 'Turn in, my lord, turn in to me; fear not.' And when he had turned in unto her into the tent, she covered him with a mantle.

In general it was not good for a man to go into a woman's tent without her husbands permission in those days.

19 And he said unto her, 'Give me, I pray thee, a little water to drink; for I am thirsty.' And she opened a bottle of milk, and gave him drink, and covered him.

20 Again he said unto her, 'Stand in the door of the tent, and it shall be, when any man doth come and inquire of thee, and say, 'Is there any man here? That thou shalt say, 'No'.

21 Then Jael Heber's wife took a nail of the tent, and took an hammer in her hand, and went softly unto him, and smote the nail into his temples, and fastened it into the ground: for he was fast asleep and weary. So he died.
She did the only right thing, and Israel won the battle by a woman, with guts.

1 Kings 19:

2 Then Jezebel sent a messenger unto Elijah, saying, 'So let the gods do to me, and more also, if I make not thy life as the life of one of them by to morrow about this time.'

3 And when he saw that, he arose, and went for his life, and came to Beer-sheba, which belongeth to Judah, and left his servant there.

4 But he himself went a day's journey into the wilderness, and came and sat down under a juniper tree: and he requested for himself that he might die; and said, It is enough; now, O Lord, take away my life; for I am not better than my fathers.'

5 And as he lay and slept under a juniper tree, behold, then an Angel touched him, and said unto him, 'Arise and eat.'

6 And he looked, and, behold, there was a cake baken on the coals, and a cruse of water at his head. And he did eat and drink, and laid him down again.

Here we see that not even Elijah was so gutsy all the time.

Jeremiah 1:

4 Then the word of the Lord came unto me, saying,

5 'Before I formed thee in the belly I knew thee; and before thou camest forth out of the womb I sanctified thee, and I ordained thee a prophet unto the nations.'

Jeremiah is one of the elect, so he earned his sanctification and ordination in the first earth age at the katabole. God knew him from then, and knew he could trust him for the work he was going to do in this earth age.

6 Then said I, 'Ah, Lord God! behold, I cannot speak: for I am a child.'

'Child' is better translated 'youth', young man.

7 But the Lord said unto me, 'Say not, 'I am a child:' for thou shalt go to all that I shall send thee, and whatsoever I command thee thou shalt speak.

Jeremiah is an 'apostle', 'a sent one.'

8 Be not afraid of their faces: for I am with thee to deliver thee, saith the Lord.

9 Then the Lord put forth His hand, and touched my mouth. And the Lord said unto me, 'Behold, I have put My words in thy mouth.

10 See, I have this day set thee over the nations and over the kingdoms, to root out, and to pull down, and to destroy, and to throw down, to build, and to plant.

Here we see that Jeremiah was not very gutsy, but God touched him, so he could do his work for the Lord.

Hebrews 13:

5 Let your conversation be without covetousness; and be content with such things as ye have: for he hath said, 'I will never leave thee, nor forsake thee.'

Your home assignment here is to find where this quote is from.
God will never forsake or leave us. He is there all the time. We can trust that, but we don't all the time.

6 So that we may boldly say, 'The Lord is my Helper, and I will not fear what man shall do unto me.'

The quote is from Psalms 118:6.

7 Remember them which have the rule over you, who have spoken unto you the word of God; whose faith follow, considering the end of their conversation.

'Follow' here means 'imitate'. It means that we shall imitate them we have learned the Word from.

8 Jesus Christ the same yesterday, and to day, and for ever.

9 Be not carried about with divers and strange doctrines. For it is a good thing that the heart be established with grace; not with meats, which have not profited them that have been occupied therein.

If we study the Word, are obedient to God, use common sense, and work, we are OK.

Chapter XXIV

How To Prepare To Be A Teacher

Ezekiel 1:

28......This was the appearance of the likeness of the glory of the Lord. And when I saw it, I fell upon my face, and I heard a voice of One That spake.

If you read the first chapter of Ezekiel you see that God, with His throne, had just appeared to Ezekiel, and God starts talking to him.
See my chapter about UFOs.

Ezekiel 2:

1 And he said unto me, 'Son of man, stand upon thy feet, and I will speak unto thee.'

God will not speak to you until you stand up for yourself.

2 And the spirit entered into me when He spake unto me, and set me upon my feet, that I heard Him That spake unto me.

First we have to stand up. Then God talks to us, and then God's spirit enters us. That's a little different picture from what we are used to see in churches, when preachers lay hands on people, and they fall backwards onto the floor, and it's supposed to mean that God's spirit struck them down. I don't believe that. I think its fake. Ezekiel fell down of himself in awe of God. God didn't strike him down in the first place. God wanted him to stand on his feet, even before He wanted to talk to him. It even says here that God's spirit set Ezekiel up on his feet, so that Ezekiel then could hear God.

3 And He said unto me, 'Son of man, I send thee to the children of Israel, to a rebellious nation that hath rebelled against Me: they and their fathers have transgressed against Me, even unto this very day.

We see here how rebellious God thinks the western Christian nations, Western Europe, USA, Canada, etc., are, and unto this very day. Ezekiel is a prophet to us today. That's why we are reading it right now. So, this chapter applies to us today about how we become teachers of God's word. Not man's words, which are the traditions of men.

4 For they are impudent children and stiffhearted. I do send thee unto them; and thou shalt say unto them, 'Thus saith the Lord God.'

5 And they, whether they will hear, or whether they will forbear, (for they are a rebellious house,) yet shall know that there hath been a prophet among them.

You see, we shall speak the word, spread the word, even if we think people do not listen. We don't know in beforehand who will listen or not. People will understand though, now or later, that there has been a prophet among them.

6 And thou, son of man, be not afraid of them, neither be afraid of their words, though briers and thorns be with thee, and thou dost dwell among scorpions: be not afraid of their words, nor be dismayed at their looks, though they be a rebellious house.

Speaks for itself.

7 And thou shalt speak My words unto them, whether they will hear, or whether they will forbear: for they are most rebellious.

God says, we shall speak His words, meaning not man's words.

8 But thou, son of man, hear what I say unto thee; Be not thou rebellious like that rebellious house: open thy mouth, and eat that I give thee.'

Here God is saying that we shall eat what He gives us, meaning of knowledge of God's word. We obviously have to study before we go out and teach.

9 And when I looked, behold, an hand was sent unto me; and, lo, a roll of a book was therein;

Here God is giving Ezekiel the word of God. The main learning tool.

10 And He spread it before me; and it was written within and without: and there was written therein lamentations, and morning, and woe.

The word of God is always complete, this means. God gave all of it to Ezekiel.

Ezekiel 3:

1 Moreover He said unto me, 'Son of man, eat that thou findest; eat this roll, and go speak unto the house of Israel.'

God is telling Ezekiel to learn the word of God before he goes out and teach. God says, 'eat it'. That means serious learning through serious studying. Two years of seminary is not enough. It takes much more than that, and with teachers that teach the truth, and not the traditions of men, as most seminaries, universities, and colleges do today. I haven't found one yet that teaches the truth.

2 So I opened my mouth, and He caused me to eat that roll.

God opened Ezekiel's mind so he could understand the word. We need God's help to understand the word. It starts with love for the truth, 2 Thess 2:10-11, from our part.

3 And He said unto me, 'Son of man, cause thy belly to eat, and fill thy bowels with this roll that I give thee.' Then did I eat it; and it was in my mouth as honey for sweetness.

We have to fill our mind with God's word before we can teach. We need to understand the whole Word, at least the basic working plan of God, from the Scriptures. Not just pieces of it. Few do that today. Then its going to be sweet like honey.

4 And He said unto me, 'Son of man, go, get thee unto the house of Israel, and speak with My words unto them.

God is emphasizing 'My' words, meaning not man's words, meaning not the traditions of men, which most churches teach today. It is sad.

5 For thou art not sent to a people of a strange speech and of an hard language, but to the house of Israel;

6 Not to many people of a strange speech and of an hard language, whose words thou canst not understand. Surely, had I sent thee to them, they would have hearkened unto thee.

God is saying that the Gentiles, the heathen, would have been more receptive than Israel, if I had sent you to them, although they don't understand your language.

7 But the house of Israel will not hearken unto thee; for they will not hearken unto Me: for all the house of Israel are impudent and hardhearted.

8 Behold, I have made thy face strong against their faces, and thy forehead strong against their foreheads.

God makes us sharp in the Word, or the Word makes us sharp, for the Word is God.

9 As an adamant harder than flint have I made thy forehead: fear them not, neither be dismayed at their looks, though they be a rebellious house.'

10 Moreover He said unto me, "Son of man, all My words that I shall speak unto thee receive in thine heart, and hear with thine ears.

God is saying, 'Listen carefully to all, not part, of My Words,' meaning divide the Word correctly, and let them sink in real good.

11 And go, get thee to them of the captivity, unto the children of thy People, and speak unto them, and tell them, 'Thus saith the Lord God;' whether they will hear, or whether they will forbear.'

It doesn't matter if they hear or not, speak the Word any way. Remember Ez 37, when Ezekiel preached to the bones, and they came alive.

This is a glimpse into how to become a true teacher of God's word.

Chapter XXV

Zechariah Chapter 14

Zechariah was murdered by the Kenites, sons of the first murderer, Cain, John 8:44, between the Temple and the altar, Matt 23:35. The name means 'remembered by YHVH.' The book of Zechariah is about how it is going to go down in the end times. It is written about 400 years before John the Baptist appeared. The period in between is not written about in the Word, but in history only. It went down bad for them that returned, around 40000, from the captivity in Babylon, see the book of Ezra, so when Jesus was born the situation was bad. We know, for example, that Caiaphas, the chief priest was a Kenite, appointed by the Roman Government, not by God.

I have chosen chapter 14 here, the last chapter of the book, for a little analyze.

Zech 14:

1 Behold the day of the Lord cometh, and thy spoil shall be divided in the midst of thee.

Christ returns when Antichrist, Satan, is in Jerusalem, 2 Thess 2:3-4, Rev 12:9.

Let's go to Zech 13:

8 And it shall come to pass, that in all the land, saith the Lord, two parts therein shall be cut off and die; but the third shall be left therein.

Two thirds of the worlds population are going to be deceived, believe Satan is Christ, and therefore be spiritually dead, cp. Rev 20:5. They never read, or understood, 2 Thess 2. One third is not deceived, and therefore spiritually alive, for they love the truth enough to study His Word.

9 And I will bring the third part through the fire, and will refine them as silver is refined, and will try them as gold is tried: they shall call on My name, and I will hear them: I will say, 'It is My People:' and they shall say, 'The Lord is my God.'

'My people' is 'Ami' in the Hebrew. They who are not deceived, they who know the truth, are going to be tested, by this situation in Jerusalem. Satan as Antichrist is going to be very convincing.

Back to Zech 14:

2 For I will gather all nations against Jerusalem to battle; and the city shall be taken, and the houses rifled, and the women ravished; and half of the city shall go forth into captivity, and the residue of the People shall not be cut off from the city.

The 'ravished women' are the 'whore' of Rev 17, the deceived Christian church, by the fallen angels in part, cp. Jude 6, Gen 6, 1 Cor 11:10. I mean 'ravish' means 'rape', and in this case I would suggest spiritual rape, for gender is not necessarily involved, or why not also 'wholly seduction' as with Eve in the Garden, cp. Gen 3 and 2 Cor 11:2-3, where 'beguiled' is the Greek word 'exapataho' that only means 'wholly seduce', which includes loss of virginity. Their can not be violence involved here, for Satan and his fallen angels, and the Kenites, can not deceive using violence. They are coming in peaceably, prosperously and flattering, Dan 8 and 11.
The 'residue' is the 'elect'.

3 Then shall the Lord go forth, and fight against those nations, as when He fought in the day of battle.

When Christ returns He is going to battle like He did in the first earth age, when Satan rebelled, Ez 28.

'Those nations' here is the Kenites' 'one world order, or poli-tical system', the first beast of Rev 13. The world is 'one' nation at this time. The battles are written about in Ez 38 and 39 and Rev. Are Hamon-gog, Ez 39, and Armageddon, Rev 16, familiar? My second book has an indepth study of this.

It ultimately comes to what is written in Rev 18 and 14, Babylon's fall, the end of this earth age, the end of confusion, which is what Babylon means, Satan's empire.

In one hour,......*for in one hour is thy judgment come,* Rev 18:10, shall all the Kenite's commerce be finished for ever,......*the merchants of the earth shall weep and mourn over her; for no man buyeth their merchandise any more:,* Rev 18:11,......*The merchants......, which were made rich by her,* her meaning Babylon, or Jerusalem in this instance, the center of the world, for Satan is reigning there in person, *shall stand......weeping and wailing,* Rev 18:15. *For in one hour so great riches is come to nought. And every shipmaster, and all the company in ships, and sailors, and as many as trade by sea, stood......and cried when they saw the smoke of her burning......and they cast dust on their heads, and cried, weeping and wailing, saying, 'Alas, alas, that great city wherein were made rich all that had ships in the sea by reason of her costliness! for in one hour is she made desolate......And the voice of harpers, and musicians, and pipers, and trumpeters, shall be heard no more at all in thee; and no craftsman, of whatsoever craft he be, shall be found any more in thee;......for thy merchants were the great men of the earth; for by thy sorceries were all nations deceived, Rev 18:17-23.*

'Sorceries' is the Greek word 'pharmakeia' from where 'pharmacy' or 'pharmacist' come. It is talking about the pharmaceutical industry. They are doing a pretty good job today, like always, trying to delude people with psychopharmacals, tranquilizers, and all other medicines, with deadly side effects, the doctors are prescribing, instead of using 'natural' medicine. They are mentioned in Rev 9:21 also, and are there called murderers, fornicators, and thieves. Thieves of souls I would say. The pharmaceutical industry are the great, rich, men of the earth today.

283

4 And His feet shall stand in that day upon the mount of Olives, which is before Jerusalem on the east, and the mount of Olives shall cleave in the midst thereof toward the east and toward the west, and there shall be a very great valley; and half of the mountain shall remove toward the north, and half of it toward the south.

Here we see how Christ is returning. The same way He left, Acts 1:11. Read it. Christ is coming by the east gate, Satan, Antichrist, by the north gate, Is 14:13-15.

5 And ye shall flee to the valley of the mountains; for the valley of the mountains shall reach unto Azal: yea, ye shall flee, like as ye fled before the earthquake in the days of Uzziah king of Judah: and the Lord my God shall come, and all the saints with Thee.

Azal means 'new place,' and is talking about the millennium, the last eight chapters of the book of Ezekiel, as well as Rev 20, and other places. Here we have all the prophets of the Bible, and other saints, may be you?, saved relatives, etc., coming 'back' together with Christ, we who sing the song of Moses, Rev 15 and Deut 32.

6 And it shall come to pass in that day, that the light shall not be clear, nor dark:

When Christ has returned, we don't live in a flesh, terrestrial, body any more, for we live in another dimension. Light and dark are different then, obviously. It is difficult to understand that now.

7 But it shall be one day which shall be known to the Lord, not day, nor night: but it shall come to pass, that at evening time it shall be light.

8 And it shall be in that day, that living waters shall go out from Jerusalem; half of them toward the former sea, and half of them toward the hinder sea: in summer and in winter shall it be.

This is the same waters as in Ez 47 and Rev 22.

9 And the Lord shall be King over all the earth: in that day shall there be one Lord, and His name one.

10 All the land shall be turned as a plain from Geba to Rimmon south of Jerusalem: and it shall be lifted up, and inhabited in her place, from Benjamin's gate unto the place of the first gate, unto the corner gate, and from the tower of Hananeel unto the king's winepresses.

This means everywhere, all of it.

11 And men shall dwell in it, and there shall be no more utter destruction; but Jerusalem shall be safely inhabited.

Satan locked in the pit, Rev 20:1-3.

12 And this shall be the plague wherewith the Lord will smite all the people that have fought against Jerusalem; Their flesh shall consume away while they stand upon their feet, and their eyes shall consume away in their holes, and their tongue shall consume away in their mouth.

This is the change of body, from terrestrial to celestial, of 1 Cor 15:52 and 1 Thess 4:17.

13 And it shall come to pass in that day, that a great tumult from the Lord shall be among them; and they shall lay hold every one on the hand of his neighbour, and his hand shall rise up against the hand of his neighbour.

People are going to blame each other for having deceived each other. There was no 'rapture', for example, are they going to see.

14 And Judah also shall fight at Jerusalem; and the wealth of all the heathen round about shall be gathered together, gold, and silver, and apparel, in great abundance.

It has no value though, for in the millennium and beyond there is no commerce any more. So if commerce is the only thing you know, start directly to learn something else also, that you can do in the eternity, if you make it there. It is going to be rather empty otherwise.

15 And so shall be the plague of the horse, of the mule, of the camel, and of the ass, and of all the beasts that shall be in these tents, as this plague.

These are all trade, commerce, carriers.

16 And it shall come to pass, that every one that is left of all the nations which came against Jerusalem shall even go up from year to year to worship the King, the Lord of hosts, and to keep the feast of tabernacles.

17 And it shall be, that whoso will not come up of all the families of the earth unto Jerusalem to worship the King, the Lord of hosts, even upon them shall be no rain.
This is the rain, the waters, of Ez 47.

18 And if the family of Egypt go not up, and come not, that have no rain, there shall be the plague, wherewith the Lord will smite the heathen that come not up to keep the feast of tabernacles.

19 This shall be the punishment of Egypt, and the punishment of all nations that come not up to keep the feast of tabernacles.

They don't receive the rain, receive the waters of Ez 47, which is the Living Water, the Truth, during the millennium. Cp. 'latter rain.'

20 In that day shall there be upon the bells of the horses, HOLINESS UNTO THE LORD; and the pots in the Lord's house shall be like the bowls before the altar.

Everything is going to be holy in the millennium.

21 Yea, every pot in Jerusalem and in Judah shall be holiness unto the Lord of hosts: and all they that sacrifice shall come and take of them, and seethe therein: and in that day there shall be no more the Canaanite in the house of the Lord of hosts.

The sacrifice is 'love'. There will be no more the Canaanite, which means no more commerce, trade, as mentioned above. This word the translators divided into two words in Zech 11:7, 11, rendered 'the poor of the flock'. It shall be 'one' word and mean 'merchant' or 'trafficker', 'sheep-trafficker' selling souls into hell. It can also be used for that which is 'unclean'.

Chapter XXVI

Kenites

You can start reading about the Kenites in Gen 4:17-24, where you have Cain's genealogy.

'Kenite(s)' is the Hebrew word 'Qayin' and means 'sons of Cain' or just 'Cain'. So, we see that they have to do with Cain, the first murderer, John 8:

44 Ye are of your father the devil, and the lusts of your father ye will do. He was a murderer from the beginning, and abode not in the truth, because there is no truth in him. When he speaketh a lie, he speaketh of his own: for he is a liar, and the father of it.

This is Jesus talking to the Kenites. They say they are Jews but they are Kenites, Rev 2:9 and 3:9. They are causing many problems for the Jewish people. They crucified Christ, and the blame came on the Jewish, the Hebrew, people. Well, it was God's plan any way. He is in control.

The Levite priesthood got lazy and employed people to shop wood for the altar, and to do other things for them. The Kenites took the job and successively took over the whole church, see Ezra 2:43 and the Nethinims. When Ezra counted the priests among the returning from the 70 year captivity in Babylon, he found no Levite among them, Ezra 8:15. Already David and king Solomon let the Kenites work in the Temple, 1 Kings 9:

20 And all the people that were left of the Amorites, Hittites, Perizzites, Hivites, and Jebusites, which were not the children of Israel,

Among these, who were supposed to be killed by Solomon, were Kenites, 1 Chr 2:

55 And the families of the scribes which dwelt at Jabez; the Tirathites, the Shimeathites, and Suchathites. These are the Kenites that came of Hemath, the father of the house of Rechab.

and some even second influx of the fallen angels of Jude 6 and Gen 6. We see here, that they were even scribes in the church. If you are a scribe, you can mess up a lot, change the Scriptures even, and certainly the liturgical traditions, and both have been done. Cp. Easter for example in Acts 12:4, which should be Passover, put there by a scribe as late as 1611.

Back to 1 Kings 9:

21 Their children that were left after them in the land, whom the children of Israel also were not able utterly to destroy, upon those did Solomon levy a tribute of bondservice unto this day.

Bondservants here are temple servants, Ezra 8:20, 2:58.
Kenites are written about in Gen 15:19, Nu 24:21, 22, Judg 1:16, 4:11, 17, 5:24, 1 Sam 15:6, 27:10, 30:29, 1 Chr 2:55. The Kenites are smart though, for they don't call themselves Kenites, but they call themselves Jews, as mentioned above from Rev 2 and 3. We have to find them with other tools.
The word 'Jews' used in this context is the Greek word 'Ioudaios', which means a resident of Judaea in the sense as a country, not the tribe of Judah. So, Kenites living in Judaea are in this sense Jews.

Jesus was addressing them a few times. Let's go to John 8:

38 I speak that which I have seen with My Father: and ye do that which ye have seen with your father.

39 They answered and said unto Him, 'Abraham is our father.' Jesus saith unto them, 'If ye were Abraham's children, ye would do the works of Abraham.

40 But now ye seek to kill Me, a Man That hath told you the truth, which I have heard of God: this did not Abraham.

I would use 'murder' instead of 'kill.'

41 Ye do the deeds of your father.' Then said they to Him, 'We be not born of fornication; we have one Father, even God'

They were born of fornication, for Cain, their father, was the son of Satan and Eve, and they were not married. Eve's husband was Adam, Gen 2:24-25.

42 Jesus said unto them, 'If God were your Father, ye would love Me: for I proceeded forth and came from God; neither came I of Myself, but he sent Me.

43 Why do ye not understand My speech? even because ye cannot hear My word.

44 Ye are of your father the devil, and the lusts of your father ye will do. He was a murderer from the beginning, and abode not in the truth, because there is no truth in him. When he speaketh a lie, he speaketh of his own: for he is a liar, and the father of it.

In the Parable of The Tares you see Jesus addressing the same object and subject, Kenites, Matt 13.

Now let's go to Nu 24:

14 And now, behold, I go unto my people: come therefore, and I will advertise thee what this People shall do to thy People in the latter days.'

21 And he looked on the Kenites, and took up his parable, and said, 'Strong is thy dwelling place, And thou puttest thy nest in a rock.

'Rock' is alluding to Tyre, which means 'rock', their headquaters on the little island by the coast of Lebanon.

22 Nevertheless the Kenite shall be wasted, Until Asshur carry thee away captive.'

'Asshur' (Assyrian) is a type of Antichrist, Satan, in the end times, latter days. Antichrist is going to carry the Biblically alliterate people away from the truth, for they don't know he is Satan, when he is coming playing Christ in the temple of God, 2 Thess 2.

24 And ships shall come from the coast of Chittim, And shall afflict Asshur, and shall afflict Eber, And he also shall perish for ever.'

'Chittim' means 'bruiser'. 'Ships of Chittim', a figure of speech, a play on the 'bruisers', Gen 3:15, who are the people in the lineage of Christ, sons of Adam and Eve, or grafted in to it through faith. They, the believers in Christ, who know the truth, are going to bruise Satan's head, with the truth, when he is coming trying to deceive people, Luke 21:12-15. He, Satan, shall perish for ever, Ez 28:18-19. He is going to be blotted out, and never be any more, and all the wicked with him. I call that bruising, and it's ultimately done by Christ in the lake of fire, Rev 20.

In Judges 1:16 we see that Moses' father in law was a Kenite. He was not a Kenite by lineage though, that will say a son of Cain, and Satan, but by living, being a resident, in the land of the Kenites. Moses father in law, Jethro, was a Median priest, Ex 3:1. Median was Abraham's son through Keturah, Gen 25:2. We have the same situation in Judges 4:11, 17, 5:24. You have to watch it. Be careful. Everybody is not a Kenite.

Jesus is addressing the Kenites of the religious community in Matt 23. See for example 23:

33 Ye serpents, ye generation of vipers,……

"Generation" is 'offspring', 'serpent' and 'viper' is Satan.

In Ezra 1:

5……and the priests, and the Levites,……

you can see that the priests and the Levites were not the same people, which they should. The priests were not Levites. They were Kenites.

In Ezra 2:3-42 you see the amount of Hebrews returning from the captivity in Babylon, and from verse

43 The Nethinims:……

you see that the names change from Hebrew names to Chaldean names, and in verse

58 All the Nethinims, and the children of Solomon's servants, were three hundred ninety and two.

you see how many they were. That is scary biscuits. Lots of Kenites slipping in among the Hebrew people. They were still there when Christ walked the earth, and are unto this day.

In Ezra 2:

59……but they could nor shew their father's house, and their seed, whether they were of Israel.

62 These sought their register among those that reckoned by genealogy, but they were not found: therefore were they, as polluted, put from the priesthood.

is the evidence. All where not Kenites of course, but there were Kenites among them.

Observe that all were not put away from the church. Read carefully. Nethinims were still left in the church.

Ezra 3:

7 They gave money......and meat, and drink......,and to them of Tyre, to bring cedar trees from Lebanon to the sea of Joppa,......

reveals Kenites also, them of Tyre, their headquaters.

You see in Ezra 7:

24 Also we certify you, that touching any of the priests and Levites, singers, porters, Nethinims, or ministers of this house of God, it shall not be lawful to impose toll, tribute, or custom, upon them.

that the Nethinims are still in the house of God.

In Ezra 8:

15......:and I viewed the People, and the priests, and found there none of the sons of Levi.

mentioned above, we see that none of the priesthood were Levite. If you read on you understand what I am saying. The Nethinims had taken over the Temple. Not good. God doesn't like that.

As you see in Ezra 9:1-2, just as an important parentheses, the People of Israel, and the priests, and the Levites had not separated themselves from the people of the lands. They did according to their abominations, even of the Canaanites, the Hittites, the Perizzites, the Jebusites, the Amonites, the Moabites, the Egyptians, and the Amorites. Perizzites were even offsprings of the fallen angels, Nephilim. Here we have five different religions represented. Cp. the five husbunds of the Samarian woman at Sychar's well, John 4:12-26.

She was not of Israel. The king of Assyria had brought men from Babylon, and from Cuthah, and from Ava, and from Hamath, and from Sepharvaim, and placed them in the cities of Samaria instead of the children of Israel, 2 Kings 17:24-41. This was when Israel, the ten northern tribes were taken captive by the Assyrian 270 years earlier.

Ezra couldn't see that the priesthood was mixed in with Nethinims, but he did see the race mixing.

In Nehemiah 3:26-27 you can see where the head quaters of the Kenites were in Jerusalem. It was in the Tower of Ophel, in the east Wall. You know what's running under the east wall. It is the 'Living' water of the water gate toward the east and the Virgin's Fountain. See cover.

The 'cancer' Ezra couldn't see, Matt 23:

2......'The scribes and the Pharisees sit in Moses seat:......

the church can still not see today.

I have explained about the Kenites, here and there, in several of my other chapters.

I must mention something very funny here. When I was typing the peoples of the land above, the Moabites came out printed Mbytes instead, which obviously is the religion today. I think God had a finger in that, for it actually printed Mbytes, just one time, and there was no typo in the file. God is in control, and He has humor. I think it's very funny.

Chapter XXVII

Obadiah

Obadiah

1 The vision of Obadiah. Thus saith the Lord God concerning Edom; 'We have heard a rumour from the Lord, and an ambassador is sent among the heathen, Arise ye, and let us rise up against her in battle.

Esau and Jacob were twin brothers. They were Isaac's sons. By the way, Saxon comes from Isaac because the ten northern tribes were scattered over the Caucasus mountains, called therefore Caucasians, after being captive by the Assyrian 200 years before Judah and Benjamin were captive in Babylon. The ten northern tribes thus became split from the two southern tribes, the former called Israel, or Ephraim (the larger of the northern tribes), and the latter called Judah. They are still split. The ten northern tribes became the western Christian nations, including the Americas. Judah we know where they are. The ten tribes mixed in with the six day creation of people, Gen 1:26. The Vikings, Anglo-Saxons, Celts, and Germans, are from the ten northern tribes. There we have all the people of Gen 17:4.

Now if we go to Gen 25:22-34, we see in verse 23, that the Lord is saying to Rebekah, that she has two nations in her womb. She had Russia and the western Christian nations in her womb. In Ez 38:2-3 you see that the chief prince of Meshech and Tubal is the leader of Rosh, Hebrew 'Ro'sh', which is Russia. Esau moved north to the land of Seir, the country of Edom, Gen 32:3. Esau he is Edom, Gen 36:8. Edom comes from 'adom' that means 'red'. Esau occupied the region Idumaea, which is Edom, which is Russia. Even the pottage Esau sold for his birthright was red. This is the reason his name was called Edom, Gen 25:30.

In Mal 1, quoted in Rom 9:13, you see that God hated Esau and Jacob He loved. God hated Esau even before he was born, Rom 9:11. How can that be? Is God unfair, and has favorites? No! He hated Esau for what he did in the first earth age, when Satan rebelled, the katabole, Ez 28:16-18. That is what predestination is about in Rom 8 and 9. The called, the elect, stood up for God, against Satan, in the first earth age. That is why they are justified, Rom 8:30, and called.

2 Behold, I have made thee small among the heathen: thou art greatly despised.

3 The pride of thine heart hath deceived thee, thou that dwellest in the clefts of the rock, whose habitation is high; that saith in his heart, 'Who shall bring me down to the ground?'

The false 'rock', Tyre, Antichrist, Ez 28.

4 Though thou exalt thyself as the eagle, and though thou set thy nest among the stars, thence will I bring thee down, saith the Lord.

'Eagle' is alluding to USA, and 'nest among the stars' could be alluding to 'sputnik.'
See Gen 25-27. We are talking about Russia here, where Esau while mixing into other tribes moved, contra Jacob, which are the western Christian nations.

5 If thieves came to thee, if robbers by night, (how art thou cut off!) would they not have stolen till they had enough? if the grapegatherers came to thee, would they not leave some grapes?

Russia has ripped off its own people. The system that should protect the little man!?

6 How are the things of Esau searched out! how are his hidden things sought up!

There is nothing hidden anymore. Even the archives of KGB are become public now.

7 All the men of thy confederacy have brought thee even to the border: the men that were at peace with thee have deceived thee, and prevailed against thee; they that eat thy bread have laid a wound under thee: there is none understanding in him.

Here we have the Warsaw Pact, Kuba, Nicaragua, etc., that has received ship load after ship load from Russia.

8 Shall I not in that day, saith the Lord, even destroy the wise men out of Edom, and understanding out of the mount of Esau?

All wisdom comes from God. Russia is without God, and therefore without wisdom.

9 And thy mighty men, O Teman, shall be dismayed, to the end that every one of the mount of Esau may be cut off by slaughter.

Teman is southern Russia. It is talking about spiritual slaughter by deception, not physical, no blood bath, for we are in a time of peace, trying to create peace, cp. Mark 13:7, Dan 11:21. The Devil, Spurious Messiah, is coming peaceably and by flatteries. He can not play Christ, 2 Thess 2, and win souls, deceive, if he is cruel physically. He is very convincing, and an expert on deceiving, and he is going to deceive the whole world, Rev 13:3.

10 For thy violence against thy brother Jacob shame shall cover thee, and thou shalt be cut off for ever.

There shall never be any Warsaw Pact or like any more. But there shall be a religious pact within the One World System, which has been around and developed pretty long time now. Have you heard about it? The government officials are talking about it now. IMF, The International Monetary Fund, is one appearance. Even the Federal Reserve bank, which is not a government bank, but a private, owned by the riches families in USA, including the Kenites, is going more international now. You have certainly heard about UN, United Nations, and peace, peace. That's it, along with the European Union, and much more. Have you heard about The Four Hidden Dynasties, which are Politics, Religion, Education, and the Economy? That's the whole 'Pact', friend, and it's ruling the whole world by the Kenites, Satan's children umbilical cord to umbilical cord from the Garden of Eden.

The religious system shall come against Israel, the natural seed of Jacob, all twelve tribes, the Hebrew people, in the end times. That is now and forward.

11 In the day that thou stoodest on the other side, in the day that the strangers carried away captive his forces, and foreigners entered into his gates, and cast lots upon Jerusalem, even thou wast as one of them.

This is talking about the ten northern tribes, scattered all over the world, settling Europe, and the Americas, becoming the western Christian nations. Esau was not there to help, when they were taken captive by the Assyrian, around 600 BC.

Today we have many gangs and Mafias we never had before, also.

12 But thou shouldest not have looked on the day of thy brother in the day that he became a stranger; neither shouldest thou have rejoiced over the children of Judah in the day of there destruction; neither shouldest thou have spoken proudly in the day of distress.

Judah and Benjamin were taken captive into Babylon 200 years after the ten northern tribes were taken by the Assyrian.

Judah is also the nation Israel today, both the good and the bad figs, Jer 24, Mark 13:28. That means there are both Hebrews and Kenites there now.

This is also when they shall mock the elect, when they stand against The One World Order, and Satan, in the synagogues of Satan, Matt 24:9, 14, Mark 13:9-11, Rev 2:9 and 3:9, Luke 21:12-15, and many other places. It is yet to come. Satan is going to be here five months disguised to Christ, 2 Cor 11:14, just before Christ returns, Rev 9:5, 10, 2 Thess 2, Mark 13:14, Matt 24:15, Luke 12:11, 21:12-

15, Rev 12:9, Rev 9, Dan 8-11, Is 57:8, and many, many other scriptures, major and minor prophets.

13 Thou shouldest not have entered into the gate of My people in the day of their calamity; thou shouldest not have looked on their affliction in the day of their calamity, nor have laid hands on their substance in the day of their calamity;

14 Neither shouldest thou have stood in the crossway, to cut off those of his that did escape; neither shouldest thou have delivered up those of his that did remain in the day of distress.

I think we have the Berlin wall here!

15 For the day of the Lord is near upon all the heathen: as thou hast done, it shall be done unto thee: thy reward shall return upon thine own head.

Russia, acting like the heathen, although Esau was a Hebrew, brother of Jacob, has spent there resources on weapon and tried to buy friends, instead of taking care of their own people, all to play superpower. They will pay for it.

16 For as ye have drunk upon My holy mountain, so shall all the heathen drink continually, yea, they shall drink, and they shall swallow down, and they shall be as though they had not been.

They are going to drink the cup if God's wrath, Rev 14:10, the cup that Jesus, in the garden of Gethsemane, before He was crucified, asked Father to pass if it were possible.

In Amos 2:1 we read......*because he burned the bones of the king of Edom into lime.*

What does it mean? In 1917 the Bolsheviks took the Romanov family, the last Russian king Nicholas and his wife Alexandra, murdered them, and burned them. There is DNA test made comparing prince Philip's DNA, for he is related to the Romanovs, with the DNA of the remains of the bones. DNA fits. Alexandra wrote Obadiah verse 4 in her diary that day.

Now when we have read about the destruction of Edom, let's go to the restoration of Israel, Obadiah

17 But upon mount Zion shall be deliverance, and there shall be holiness; and the house of Jacob shall posses their possessions.

On one of these mounts, Golgatha, was the price paid by Christ. There shall be deliverance also in the end upon Zion.

18 And the house of Jacob shall be a fire, and the house of Joseph a flame, and the house of Esau for stubble, and they shall kindle in them, and devour them; and there shall not be any remaining of the house of Esau; for the Lord hath spoken it.

The house of Jacob are all twelve tribes. The house of Joseph are the ten northern tribes.

Of the house of Esau, Russia, shall only be stubble left. Every knee shall bow when Christ returns, Is 45:23.

19 And they of the south shall possess the mount of Esau; and they of the plain the Philistines: and they shall possess the fields of Ephraim, and the fields of Samaria: and Benjamin shall possess Gilead.

God owns the world, and He will give it to His people, as He promised Jacob, Gen 28:13-15, because Jacob cared about God. Esau didn't, not in the first earth age either......*"Jacob have I loved, but Esau have I hated",* Rom 9:13.

20 And the captivity of this host of the children of Israel shall possess that of the Canaanites, even unto Zarephath; and the captivity of Jerusalem, which is in Sepharad, shall possess the cities of the south.

'The Canaanites' means 'the unclean,' or the 'merchants,' or the 'traffickers,' which is 'the sheep-traffickers' selling souls unto hell. It is the Kenites with their Four Hidden Dynasties.

Zarephath is the 'smelting place,' where the lake of fire shall take place, the blotting out process, of all evil, by God's Shekinah Glory, Rev 20. Sepharad means separated. As we see there is a separation taking place here.

21 And saviours shall come up on mount Zion to judge the mount of Esau; and the kingdom shall be the Lord's.

This is about the millennium, Ez 40 and forward, and the elect, the Zedek or Zadok, in English, but more correct 'tsaddiyq' in the Hebrew, the just, Rom 8:30. The elect are the saviours.

Chapter XXVIII

Malachi

Malachi was written to the scattered ten northern tribes, called Israel, about 400 years before Messiah and the Messenger John the Baptist were born. Malachi means messenger. It can also mean angel. If we add 'ah' to the name, with which it could be its original form, it means messenger of God.

The book is a warning to Israel still in effect today. I said Israel, and who are they. They are the major part of the Hebrew People of the Western Christian nations, Gen 15:5......*and tell the stars, if thou be able to number them:......So shall thy seed be.* That's a lot of people, and it was God's promise to Abraham. Where are they? I just told you.

Malachi 1:

1 The burden of the word of the Lord to Israel by Malachi.

2 I have loved you, saith the Lord. Yet ye say, "Wherein hast Thou loved us?' Was not Esau Jacob's brother? saith the Lord: yet I loved Jacob,

Jacob is the natural seed of all twelve tribes.

3 And I hated Esau, and laid his mountains and his heritage waste for the dragons of the wilderness.

'Dragons' here is the Hebrew word 'tannah', which means 'female jackal' and has to do with the women Esau chased. He chased heathen, Gentile, women. He didn't care about his heritage as a Hebrew. God didn't like it. The seed of Christ was supposed to come through him, he was the first-born, but he sold it for a meal of 'red pottage'. That's why he couldn't be the seed line for Christ, and therefore his mother had to go through with the covert activity with Jacob. It starts in Gen 25.

4 Whereas Edom saith, 'We are impoverished, but we will return and build the desolate places;' thus saith the Lord of hosts, They shall build, but I shall throw down; and they shall call them, The border of wickedness, and, The people against whom the Lord hath indignation for ever.

Observe it says 'for ever.'

Edom means red and is Russia. Esau's name was called Edom, Gen 25:30......*Esau is Edom,* Gen 36:8. Esau's people mixed in with the heathen, Gentile, peoples and moved north. I have explained this, touching on Ez 38 in part, in another chapter.

You see, that if you leave God out, which Russia has done, it doesn't matter how much you build.

'The border of wickedness' sounds like the Berlin wall, or the Iron curtain, for me.

5 And your eyes shall see, and ye shall say, 'The Lord will be magnified from the border of Israel.'

The border of Israel is Alaska, which is Hamon-gog. USA who owns Alaska, after buying it for little over seven million dollars, is part of Israel. This has to do with the final battles of Ez 38 and 39. God is going to win the war for Israel by *an overflowing rain, and great hailstones, fire, and brimstone......Thus will I magnify Myself......*Ez 38:22-23.

6 A son honoureth his father, and a servant his master: if then I be a Father, where is Mine honour? and if I be a Master, where is My fear? saith the Lord of hosts unto you, O priests, that despise My name. And ye say, 'Wherein have we despised Thy name?'

God is criticizing the priesthood of Israel, effective even today. Why? The priesthood is not doing their duties. They don't revere (fear) God through teaching the word of God, but the traditions of men. Take Easter for example, which should be Passover, as you know by now, mistranslated one time in the King James Bible, in Acts 12:4, and in all other 76 instances correctly translated Passover. Just for that one time 'deliberate' typo by a false scribe in 1611, the majority of the churches of the world are 'celebrating' Easter with eggs and 'quick like a bunny', in stead of Passover. Easter is fertility rites, as you know. It has absolutely nothing to do with Christ's death and resurrection. I have talked to priests about it, and they don't see any big harm with this. Just an unfortunate mixing, they say, of heathen and Christian feast days. Hmmmm!? Not much fire for Christ in them. Think about it.

The majority of the priesthood today also teach 'the rapture theory', which is 180 degrees from the truth of the Scriptures. It is very strange, but the ten northern tribes have been like that from the beginning. They love to worship, but worship traditions of men rather than their heavenly Father.

7 Ye offer polluted bread upon Mine altar; and ye say, 'Wherein have we polluted Thee?' In that ye say, 'The table of the Lord is contemptible.'

They do not teach that Satan comes first, playing Christ, the false bread, before the true bread, Christ, returns, 2 Thess 2, Rev 9, Mark 13, Matt 24, Luke 12, 21, etc.

8 And if ye offer the blind for sacrifice, is it not evil? and if ye offer the lame and sick, is it not evil? offer it now unto thy governor; will he be pleased with thee, or accept thy person? saith the Lord of hosts.

They offered mite-infested doves bought at the Temple. Give that to your governor and see if he likes it.

Today they, the priest, offer false love, they don't teach the truth, for they are Biblically illiterate. How can you be Biblically illiterate if you truly love God? You can't. God will give you the truth if you love Him, truly, 2 Thess 2:10-11, unless you are among them that God has blinded, Rom 11:7-8. I have explained this in another chapter.

Otherwise He will send you *'strong delusion'*, false teachers etc. Isn't it strange that it is impossible today to find a University, College, or Seminary that teach the true Word of God? I think so. Try yourself to find it, and you will see. Well, Rev 13:3 states, that *all the world wondered after the beast,* so God new. We have the millennium for this reason to teach the truth, Rev 20:6, and most people are going to be 'saved' then. You can see in Zech 13:8 that *two parts therein shall be cut off and die; but the third shall be left therein.* Two thirds are going to be deceived. We are going to teach the truth to these 66% in the millennium. They have their chance then.

9 And now, I pray you, beseech God that He will be gracious unto us: this hath been by your means: will He regard your persons? saith the Lord of hosts.

Said in irony.

10 Who is there even among you that would shut the doors for naught? neither do ye kindle fire on Mine altar for naught. I have no pleasure in you, saith the Lord of hosts, neither will I accept an offering at your hand.

If the priesthood do not teach the word of God but traditions of men, that will say lie, as is mostly done today, God will not accept our love even, because love is the main offering, or sacrifice. Shut the temple down and don't light the altar fire in vain. You can just as well close the church and go home. You are preaching in vain any way, God is saying.

11 For from the rising of the sun even unto the going down of the same My name shall be great among the Gentiles; and in every place incense shall be offered unto My name, and a pure offering: for My name shall be great among the heathen, saith the Lord of hosts.

Even the Gentiles are more obedient than you are, God is saying.

12 But ye have profaned it, in that ye say, 'The table of the Lord is polluted; and the fruit thereof, even his meat, is contemptible.'

13 Ye said also, 'Behold, what a weariness is it!' and ye have snuffed at it, saith the Lord of hosts; and ye brought that which was torn, and the lame, and the sick; thus ye brought an offering: should I accept this of your hand? saith the Lord.

Of course not. God is still talking to the preachers, and even the ones today.

14 But cursed be the deceiver, which hath in his flock a male, and voweth, and sacrificeth unto the Lord a corrupt thing: for I am a great King, saith the Lord of hosts, and My name is dreadful among the heathen.

'Dreadful' is better translated 'awesome.' 'Heathen' is better translated 'nations'.

Malachi 2:

1 And now, O ye priests, this commandment is for you.

2 If ye will not hear, and if ye will not lay it to heart, to give glory unto My name, saith the Lord of hosts, I will even send a curse upon you, and I will curse your blessings: yea, I have cursed them already, because ye do not lay it to heart.

'Heart' is better translated 'mind.' The curse is written in Zech 5:

3......'This is the curse that goeth forth over the face of the whole earth: for every one that stealeth shall be cut off as on this side according to it; and every one that sweareth shall be cut off as on that side according to it.

'Stealeth' here is about 'stealing souls' for Antichrist, through deception, with the 'rapture theory', see Ez 13:18-20, and 'sweareth' is of course 'swearing' to false gods, Antichrist, the Spurious Messiah, 2 Thess 2, the son of perdition. God is still talking to the priesthood, effective even today.

4 I will bring it forth, saith the Lord of hosts, and it shall enter into the house of the thief, and into the house of him that sweareth falsely by My name: and it shall remain in the midst of his house, and shall consume it with the timber and the stones thereof.'

'Thief' is 'deceiver'. Now back to Malachi 2:

3 Behold, I will corrupt your seed, and spread dung upon your faces, even the dung of your solemn feasts; and one shall take you away with it.

God is going to throw the dung from the sick animals they sacrifice back in their faces. We have to think equivalent to that today, for these ordinances don't apply today of course, because of the Cross. That will be false love as mentioned above. You can't say you love God and never study, or understand His Word. That is not trustworthy.

4 And ye shall know that I have sent this commandment unto you, that My covenant might be with Levi, saith the Lord of hosts.

The priesthood shall come out of the lineage of Levi. This is through Christ by Mary, a full Levite, cousin to Elisabeth, their mothers were sisters, see Luke 1.

5 My covenant was with him of life and peace; and I gave them to him for the fear wherewith he feared Me, and was afraid before My name.

'Fear' is better translated 'revere'.

6 The law of truth was in his mouth, and iniquity was not found in his lips: he walked with Me in peace and equity, and did turn many away from iniquity.

He was a good teacher.

7 For the priest's lips should keep knowledge, and they should seek the law at his mouth: for he is the messenger of the Lord of hosts.

8 But ye are departed out of the way; ye have caused many to stumble at the law; ye have corrupted the covenant of Levi, saith the Lord of hosts.

The priesthood has caused many to misunderstand the Word and go wrong, for they teach lies.

9 Therefore have I also made you contemptible and base before all the People, according as ye have not kept My ways, but have been partial in the law.

Their creditability is not very solid. Isn't that true today, if we really think about it.

10 Have we not all one Father? hath not one God created us? why do we deal treacherously every man against his brother, by profaning the covenant of our fathers?

11 Judah has dealt treacherously, and an abomination is committed in Israel and in Jerusalem; for Judah hath profaned the holiness of the Lord which He loved, and hath married the daughter of a strange GOD.

'An abomination' is alluding to Antichrist and his tribulation, cp. Mark 13:14.

'Married the daughter of a strange GOD' is alluding to the 'whoring', Rev 17, after Antichrist, the wrong husband. That's what it means in Mark 13:

17 But woe to them that are with child, and to them that give suck in those days!

They think Antichrist is Christ. The bride only has one true husband, and that is Christ, not the in stead of Christ, who is Antichrist, who is Satan playing, disguised to, Christ, 2 Thess 2.

It is also alluding to that Tamar had to play the harlot to be impregnated, so the lineage of Christ could continue without interference, Gen 38. We know who Judah married, and about his sons. Read it.

Cp. also Col 2:

14 Blotting out the handwriting of ordinances that was against us, which was contrary to us, and took it out of the way, nailing it to His cross.

What did Christ change? He changed the ordinances, not the law. He fulfilled the law, Matt 5:

17 Think not that I am come to destroy the law, or the prophets: I am not come to destroy, but to fulfill.

18 For verily I say unto you, Till heaven and earth pass, one jot or one tittle shall in no wise pass from the law, till all be fulfilled.

19 Whosoever therefore shall break one of these least commandments, and shall teach men so, he shall be called the least in the kingdom of heaven: but whosoever shall do and teach them, the same shall be called great in the kingdom of heaven.

20 For I say unto you, That except your righteousness shall exceed the righteousness of the scribes and Pharisees, ye shall in no case enter into the kingdom of heaven.

Now back to Malachi 2:

12 The Lord will cut off the man that doeth this, the master and the scholar, out of the tabernacles of Jacob, and him that offereth an offering unto the Lord of hosts.

Jacob is the father of all twelve tribes.

God is still talking to the priesthood of Israel, the scattered ten northern tribes, which are the leaders of the Christian church in the Western Christian nations.

13 And this have ye done again, covering the altar of the Lord with tears, with weeping, and with crying out, insomuch that He regardeth not the offering any more, or receiveth it with good will at your hand.

You left your own women for strange women, and them you left are crying and weeping. God is not going to bless you therefore.

14 Yet ye say, 'Wherefore?' Because the Lord hath been witness between thee and the wife of thy youth, against whom thou hast dealt treacherously: yet is she thy companion, and the wife of thy covenant.

This is meant physically and spiritually. They left their wives and took wives from the land, Ezra 10:10.

15 And did not He make one? Yet had He the residue of the spirit. And wherefore one? That he might seek a godly seed. Therefore take heed to your spirit, and let none deal treacherously against the wife of his youth.

'One' refers to Adam and Abraham. The seed, the lineage, of Christ had to be 'clean', not mixed with the Gentile's. We have to know the truth so we keep to the true Christ, and not to Antichrist. This is not meant as a racist statement, for God created all races as they are,.......*and......it was very good......*, Gen 1:31, but it is meant as a metaphor to emphasize, that we have to study God's word, because we love Him, to understand the truth, so we don't be deceived, led astray.

16 For the Lord, the God of Israel, saith that He hateth putting away: 'for one covereth violence with his garment,' saith the Lord of hosts: therefore take heed to your spirit, that ye deal not treacherously.'

God took Israel to wife but divorced her, Jer 3:8-9, because of her adultery, meant idolatry, worshipping stones and stocks.

To cover a lady with your garment is to marry her.

(Today if we truly repent our part for the reason of a divorce, we are forgiven by Christ, because of the Cross, and can marry again.)

17 Ye have wearied the Lord with your words. Yet ye say, Wherein have we wearied Him?' When ye say, 'Every one that doeth evil is good in the sight of the Lord, and He delighteth in them;' or, 'Where is the God of judgment?'

'Words' with false teaching, false words, by the preachers, the priesthood. They say, 'it is OK, don't worry,' instead of teaching the congregation discipline in the Word.

Malachi 3:

1 Behold, I will send My messenger, and he shall prepare the way before Me: and the Lord, Whom ye seek, shall suddenly come to His temple, even the messenger of the covenant, whom ye delight in: behold, He shall come, saith the Lord of hosts.

The messenger is Elijah or John the Baptist, it depends, see Matt 11:10, and

14 And if ye will receive it, this is Elias, which was for to come.

They did not receive it. John the Baptist was beheaded, and Christ was crucified, so John the Baptist was not Elijah. Therefore Christ has to come again, which is the Second Advent.

Back to Malachi 3:

2 But who may abide the day of His coming? and who shall stand when He appeareth? for he is like a refiner's fire, and like fullers' sope:

There is going to be a cleansing de luxe. They who know the truth will abide at the Second Advent.

3 And he shall sit as a refiner and purifier of silver: and He shall purify the sons of Levi, and purge them as gold and silver, that they offer unto the Lord an offering in righteousness.
Judgment starts at the pulpit. God is going to put the heat to the priests.

4 Then shall the offering of Judah and Jerusalem be pleasant unto the Lord, as in the days of old, and as in former years.

This is going to happen in the millennium.
'The days of old' and 'former years' is the first earth age.

5 And I will come near to you to judgment; and I will be a swift witness against the sorcerers, and against the adulterers, and against false swearers, and against those that oppress the hireling in his wages, the widow, and the fatherless, and that turn aside the stranger from his right, and fear not Me, saith the Lord of hosts.

Judgment is both positive, rewards, and negative, punishment.

Sorcerers is the Hebrew word 'kashaph', which means 'to whisper a spell, to inchant or practice magic, use witch craft.' I think it's proper to connect this Hebrew word with the Greek word 'pharmakeia' used in Rev 9:21 and 18:23, from where our word 'pharmaceutical' is coming. The pharmaceutical industry is deluding a lot of people with tranquilizers and psychopharmicals today, really 'killing' souls that way making people die spiritually.

We all know about wages and cash cow systems by the merchants, the Canaanites, the sheep-traffickers selling souls, the Kenites. 'Oppress' is better translated 'defraud'.

6 For I am the Lord, I change not; therefore ye sons of Jacob are not consumed.

Because of the covenant.

7 Even from the days of your fathers ye are gone away from Mine ordinances, and have not kept them. Return unto Me, and I will return unto you,' saith the Lord of hosts. But ye said, 'Wherein shall we return?

'Ordinances' here is the Hebrew word 'choq', and it means like 'to do the will of God.' We have another word 'ordinances' in verse 14, and we get to that then.

8 Will a man rob God? Yet ye have robbed Me. But ye say, 'Wherein have we robbed Thee?' In tithes and offerings.

'Rob' is better translated 'defraud.' If we give tithes and offerings to churches that do not teach God's word, but the traditions of men, we are robbing God. The whole world is, Rev 13:3.

9 Ye are cursed with a curse: for ye have robbed Me, even this whole nation.

There we have 'the whole world,' and specifically the 'nation' of Israel.

10 Bring ye all the tithes into the storehouse, that there may be meat in Mine house, and prove Me now herewith, saith the Lord of hosts, if I will not open you the windows of heaven, and pour you out a blessing, that there shall not be room enough to receive it.

Remember Amos 8:

11 Behold, the days come, saith the Lord God, that I will send a famine in the land, not a famine of bread, nor a thirst for water, but of hearing the words of the Lord:

'Meat' means the meat of the word of God, not milk, Hebr 5:

12......and are become such as have need of milk, and not of strong meat.

13 For every one that useth milk is unskillful in the word of righteousness: for he is a babe.

14 But strong meat belongeth to them that are of full age, even those who by reason of use have their senses exercised to discern both good and evil.

When we tithe to a church where we are taught God's word, we are going to be blessed, and because of our tithe the teaching of God's word can continue, not the traditions of men. It is so simple.

Now back to Malachi 3:

11 And I will rebuke the devourer for your sakes, and he shall not destroy the fruits of your ground; neither shall your vine cast her fruit before the time in the field, saith the Lord of hosts.

God will protect us from the devourer, Satan, and his evil spirits. Cp. Job 1:9-11.

12 And all nations shall call you blessed: for ye shall be a delightsome land, saith the Lord of hosts.

The Western Christian nations are blessed, despite the short-fall by its priesthood, because of the covenant with Abraham, Isaac, and Jacob. There are good churches of course also, teaching the Word, and it's keeping the blessings flowing. Not all are bad.

13 Your words have been stout against Me, saith the Lord. Yet ye say, 'What have we spoken so much against Thee?'

How about the 'rapture'? dear priesthood. This is talking about apostasy, 2 Thess 2, which means falling away from the true doctrine of Christ, and falling away to Antichrist.
14 Ye have said, 'It is vain to serve God: and what profit is it that we have kept His ordinances, and that we have walked mournfully before the Lord of hosts?

We have to divide the Word correctly and be watchmen. The word 'ordinances' here is different from that in verse 7. Here it is the Hebrew word 'mishmereth' and means 'safeguard, ward, watch, charge, keep, sentry, preservation, observance, duty.'
Walk 'mournfully' means 'in black,' just like priest mostly do.

15 And now we call the proud happy; yea, they that work wickedness are set up; yea, they that tempt God are even delivered.'

'......and all the world wondered after the beast', Rev 13:3. All the world worship the One World Order, the One World Economy, the Four Hidden Dynasties, without even knowing it, ruled by the Kenites, the 'sheep-traffickers', the merchants, the pharmaceutical industry, the Mbytes (cp. Moabites, and other '-ites' -peoples of the land of heathen religions), the Internet, etc., etc. They don't give a 'hoot' for God, if I may use that expression to emphasize their level.

Ultimately they are going to worship Antichrist, Satan, Rev. 13:11, for their own good, for it will ultimately wake them up, when they see the true Christ return, every knee shall bow, for they are Biblically illiterate. They never studied the word of God. How can they know? They can't. Read Rev 6:15-17 and see how they are going to act at that point.

Also, God doesn't send out beggars, tempters of God therefore, to preach. See Luke 9:3, Matt 10:10, where 'scrip' is the word 'pera' in the Manuscripts, which means 'begging bag', according to an inscription at Kefr-Hauar, in Syria, where the word 'pera' is used for 'begging bag.' That's why the Lord used this word here. Disciples, that will say sent ones from God, shall not beg, period, but many who claim they are do. Are they really from God? I doubt it strongly. Lot of 'church business' going on, by the 'sheep-traffickers', the 'soul-sellers', the Canaanites, merchants, the Kenites, and their helpers. Be careful.

16 Then they that feared the Lord spake often one to another; and the Lord hearkened, and heard it, and a book of remembrance was written before Him for them that feared the Lord, and that thought upon His name.

Here is the Book of Life, Rev 20:12.

Check out for yourself what God's name really is. It is an interesting study.

17 And they shall be Mine, saith the Lord of hosts, in that day when I make up My jewels; and I will spare them, as a man spareth his own son that serveth him.

The 'jewels' are the elect. God is their inheritance, Ez 44:26-29......*I am their inheritance: and ye shall give them no possession in Israel: I am their possession......and every dedicated thing in Israel shall be their's.*

Back to Malachi 3:

18 Then shall ye return, and discern between the righteous and the wicked, between him that serveth God and him that serveth Him not.

This is referring to the teaching by Christ and the elect in the millennium. Rev 20:6, and Ez 44:

23 And they shall teach My People the difference between the holy and the profane, and cause them to discern between the unclean and the clean.

24 And in the controversy they shall stand in judgment; and they shall judge it according to My judgments: and they shall keep My laws and My statutes in all Mine assemblies; and they shall hallow My sabbaths.

Back to Malachi and chapter 4:

1 For, behold, the day cometh, that shall burn as an oven; and all the proud, yea, and all that do wickedly, shall be stubble: and the day that cometh shall burn them up, saith the Lord of hosts, that it shall leave them neither root nor branch.

'Neither root nor branch', nothing to grow from.
God's Shekinah Glory shall burn all evil, 2 Pet 3 and Hebr 12:29. 'Shekinah' means 'God is there.'
There is a day coming with judgment, 2 Pet 3, Matt 13:37-42, Hebr 12:29, Rev 20:11-15, just to mention some addresses.

2 But unto you that fear My name shall the Sun of righteousness arise with healing in His wings; and ye shall go forth, and grow up as calves of the stall.

Calves that are turned loose and running out into the pasture after being in the stall all winter, they happily jump and run. So will we, or are we already.

23 And ye shall tread down, the wicked; for they shall be ashes under the soles of your feet in the day that I shall do this, saith the Lord of hosts.

Ex 28:18-19......*therefore will I bring forth a fire from the midst of thee, it shall devour thee, and I will bring thee to ashes upon the earth in the sight of all them that behold thee. All they that know thee among the people shall be astonished at thee: thou shalt be a terror, and never shalt thou be any more.*

Satan is going to be blotted out, Rev 20:10. The same will happen to his friends, Rev 20:15.

Back to Malachi 4:

4 Remember ye the law of Moses My servant, which I commanded unto him in Horeb for all Israel, with the statutes and judgments.

You see the statutes and the law are still in effect, but not ordinances.

5 Behold, I will send you Elijah the prophet before the coming of the great and dreadful day of the Lord:

Here is Second Advent, and Elijah will announce It, so everybody who has ears to hear will know.

6 And he shall turn the heart of the fathers to the children, and the heart of the children to their fathers, lest I come and smite the earth with a curse.

This is not Luke 1:16-17, cp. John 1:21 and Matt 11:14.
Observe that 'fathers' is in plural. Why? There are two fathers, the true Christ and Antichrist, who is Satan, who is the false Christ, 2 Thess 2, who is 'the son of perdition.'
The curse is in Zech 5.

Printed in the United States
42558LVS00005B/91

9 781410 758415